TAR HEEL BRED

HOW BASKETBALL MADE A MAN OUT OF ME

SCOTT WHISNANT

Tar Heel Bred:
How Basketball Made a Man Out of Me
© 2024 by Scott Whisnant
Cover photo by grapix
Designed by Izabell Slade

For more information on this work please contact
TarHeelBredbook@gmail.com
ISBN-13: 979-8-218-59881-5
Printed in U.S.A.

To Celia

My pal, my confidante, my fellow schmuck who understood the gravity of the situation. I couldn't have shared this with anyone else.

FOREWORD

Many years ago, a Philadelphia native moved here to Wilmington, N.C, and became my good friend. A basketball connoisseur, he impressed me as someone able to detect techniques, fundamentals, schemes and execution as well as anyone I know.

Having landed in the heart of ACC basketball country, he felt compelled to choose a rooting interest. To my abject horror, he picked Duke.

"Why?" I asked, or possibly shrieked.

"I think they play harder," he said.

(This assessment provoked a huge argument in 2016, when Carolina went into Cameron Indoor Stadium to face a ranked Duke team and outrebounded the Blue Devils, 64-29, to win by four. Yes, let's talk about "effort.")

"But what about what Carolina stands for?" I continued. "Team basketball. The sum greater than the parts. Point to the passer. Innovations that changed the game. Sustained historical greatness from playing the game the right way.

"And what about the culture? We're the oldest state school in the nation, the place where North Carolinians can go and make something of themselves, even if they come from nothing. We're diverse - we basically integrated college basketball in the South. We represent the best of what our state can be...

"And Duke? They artificially aged their buildings so they could look like an Ivy League school! They're fake. They're transplanted Yankees – didn't you move to get away from that? They didn't start a black player until 1977. They were really crappy back when UCLA ruled and college basketball was really trying to grow. And now they finally got good and you want to tell me they 'play harder?' Don't you recognize they're imposters?"

That's the toned-down version. I may have gone on for a while. Louis looked at me after I finally stopped.

"I don't care about any of that other stuff," he said.

My friend is a basketball fan. But he is not an ACC basketball fan.

There is a difference. That "other stuff" is the culture, heritage and life experience of Southerners like me who grew up when hardly anything else mattered. There were no Panthers, Hurricanes or, God help us, Charlotte Hornets. Our major league cities were places like Clemson, Charlottesville, and Columbia. How many NBA arenas, as the home team is sealing a win, break into the "Amen chorus," as so often happened when we lost a game in College Park, the Maryland outpost that represented the northern boundary of our sports world?

Oh, this stuff matters. To millions like me, it matters a lot. Yes, I grew up a Carolina fan, as did the majority of us. We got used to fans of other teams hating us, renting our opponents as their favorite team for two hours at a time. We were a bit like Israel in a hostile Arab world, always a power to the utter dismay of our rivals.

But there are so many who can substitute details of these pages with foundational memories of their own team. My N.C. State friends can point to a time – now long ago, as I remind them – when they were not only the class of the league, but the toast of college basketball. Carolina once sent ranked teams nine consecutive times up against State and lost every damn one of them. That happened.

Maryland fans will remember historically great programs that never were quite the best. Wake Forest fans can recall wandering through the desert, occasionally tasting greatness. Duke fans can boast about camping out for months at a time so they could attend a game dressed as a banana in their high school gym, trying to convince the rest of us they won because their players loved their school more, and effortlessly pivoting when Duke became the leading proponent of the "one-and-done" whoredom rental system that paved the way for college basketball's eventual ruin.

But I digress. These pages are about my journey as told through the prism of Carolina basketball games. Yes, I grew up in a loving home with wonderful parents. But there were times when it felt like the Tar Heels were about all this awkward, skinny buck-toothed kid had going for him.

They didn't always win the biggest game, but they never let me down. This is my story, but my hope is you will find some of yours within these pages as well.

ACKNOWLEDGEMENTS

My list of people to thank starts, of course, with my wife, Celia Rivenbark, and daughter, Sophie Whisnant, the co-stars of my life's journey. Celia not only encouraged, supported and uplifted, as she has always done, but wielded a critical and needed editor's pen. She also has sat next to me and invested in these games for close to 40 years.

I once casually told Sophie, "My life's story could be told through a series of Carolina games." She then encouraged me to make that vision a reality, the single biggest reason we have this publication today.

Special thanks also to my sisters, Linda Whisnant and Judy Whisnant, who not only allowed me to dredge up some tender childhood memories, but edited in factual ways only they could offer. For example, they filled in missing details of the mayonnaise grilled cheese story and graciously consented to my detailing their villainous roles within it.

My deepest thanks again to Pam "Tiger" Sander, whose editing gave this work a much-needed perspective, just as she did with *Innocent*

Victims. I also want to thank early readers, including Laura Powell Hicks, Gray Wells, Lisa Noecker, Rich Novak and David Tugwell, who kept me encouraged just enough to keep going. Special shout out to Kevin Parker, who not only gave an early read but allowed himself to bear the brunt of my N.C. State jokes.

Heartfelt thanks to the Willard family for their love and support from teenage years to this day, as well as their early feedback on this story. Love you, Dave and Patsy. And RIP Rick, Laura and Lee "Pee-Heed" Willard.

Thanks to my high school and college friends who allowed their names to be used alongside anecdotes in these pages. Names were changed on just a handful of occasions. This process prompted me to reach out to many old friends—some of whom I hadn't spoken to for 40 years—and led to some truly warm conversations. I appreciate their cheerful willingness to be included.

I cannot thank Amy Gary and Izabell Slade enough for their work in laying out this book and chasing down the components needed for publication. I am so fortunate my nephew married into the Gary family.

Finally, a posthumous thanks to my parents, Bob and Nancy Whisnant. To grow up in a loving and supportive home is a gift beyond expression. On behalf of my sisters, you made us who we are, and we miss you every day. I wish they had lived to read these pages. Well... most of these pages.

1
COMING OF AGE

February 28, 1968

South Carolina 87, North Carolina 86

I am 6 years old, I'm in bed and I'm crying.

This is a theological crisis. To date I've been taught that God is great, and God is good. That Jesus loves me. This I know.

Yet it doesn't square. The brooding thugs from South Carolina have defeated the 22-1 Tar Heels. Had they not heard about Dean Smith? And, worse, this was in front of our own fans, the true believers for whom Carolina basketball is not about wins or losses, but performance art. The winning part is understood. Or at least I thought it was.

Now I don't know what to think. Is God even real?

My earliest memory of both religion and Carolina basketball are the same. This is not an accident. Millions like me are raised on the steady diet that Carolina[1] stands for something, that we (yes "we") win because we believe in something greater than ourselves. We're too young to remember when we were just another ACC team, when Carolina players shaved points (!!!), or when Coach Smith was promoted from assistant coach, at age 30, to basically de-emphasize basketball.

He has failed spectacularly. Nothing has more emphasis. Winning, or more precisely, the smug confidence that we can trust we will win because we're supposed to, makes going to school easier, smooths the hard edges of daily home life and provides a salve for my father, who is, to put it mildly, all in. It's easier to get up on Sunday morning after a Carolina win and go to church, which often serves as a Carolina debrief session wrapped around a sermon.

And now this South Carolina thing. I'm a little too young to cope. But a coming Revelation, a redemption story gives us hope even in the depths of despair. Our God is a God of second chances.

The ACC Tournament starts in a week.

March 8, 1968
North Carolina 82, South Carolina 79 (OT)
ACC Tournament Semifinal

We're at Aunt Alice's, and why is a mystery to me. We typically cocoon in our own living room for these, with no outsiders trying to take the conversation elsewhere. We might as well be engaged in group prayer.

But we're here, and it might be because Alice and my Uncle Charles have a color TV. Nonetheless, the game is as tight as Dick's hatband, as we like to say down here. Dick Grubar fouls out, and my father slams his fist in disgust on the armrest of his chair.

---

1   Let's be clear about something: "Carolina" refers to the University of North Carolina at Chapel Hill. Even though this note concerns a game including South Carolina, the Gamecocks have no valid claim to "Carolina." In fact, we like to say South Carolina is neither "Carolina" nor "USC" (that's Southern Cal). Hey, I don't make the rules; it's just the way it is.

The thud silences the house. No muscle moves. No lung expands or contracts. Stillness.

"Bob!" Aunt Alice finally shouts. How dare she question my father? She must have cooties. The rest of us are frozen. It's not that we're surprised. We've seen this before from our father. We're shocked it's been called into question. We aren't sure where this is headed.

We know it's inexcusable. We know there is no rational explanation. We know better than to question it. It shouldn't have happened. Dick Grubar should not have committed his fifth foul.

Carolina prevails in overtime. We can be a family again. As bemused onlookers, we watch Duke do nothing to stop N.C. State from holding the ball in the second semifinal. Long stretches give us nothing but State center Bill Kretzer dribbling, dribbling and more dribbling. Television goes to commercial during live action, only to return to more dribbling.

Years later, I will read about this game and learn that Bill Currie, Carolina's colorful play-by-play announcer with the duty of broadcasting all tournament games, almost ran out of things to say.

"This game has all the thrill of artificial insemination," he would say.

Final score: N.C. State 12, Duke 10, the lowest-scoring game in ACC history, a record unlikely to be broken. We watch every second. We are scouting our next opponent, the 12-point-scoring N.C. State.

And we will beat them by 37 points.

March 23, 1968
UCLA 78, North Carolina 55
NCAA Tournament Final

To my utter dismay, my parents will not let their 6-year-old son watch a game that starts past 11 p.m. on the East Coast. I thought I had put in the sweat equity to earn this, but instead I get a life lesson.

"You can't win 'em all," my father tells me, "unless you're UCLA."

So they let me watch the tip. Now keep this in mind: Sixteen months later, our family will be over at the Madisons' house watching Neil

Armstrong taking his small step for man. I'll be five days short of my 8th birthday. And I will fall asleep. No one will bother to wake me up, so I'm destined to see this on ESPN, or wherever replays were shown at that time.

But for the opening tip of the 1968 final past 11 p.m.? I'm wide awake. Neil Armstrong is no Lew Alcindor, who controls the tip for UCLA. And I go to bed with the scant beginning of what will become perspective, understanding that nothing is inevitable. Carolina can't win them all. But UCLA can.

March 20, 1969
North Carolina 87, Davidson 85
NCAA Tournament East Regional Final

Another victorious cruise though the ACC schedule has led us to this moment, playing tiny Davidson College from nearby Charlotte in Maryland's Cole Field House. The winner goes to the Final Four.

The gang my father had at his disposal for Saturday chores, posing here for a photo only a church directory could love. I'm looking off to the left, presumably for my dignity.

It's Saturday afternoon, or in our home, the hardest-working day of the week. Daddy is home, so we're doing housework, chores, yardwork and projects, projects, projects. Today my sisters' bedroom is to be painted, and all of us will pitch in.

However, the rhythm of the day comes to a grinding halt during the two hours of the Carolina game, especially this one. We can't lose to a runt of an in-state school in a win-or-go-home game. We have a rematch with UCLA on the horizon.

Yet it's not looking good. Davidson, led by its young coach, Lefty Driesell, is actually quite good. It's taut. My sister, not quite 13 and closest to me in age, gets her period for the first time, an oddly appropriate metaphor for this game. Dean Smith's program is reaching full adulthood, and the Whisnant family rhythms are fully synched.

It's tied but we have the ball. It goes to the capable hands of Charlie Scott. He fakes left, then pulls up from about 17 feet. Swish. Buzzer. Carolina moves on. Dancing in the living room. We are high on life, or maybe it's just the paint fumes. No matter.

Years later I would discover Charlie Scott is black. At the time, all I saw was light blue. No one told me otherwise.

2

A TOUGH WAY TO LOSE ONE

March 13, 1971

South Carolina 52, North Carolina 51

ACC Tournament Final

The great Charlie Scott has graduated. As with all good Christian repressed Southern families, no one mentions what he meant to Carolina, the ACC or society in general. Now would have been a good time for the anecdote about how Dean Smith integrated Chapel Hill itself by bringing a black theology student to a segregated restaurant in 1959 and basically daring the place not to serve them. Turns out, they had a table for four.

The thing about that story almost no one considers is that Coach Smith was but an unknown assistant coach at the time. He had no *power*, nothing like he would later achieve. By 1980, he could have brought a goat to a Chapel Hill restaurant and it would have been served.

No, he put it out there when it was risky to do so. More than a decade later, Alabama's Bear Bryant, as close to a god as one can reach in his home state, would remark that he did not want to be the first coach to integrate Southeastern Conference football—but he wasn't going to be the third, either. Translation: He knew racism was wrong, especially after Sam Bam Cunningham with USC (remember, that's Southern Cal) ran all over Alabama in 1970 right there in the heart of Dixie. But he wasn't willing to address it in any groundbreaking way.

I doubt my parents know the Chapel Hill desegregation story, as it wouldn't be often told until much later. But it isn't their style to discuss societal issues out loud. My father doesn't tell me about sex, either, and our family rarely discusses politics, other than to argue about Vietnam ("those countries will fall like dominoes if we don't fight") or to despise Richard Nixon.

His lack of vitriol, or any social position on race, does say something of the character of our father. He grew up in tiny Polkville, North Carolina, with Confederate soldiers in his lineage. His family included a binge drinking father, a saintly mother and five boys. The family survived by running a corn mill in Western North Carolina through the Depression, with my grandmother taking in sewing to make a little money. The corn mill faded as the boys got older and they survived on what they could farm behind their home, never knowing what it was like to be so full you couldn't eat more. Yet a man with that past never engaged in any of the racial language, race-baiting or assumptions that marked his generation and his region. He wasn't *totally* there racially, at least not by 21st century standards, but we grew up knowing better than to put anybody down.

Charlie Scott was a Tar Heel and we loved him. There was no qualifying language about him, just that we were better off with the ball in his hands.

When he graduates, we believe the Tar Heels are doomed in 1971, picked by some writers to finish seventh in the ACC. Coach Smith has brought in some promising sophomores but several teams appear better, especially the last remnants of an awful bunch at South Carolina.

Yet the Tar Heels finish 11-3, split with South Carolina and somehow win the regular season. South Carolina is a game back, but still considered a national power and the biggest threat to UCLA, the four-time defending champion. When the teams prepare for an ACC Tournament final that will truly settle the league championship, the Gamecocks are ranked sixth and the Tar Heels 13th. Even at 9 years old, I'm sophisticated enough in my fandom to know that Carolina will be an underdog. I almost dread watching what I believe will be inevitable.

The Elliotts, the kindest of neighbors down the street, invite us to watch—again the lure of the color TV. My mother is a better fan than 90% of the fanbase, but this is a boys-only event. Art Sullivan, our piously Quaker next-door neighbor, and Sam Stern, the highway patrolman who is prone to writing tickets for so much as inching past a stop sign to get a better look, are joining us. (It's rumored he once wrote his wife a speeding ticket but none of us have the courage to confirm it.)

My father is on best behavior, and why not? The Tar Heels are actually managing to stay ahead. It's 46-40 with 4:30 left and we're in Four Corners, our classic stall offense with a player in each corner and a dribbler in the middle. With a good middle man, it can look like a spirited game of tag.

South Carolina is forced to foul to try to catch up and the room grows tense as the Tar Heels miss five one-and-one free throws down the stretch. South Carolina has the ball, down one, as time winds down. A shot is blocked, and the ball is loose under the basket. The ref blows a quick whistle and calls a jump ball.

Under 1971 rules, this means a tipoff will take place at the South Carolina foul line. The players will be 6-foot-10 Lee Dedmon for Carolina, a senior and our best player this night, and 6-foot-3 Kevin Joyce for South Carolina, a sophomore.

If you're scoring at home, that's a 7-inch difference. Only six seconds remain.

The TV announcer is talking about South Carolina Coach Frank McGuire, and there's a good bit to say about him. For the generation just ahead of mine, McGuire was a UNC icon. Recruited south from New York City to stem an early tide of N.C. State dominance (the Wolfpack won the league the first three years of its existence and defeated Carolina

15 consecutive times), McGuire brought five Yankees with him and ran the table at 32-0 in 1957, bringing Carolina, and the ACC, its first national championship. The semifinals and final were on consecutive days and both went to triple overtime, the final coming against goliath Wilt Chamberlain, forever painting this wondrous athlete as a loser on the biggest stage.

This led to even bigger things than anyone could imagine. An entrepreneur named C.D. Chesley, a TV producer who worked from home, broadcast those last two games from Kansas City back to North Carolina. He paid nothing for the rights—he basically asked permission to televise the games and the NCAA said "Sure." These broadcasts made legends of McGuire and the UNC players and staked Carolina as the enemy right then and there for many in ACC territory. It also created ACC fever as we know it today, as Chesley expanded on this success and began regularly televising games the following season.

It turns out one of the assistant coaches on that team was bad to drink, so McGuire had to replace him the following season. He hired an unknown 27-year-old coach at the Air Force Academy named Dean Smith. A few years later, McGuire and UNC soured, with recruiting scandals and point-shaving allegations dogging the program. McGuire left for the NBA and Smith was famously hired for the 1961-62 season.

McGuire would go on to coach Chamberlain in the NBA, including the 1962 season when Chamberlain *averaged* 50 points a game. But he left the NBA and returned to college to an ACC rival of North Carolina. Before he was first introduced in Chapel Hill as South Carolina's new coach, Coach Smith implored the faithful to be courteous to the former coach. They were, but the goodwill didn't last long. McGuire brought in more Yankees to build South Carolina into a formidable, entirely hateable, force. The tension between the programs was palpable.

But for now, the announcer is simply reporting that McGuire is griping.

"McGuire is questioning why Dedmon is jumping for UNC," he says.

"Because he's our tallest player," Sam Stern says. We all laugh. South Carolina calls timeout and we finally relax. This one is ours.

Then the jump ball. Defying physics as we know them, Joyce outjumps Dedmon, tapping the ball to Tom Owens, inexplicably left open under the South Carolina basket. He lays it in and the clock runs out.

South Carolina, a team we hated more than we would ever hate Duke, is ACC champion, and North Carolina is headed to the NIT.

The Elliott living room is stone silent. Each of us is lost in thoughts on how such a dark, dystopian world can exist. Did that just happen?

A chipper voice breaks in. Way too chipper.

"Well, it's a tough way to lose a ball game, but you can't win them all."

We glare at Art Sullivan. Most juries in North Carolina would acquit, even if a prosecutor would bother to charge. But we resist the temptation to strangle him with our bare hands.

My father and I walk home, and I go to bed not questioning whether God exists, but why Art Sullivan has to. So I'm making theological progress.

3

BECAUSE WE'RE CAROLINA

March 23, 1972

Florida State 79, North Carolina 75

NCAA Tournament Final Four

Puberty is running a three-on-one break and I am powerless to stop it. So many options to score against my sagging childhood.

By fifth grade, my overbite has grown from "impish feature that prompts adults to smile at the innocence of youth" to "cosmetic emergency that needs to be addressed." After my third-grade school pictures portray an expression only a mother, under duress, could love, my sister advises me to never smile again for a photo. I am the proverbial mule eating apples through a picket fence.

A growth spurt decides to concentrate its energy on my neck, so I grow there about four inches, adding height and no bulk anywhere else. I'm about 75 pounds and begin to hear skinny jokes, which I can't understand because I know enough not to make fat jokes.

Girls don't like me, and for now, I'm ok with it. I still have my Tar Heels.

The buck-toothed aesthetic disaster on the left prompted my sister to tell me to never again smile with my mouth open for a photo. Which led to efforts like the one on the right.

The 1972 season is another raging success with Bob McAdoo, the Greensboro native who transfers in from junior college. Why had I not heard of Bob McAdoo, who went to high school in my hometown? Did the local newspaper write much about a 6-foot-9 black guy from Smith High School? I can't be sure.

I do know I am somehow alone in the house for the Final Four semifinal against Florida State, a team we have never heard of. It is assumed this is a tune-up for another match against UCLA in the final, and this time we have a team worthy of taking down the Bruins.

My parents have gone to a Sunday School class party to watch the game and I'm not sure where my sisters are. This is unconscionable. Could it be that my father truly valued the ACC Tournament win over Maryland and the NCAAs are an afterthought?

Not to me. For the rest of the nation to appreciate Dean Smith as much as I do, he needs to win one of these. His program has so consumed my life to this point that it seems impossible he is only 41 years old. It feels like we've been trying to get past UCLA forever.

But first Florida State. They don't even play in a conference. And we all know the ACC is the best in the land. Right?

But wait. Bill Chamberlain, a key starter for UNC, shows up late for a pre-game dinner and therefore is benched to start the game. The Seminoles seize, and they are lightning quick. Some guy named Otto Petty, about my 10-year-old height, runs circles around us, pestering us on defense and creating layups at the other end.

We're 23 points behind midway through the second half. And I'm absorbing this alone. I act out the way I've seen my father do it, ranting aloud about heart, passion and commitment. At some point, I grab a towel from the bathroom and watch the game with it over my head, peeking at intervals. Thanks, Otto Petty.

Carolina rallies. It's starting to look good, but McAdoo fouls out. Still, it gets better. We're down five with 5 minutes to go but miss four chances to cut the lead further. Florida State wins by four.

Then when Daddy gets home, we get to relive it. Not just that night, but for many to come. The Tar Heels have let us down. That Florida State goes on to play UCLA close in the final—closer than any of its 10 championships during this run—does not help. It just means UCLA was vulnerable. Carolina should have won.

This was an unforced error. Puberty scores an easy lay-up as my teeth inch forward another two millimeters. Childhood needs a time out.

March 2, 1974
North Carolina 96, Duke 92 (OT)

The Tar Heels of 1973 and 1974 have a problem and it's no longer South Carolina. We took care of them last year, when they made the NCAA Tournament through the cowardly route of an independent, having left the ACC the year before. We beat them by 23 points in the first round, and South Carolina basically will not be heard from again.

A guy named David Thompson has signed to play for N.C. State, a recruitment that earns probation for two programs. Cue the howling from State and Duke fans at this point. It's a sore subject.

When Thompson was at Shelby's Crest High School, he was essentially an urban legend. No one had seen Crest play—they weren't even part of the state's high school athletic association. But the coaches from UNC, State and Duke sure had, and they were desperate to get Thompson. Duke apparently bought a sports coat for Thompson, the youngest of 11 children living in abject poverty, earning a year's probation for that benevolence. But they didn't even sign Thompson. N.C. State did. And that year, our state government based in Raleigh paved the road that led to Thompson's house.

Oh, how the allegations flew. But the *Raleigh Times* established the road had been scheduled for paving three years earlier, while an unaware Thompson was still playing blissfully on his dirt driveway. The actual cause of N.C. State's probation? According to the seminal *ACC Basketball: An Illustrated History,* an assistant coach played in an informal basketball game alongside five prospects. Two prospects were given financial aid to attend summer school and one had free housing in a dorm used by camp counselors. Additionally, three prospects were hired as counselors for Coach Norm Sloan's summer basketball camp.

For this, State got sacked for the 1973 NCAA Tournament, Thompson's sophomore year (he couldn't play as a freshman back then). The team went 27-0, outscored opponents by almost 22 points a game and could have seriously challenged UCLA, which was busy going undefeated in winning its seventh title in a row. Who knows what slice of greatness fans were robbed of by denying the post-season to Thompson, still the greatest player in ACC history.

The '74 team had been on its way to take on, and take down, UCLA after seven consecutive national championships, a breakthrough that college basketball, and especially ACC basketball, sorely needed. Such is the nature of UCLA's dominance that Tar Heel fans can't even work up a healthy hatred of N.C. State at this point—even though by this date we have lost to Thompson's 'Pack by 7, 3, 4, 1, 3, and 11 points. Just as Jewish people can speak of a time in their culture when they lived in the Promised Land of milk and honey, State fans can point to a time when they counted on winning any close game against Carolina. That happened.

The State rivalry will define our childhoods and it will take Duke longer than you may think to replace it. Because, rest assured, Duke was not our problem on March 2, 1974.

Yes, we beat Duke by two at the buzzer earlier that year in Cameron when Bobby Jones stole an inbounds pass at midcourt, glided in for a left-handed layup, and continued on to the locker room, as if he had to shower and dress quickly to make Bible Study. Which may have been the case with Bobby Jones.

No, Duke was on its way to a 2-10 last-place finish, and Carolina was at home and ranked fourth nationally. It's Senior Night, for goodness' sake. I allow myself the luxury of a play date with Peter Povich, where we shoot baskets in his back yard while the sport's "greatest rivalry" takes place in his living room.

Peter is about a foot shorter than I and wrestling is his top sport. Even at 70 pounds, I'm able to get to his basket at will. We tire of this inequity after a while and go inside to check on the game.

To my horror, Duke is beating Carolina without mercy.

Some forgotten Blue Devil scores to put Duke eight ahead in the closing seconds. Bobby Jones draws a shooting foul with 17 seconds to play.

Peter asks about going outside to play, presumably to grow more from height-challenged adversity. I say, no, Carolina fans stay until the end, a bit of rubbish belied by the fact that fans are already streaming out of Carmichael Auditorium.

Jones makes his free throws. Walter Davis steals the inbounds pass and feeds John Kuester for a lay-up. Timeout, Carolina. We're down 86-82.

"See, this is why you don't leave," I tell Peter. He's still laughing at Carolina for losing to Duke.

Duke throws away the inbounds pass again. Davis misses, but Jones puts in the rebound to cut it to two with six seconds left. Timeout, Carolina.

Duke University finally successfully completes an inbounds pass, and Carolina fouls.

Poor Pete Kramer. Here's the thing about being a Carolina fan in the Dean Smith era and, to a large part, even today. Pete Kramer may be a 58% foul shooter, but right now he has a zero point zero chance. Too much has already happened. The Carolina Mystique, or as detractors will call it, The Carolina Piss Factor, is fully engaged.

Even Peter Povich is intrigued. Kramer misses. Timeout, Carolina. For eons to come, announcers will point to this game to explain why Coach Smith and many others save their timeouts.

The next moment is one of the most iconic in Carolina history, yet it's almost anti-climactic. Davis gathers the inbounds pass, somehow alone, and dribbles to within 35 feet. He hoists a jumper that misses so badly that it banks off the glass and in. We have overtime, we have pandemonium and we have a new Carolina fan in Peter Povich.

Duke actually pulls ahead in overtime, as if the Blue Devils had not properly read the script. Because this one is ours. Carolina surges ahead for its most famous victory over a 10-15 team.

Peter and I play hoops in the back yard with renewed vigor, his size no longer a handicap. Anything is possible. And I come to believe some games Carolina is destined to win because we are Carolina. I'm not yet able to assess if this attitude is healthy, but it's working for me now.

4

JUMPING THE SHARK

January 18, 1975

N.C. State 88, North Carolina 85

I have been accepted at the University of North Carolina at Chapel Hill.

This will become a defining moment in my life, a root cause for much of what is to follow. This happens when I'm 12 years old, not because I am a genius but because my teeth are such a shipwreck that Carolina accepts my parents' petition that I become a "guinea pig" student for its renowned School of Dentistry.

That's right. Some wannabe orthodontist's final exam will be making me presentable in civilized society.[1] My parents will move heaven and earth for any of their three children, but paying for braces on the private

---

1   Forty years later at a social gathering in Raleigh I meet the supervisor of that orthodontist program. I remember him because I would look up from the chair and see his one eyebrow. I tell Dr. Hershey who I am and, after a career of supervising the care of thousands of young patients, he says "Oh I remember you." And it wasn't because of my good looks or snappy wit.

market is a real world practicality beyond love. UNC offers to clean me up for about $200, which even in 1973 is cheap.

While this is the break my childhood has been looking for, it comes at a cost. For my front teeth to return to the rest of my mouth's zip code, I will have to wear one of those outside retainers resembling the facemask of a 1960s quarterback. And by "wear one" I mean 24 hours a day. I have to sleep in the goddamned thing and, as a denouement to a perfectly awkward pre-teen era, wear it through eighth grade at Jamestown Junior High School.

The good news is I don't have much social standing to lose. I don't know what to do with this curly mop of hair. I am a good bit taller than most everyone, but skinnier than all. I don't eat like I should, not because of a childhood syndrome or because there wasn't food in the house. It's because, as my mother tells me, I'm "picky-unish."

This came to a head around the age of 8 as we left my grandmother's house in Polkville. We visited every Easter, Thanksgiving and Christmas, as Daddy would announce we were going "home," an expression Mama didn't like much having established what she thought was "home" with his three children in Jamestown. These visits would produce bounteous feasts of ham, potato salad, green beans, casseroles and unlimited banana pudding. We were expected to load up on leftovers for the 2½-hour ride back to Jamestown because they were delicious and because we were cheap.

Except I wouldn't do it. I didn't like leftovers. I preferred my meals freshly prepared, within the limited range of things I would eat. On this particular visit, either Thanksgiving or Christmas, Daddy said fine, I would just have to eat when I got back to Jamestown.

About a third of the way, though, I meekly pronounced from the back seat I was hungry, knowing at some level this was a mistake. But the belly growled and I had to acknowledge it. I was so skinny that Mama was hesitant to rebuff any desire I had to eat. Under duress, Daddy stopped at a greasy spoon diner and I left with a grilled cheese sandwich and a drink.

We started down the road and, in the backseat, I unwrapped my disputed treasure. And immediately shrieked in horror.

"It's got MAYONNAISE," I wailed.

My father was unmoved. Had this been a courtroom and he a lawyer, he would have moved to strike as unresponsive.

"I can't eat it!!"

Oh, but you can, Daddy said. You will. There was a little more back-and-forth than he wanted to tolerate. Tension mounted.

Tears began to flow. This sandwich was awash in mayonnaise, a living tribute to Duke's. Who the hell puts mayonnaise all over a grilled cheese sandwich?

My sisters were not helping. From their perch beside me on the back seat, this morsel resembled something a Michelin two-star restaurant would produce on the chef's most artistic day. As my eyes watered, so did their mouths.

"We can eat it," Judy volunteered.

This was out of order. Daddy pronounced that I and I alone would eat it. Every. Single. Bite.

I may as well have tried to eat the Pentagon Papers. I tried a bite, and it swelled inside my mouth. Chewing only served to strengthen it. Meanwhile, the sandwich itself seemed to regenerate like a lizard after losing its tail. I wasn't making progress.

Next to me, the two Tiger Sharks glared, perplexed and irritated that the tiny sharkling didn't know what to do with the wounded baby seal in his lap. "JUST EAT IT," they said without talking, knowing further verbalization would be rebuked and penalized.

I carefully meted out the drink so that well-planned swigs could temper the taste. Finally, the last bite went down, a big one that almost caused a career-ending wretch all over the back seat.

The rest of the ride home was silent.

I clung to skinny and awkward a few more years. By now, my neighborhood friends no longer want to play dodgeball or do wheelies on their bikes. They are into swimming, which I can't even do, and wearing tiny bathing suits, which I just can't.

They are getting invited to parties where they "see action" in spin-the-bottle games. I am not invited, causing a mixture of jealousy and relief. By now I most decidedly like girls but have no idea what I'd do if the bottle landed on me. The girls I have crushes on are laughed at for this by other girls. The girls who do talk to me escort me to the "Friends Zone," a designation that carries a persistent tag from which escape is almost impossible.

I don't have the right friends. Some of them are smoking marijuana. This frightens me to no end. Did they not pay attention to those filmstrips in school? I imagine them making like poor Art Linkletter's daughter, stoned zombies jumping off buildings thinking they will fly.

Everybody else seems to be growing up. But at least one person has noticed I'm maturing a little as well.

My father now recognizes me as enough of a Carolina fan to address his grievances, typically in the form of questions that have no answer.

"Why'd they do that?" Daddy may ask.

"Well, I don't think they meant to."

"They've decided to go into that Sorry Game Plan. Why are they in the Sorry Game Plan?"

"They're as disappointed about this as you are. Probably more so. You know, the other team has good players, too."

"If they were, then they'd stop with this Sorry Game Plan. Why can't they do like they did earlier?"

"Every team is going to have good streaks and bad. It could be the other team has adjusted."

"Yeah, but I'm not pulling for them."

And this would become the soundtrack to each Carolina game at our home. On some nights, the Tar Heels couldn't beat Ragsdale (Jamestown's high school, not particularly distinguished for its basketball). On others, he would thrust his hands in the air and shout in a very high pitch

"Nothin'!," indicating the amount of effort Carolina has brought to the battle. And on many others, he would assert that if he were coach, he would lead the team off the court and forfeit, rather than continue in such a state of sorriness.

The passion of an otherwise awkward time is becoming a chore. I watch the Tar Heels because that's who I am, but the price is getting steeper.

It comes to its first major turning point in January 1975. By now, the N.C. State thing has ceased to be funny. The Wolfpack won its national championship the year before, and good for them. The 'Pack tacks on another win against Carolina in the Big Four Tournament, an annual early-season event that serves no purpose other than to make money, over-expose the in-state rivalries and give Wake Forest a chance to win games it can't during the regular season.

That makes eight in a row for State over Carolina. Like *Happy Days* in the final seasons, the Thompson Era has lasted too long. Cancellation is past due. We need to return to the narrative where Carolina wins the games that matter most.

It's just Daddy and me in the house as we play on a Saturday afternoon in Raleigh. I'm having to debate him on whether Thompson is "that good," putting me in the untenable position of defending and hating him at the same time.

I need my mother in the house. It's not that she has any power to stop or correct him, but her presence seems to absorb some of it. She's an uncredited ally during these times, and reserves the right, when it gets really bad, to groan, harrumph or even tell him to slow down.

Mama is a sneaky good Carolina fan, often pretending not to notice but actually taking in every detail. During most games, especially those not involving Carolina, she's puttering in the kitchen. By "puttering," I mean cleaning house, organizing meals or, most often, canning, freezing or preserving vegetables from our garden so that we can eat better through the winter or, maybe more to the point, we can eat cheaply.

But it is not her role in life to challenge my father. When the game was on, any game, and she needed to walk into the den where the TV was, she would instead circle through the living room and approach the other way, so as to not interfere with his watching the game. During Carolina games she would sit, mostly quietly, in her chair until the Tar Heels did something wonderful, when she would giggle like a schoolgirl.

After the games, she absorbed the replay, courtesy of Daddy, and helped him wind down. I suspect I never even got the worst of it. Her very presence seemed to make things better, especially when the Tar Heels played.

I need some of that today, as this one promises to be tense. State is ranked fourth and UNC 14th, so we have the benefit of low expectations. Norm Sloan, the smugly paranoid State coach who enjoyed it a little too much during the championship run the year before when he claimed the media saw things through "pale blue eyes," is wearing the tackiest of sport jackets. His wife "sings" the national anthem. Was Kate Smith busy?[2]

We have a new crop of younger players, notably freshman phenom Phil Ford who has become Coach Smith's first starter as a freshman (they weren't allowed to play varsity until 1973). Everybody had recruited him and promised him the moon, but when Coach Smith went to Rocky Mount, N.C., he talked about academics and the possibility of Ford starting out on the junior varsity. The family loved him for it.

And now we love us some Phil Ford. We're up six, in Raleigh, against David Thompson, with just over a minute to play.

---

2   Kate Smith sang "God Bless America" before Game 6 of the 1974 NHL Finals, then the Philadelphia Flyers went out and clinched the Stanley Cup. From then on, she became a human good luck charm, singing this instead of the national anthem before big Flyer games. Later the Yankees adopted her rendition as part of their seventh-inning presentation. Then in 2019, she was canceled, in today's parlance, as it was discovered she sang songs in the 1930s with racist lyrics. She literally sang a song out loud called "That's Why Darkies Were Born." In 1974 she would have been a great get for any sporting event. Mrs. Sloan had a voice only a Wolfpack coach could love.

And we start missing free throws. Ford misses a huge one-and-one. Daddy claims he would make his free throws if he played, and on this count I believe him. He is practical beyond belief. If free throws were a matter of routine and common sense, he would make every one. Especially in times of need.

This no doubt stems from my father's ability to figure out how to do anything. He can wire or plumb a house. Lay brick. Build a house, craft cabinets, flash a roof. He can tear apart a car and put it back together. No odd job is one he can't do, and he uses this skill to support his church and his friends in need. Had he had an entrepreneurial bent, there is no telling what he could have earned. That's not how he chose to use his gifts.

Once he learned something, his confidence in his skill bordered on preternatural. He could split wood like nobody's business. He would have me, around age 11 or 12, hold the wedge on top of the block of wood to help get it started. Then he would take a full swing, all 250 pounds of might, onto that wedge.

He could hit it hard. I wasn't there the day he had started a wedge into a wood chunk when he drove it into a solid knot within the log. The wedge popped out so hard it hit his eye and knocked him on his back, giving him a grievous black eye. The witnesses who were there retold this with amazement.

So if I waver, we have a glancing blow, and we're replaying Abraham and Isaac. Or, more to the point, if he misses by more than an inch, his only begotten son is disfigured.

He never missed. He would have made his free throws.

But that temper! His youngest brother, Gene, loved to tell a story of growing up in the 1930s in Polkville. My father, the middle child of five boys, had the task of installing the head of the shower, which was outside the house. He did it not from following the instructions, but from common sense. He couldn't have been more than 16.

After he finished, he bent down to pick up his tools and when he stood up, he hit his head on the newly installed plumbing. That so enraged him that he took his hammer and smashed the shower head.

Then he calmly picked it up, put it back together and re-installed it, without so much as one complaint. And there you have the yin and yang of my father.

The missed free throws and turnovers down the stretch end predictably. State has won its ninth straight over Carolina.

And rage is roiling the Whisnant home. My father is ranting and pacing about the house. And he's joined by... me. I throw a mop in the kitchen. Daddy knocks around some chairs.

Are we bonding, or is something else happening here? I stop and begin to think about what I am becoming.

Time to reassess how to process Carolina basketball. Because just as Fonzie's absurd water-skiing theatrics signal that *Happy Days* has lasted too long, I, too, have jumped the shark.

February 25, 1975
North Carolina 76, N.C. State 74

We've lost to these bastards nine straight times over four seasons, long enough for me to grow into using words like "bastards."

Carmichael Auditorium is rocking. There was a time when every ACC team played in a pit of a home arena. Clemson, Virginia and Wake Forest were really hard places to win. N.C. State's Reynolds Coliseum, with its fake "noise meter," was terrifying.

And don't get me started on Cole Field House in Maryland. Lefty Driesell had migrated over from Davidson promising to build the "UCLA of the East," a reference to Maryland's paltry record of never finishing first in the ACC (the Terps' only tournament win coming when a fourth-place team won it in 1958), as well as to UCLA's dominance of college basketball that would reach seven consecutive NCAA titles and 10 in 12 years. It was somewhat akin to the new president of a third-world nation declaring he's going to build it into the Soviet Union.

Driesell also brought with him a most annoying tradition. Nothing was more dispiriting than falling hopelessly behind the Terps only to have the crowd sing the "Amen chorus" over and over, a Southern-style revival in the Yankee North fed by an offering of turnovers and missed shots. If ever life needed a fast-forward button, it was those closing moments of a Maryland loss. You were certain it would never end.

Duke had Cameron Indoor Stadium. It was one of many.

And Carolina had Carmichael, built as an addendum to the old Woolen Gym. The building had one side of bleacher-style student seating, which is what the TV cameras saw (not unlike Cameron) and plenty of antiquated, not good-for-viewing seats. When the pep band played, the noise had nowhere to go. It was deafening.

On this night, the band is not needed. During the starting line-up introductions, you can't hear the PA announcer say the names. Just higher pitches of hysteria as each player runs out to midcourt.

Before the game, Coach Smith reviews defensive assignments with his team when they hear a sound that hits them much the way the song of Whoville hit the Grinch. It's the deafening roar of the Carmichael crowd. "'Do you hear them?" Coach Smith asks his team. "They're ready. Are you?"

They are. At this point, strategy is not needed, anyway. We know State all too well. Just keep David Thompson somewhat connected to reasonable human output, and make sure the others stay in their lane. We can't lose to them again.

And Carolina plays brilliantly. The crowd is insane. We're ahead late when Phil Ford fouls out. Daddy starts bitching. I have resolved to stay positive. These guys are my guys and they are trying to keep it together, but, again, State is really good.

State, down two late, somehow gets the ball back and calls what becomes the longest timeout in history - because we know what's going to happen next. Thompson, or one of his minions, will score to force overtime, and then we have no shot. Because this is what N.C. State does.

Tim Stoddard gets a wide-open shot from the wing that he always makes. See, what did I tell you?

But it misses! Carolina finally wins. Daddy says it never should have come to this, establishing a pattern that continues for years to come. It's not the losses that trouble him the most, but the near-losses that cause unnecessary grief.

I have taped the final few minutes of Woody Durham's radio play-by-play on a cassette tape recorder back in my bedroom. The tape might be worth something today, except it also contains several of my best farts. I am still 13 years old.

March 6, 1975
North Carolina 101, Wake Forest 100 (OT)
ACC Tournament First Round

Before the State win, we were 6-4 in the league and threatening an introduction to mediocrity, or to "How the Others Have to Live." After beating State, we win at Duke, now in the throes of finishing last four consecutive years.

We wind up in a three-way tie for second behind a powerful Maryland team ("Ayyy-A-men, Amen, Amen"). A drawing goes Carolina's way—it's great to be a Tar Heel—and we draw the second seed, earning us the right to play last-place Wake Forest, 2-10 in the ACC after winning the silly Big Four tournament (and handing State its first loss to an ACC team in three years).

By contrast, State winds up in fourth place and has to play an improving Virginia team, followed by the first-place Terrapins.

Wake Forest. That's hilarious. I tuck a transistor radio into my coat pocket at school and run an earplug through the sleeve. There's nothing my eighth-grade math teacher has to say regarding what "x" may or may not be equal to that supersedes this.

So I get a real time account of Woody Durham saying "that should about do it" when a Wake player scores to put the Deacons ahead 90-82 with 50 seconds to play.

Carolina scores, steals the ball, and scores. They're doing a store label version of the Duke comeback a year ago. Now we're down four with 34 seconds left.

Wake runs a clever inbounds play. Jerry Schellenberg, a long-time Carolina thorn, throws it the length of the court to Skip Brown, who is immediately fouled. He's an 80-percent free throw shooter and Wake's best player. Hello, NIT.

But wait. The entire Carolina bench has stood up to point out something odd about this pass. Referee Fred Hikel agrees.

The ball has nicked the scoreboard hanging over the court. For the next 60 years or so, fans and media (hint: Billy Packer) sitting high in Greensboro Coliseum will say the ball came nowhere close to the scoreboard. Skip Brown claims after the game that he never would have caught the pass, which came directly to him, if it had hit the scoreboard.

Let's appeal this up to Coach Smith. His ruling on the call: "No one could make that one up."

That should settle it. The ref saw what he saw. Our ball. We score to cut it to two and foul Brown for real, this time with 11 seconds left. Now he can make the whole scoreboard thing moot, something to tell his grandchildren as he regales beating Carolina in the ACC Tournament.

Did I say 80-percent shooter? Did I also say that when things start happening for Carolina, none of this matters? Brown misses. Wake misses nine of 10 free throws down the stretch. Brad Hoffman scores at the buzzer for UNC, and we have overtime.

I'm on my way to the school bus and suddenly erupt. We're going to overtime against last-place Wake Forest! My spin-the-bottling, dope-smoking peers wonder what in the world has gotten into the gawky guy who wears a helmet to school.

Another suspicious call—a technical foul against Wake Forest for not "forcing the action" in a tie game as Carolina dribbles in Four Corners —puts Carolina ahead and Ford makes a bunch of free throws down the stretch. We live to fight another day.

March 7, 1975
North Carolina 76, Clemson 71 (OT)
ACC Tournament Semifinal

Our extra day of life is being squandered. An unusually strong Clemson team has the ball with the score tied. The shot misses but rebounds to 7-foot-1 Wayne "Tree" Rollins. He puts up a simple hook shot from about 3 feet at the buzzer. It is Carolina's death warrant.

And it rims out. Rollins hurls himself to the floor and lies prone, arms extended, as apt an analogy of Clemson basketball as has ever been given. Ford executes Four Corners and makes free throws, so many free throws, in overtime.

But in the other semifinal, N.C. State blows a big lead to Maryland, then scores at the buzzer as the final jab in one of the great rivalries of the '70s. The joke was always on Maryland. Amen, Terps.

All our miraculous death-defying work has led us back to N.C. State, where they will surely kill us after beating them the week before and move on to the national championship. This is a crossroads game. Is it true that sometimes we win because we're Carolina? We'll find out soon enough.

March 8, 1975
North Carolina 70, N.C. State 66
ACC Tournament Final

It's hard to overstate what this means to the program and its fans. To the outsider, Carolina could seem like a five-year phenomenon—driven by a really good recruiting class or two from 1967-69, then the wonder that was Bob McAdoo in 1972. But for three years we seem to have fallen behind N.C. State and Maryland.

Coach Smith is even losing some recruiting battles. We're looking at you, Tom McMillan. The top high school senior in the nation, McMillan became the subject of an intense recruiting battle between Carolina and Coach Smith and Maryland and Coach Driesell. He basically committed to Carolina, but his mother just couldn't bring herself to like Dean Smith, an odd position for any thinking member of the human race. At the end, McMillan de-committed and went to Maryland, giving Coach Driesell payback for a recruitment of Charlie Scott that he thought he had won while still at Davidson. As with Scott, McMillan turned out to be really good.

Suddenly it makes sense to ask, "Is Carolina here to stay?"

Yes. Yes we are. This ACC Tournament run seals it for life. We play even and a little ahead of State, which is hanging tough even as Thompson struggles with cramps. When State bursts to a three-point lead with about 10 minutes to go, it feels insurmountable. But Carolina scores the next 11.

Then it's Four Corners and Phil Ford. State cuts it to two with just under a minute left, but Ford scores once on a driving lay-up and feeds Mitch Kupchak for another lay-up. The image of Ford wearing the net around his neck after the game is indelible.

Everything we want to believe about Coach Smith and the inevitability of Carolina basketball is true. This is my school. They are fixing my wretched teeth. Even my father is proud, as we lapse into early iterations of our Dean Smith imitation. Daddy gives him a prissy affect, likely a riff from Coach Smith's bland and deferentially humble stance on the weekly *Dean Smith Show,* which we catch at noon each Sunday if we can shut down the post-church conversations efficiently. Judy comes home, not quite as committed to the cause as little brother but having had enough sense to watch it wherever she was. We re-live it, over and over.

We have beaten State twice in a row, the second time when it really, really matters. This is the first year the NCAA allows two teams from a conference to its tournament, but Maryland, the regular-season winner, gets the other bid alongside ACC Champion North Carolina. N.C. State is done. The Wolfpack turn down a bid to play in the NIT, calling it a "loser tournament."

David Thompson will never play in college again. He cannot hurt me anymore.

And I have thrown my last mop. I cannot, will not, be that fan again. Even if it places me at odds with my father.

5
ONE FOR THE ZEBRAS

March 6, 1976

Virginia 67, North Carolina 62

ACC Tournament Final

The break that changes everything comes courtesy of the alphabet.

Assigned to ninth-grade homeroom by last name, my "Whisnant" sits just in front of David Willard. I actually knew him from kindergarten, but he went to the traditional Jamestown Elementary while I went to upstart Millis Road. Jamestown people actually talked this way.

He's a jock but not a meathead, so he understands the language, my only language, of games, games, games. I am not an athlete, as I am too skinny to think about school teams. Well, maybe I'm too lazy and timid. The only time I so much as threaten organized sports comes when Coach Hankins, Ragsdale's basketball coach, notices I stand about 6-foot-4. He can barely see me when I turn sideways but figures he can find a way to add muscle. He invites me to his summer basketball camp and I give it a try.

Hankins, a 6-foot-7 Vietnam vet with a Marine's sensibility, a wisdom for how to live in the world and a marked deck of playing cards, is a good guy doing the right thing. He throws me a medicine ball and dares me to throw it back so hard he can't catch it. I can't. I can't finish the drills. The athletic regulars roar past me. And I'm too embarrassed to return the next day, or any day.

Dave accepts me for what I am. His weakest sport is basketball, which is my best, honed from hours of shooting alone on the goal on a pole my father installed in the back yard, imagining winning Carolina games at the buzzer. This means I can compete against him and alongside him in off-season pickup games.

He's First Family of Jamestown, so to speak, well known throughout town as part of outstanding upbringing. Patsy, his mama, keeps Dr. Fortney's general practice together as office manager. The doctor is a common denominator that ties us tighter as the Whisnants go way back with him. He is not merely our family's doctor. He cared for my grandmother Scott in her final years, before I was born, holding his head in his hands and weeping when she died.

He taught my parents' Sunday School class. My father built the cabinets in his office, and Dr. Fortney correctly diagnosed his massive heart attack in 1971, a life-defining event.

When it happened, Daddy had been playing in the annual church youth vs. Methodist Men basketball game at Jamestown Elementary School, a sweatbox of a gym that smelled of dust, urine and bleach. Most of its windows were either broken or stuck, so illegal entry to play some hoops was never a problem.

On this night, Daddy was a 47-year-old power forward, a rock at a rotund 250 pounds. When he set a screen, the kids knew better than to try to go through Mr. Whisnant, the man they knew as the jovial catbird who made people laugh and the church elder who seemed to know how to do everything. He dabbled some in formal basketball as a child, playing on some school teams, but had long ago drifted out of shape even by the standards of this game. But he hit a few set shots and was oddly effective. As my sister, Linda, and I sat on those hard bleachers, my 9-year-old self was proud of the old man.

After it was over—I think the old men won—Linda and I walked with him back to the car. Before we climbed in, Daddy started having trouble breathing and claimed he had indigestion. He asked Linda, then 17, to drive us home.

Had I been older, I would have recognized this as the red flag it was. My father never let anyone else drive. He loved driving and he loved cars, perhaps the one indulgence he allowed in life. As a younger man, he would pay in cash for new cars, usually Mercurys, as soon as they came out. He knew how many horses each had and could identify them on the road at a glance, really up until he died.

He would drive them fast. He would tell the story, without judgment or shame, of placing 1-year-old Linda on the front seat (Seatbelt? Car seat? No, this was 1954), finding a flat spot of South Carolina highway and driving 110 miles an hour. The only reason he didn't go 120 was because the car wouldn't. And Linda would sleep without stirring the whole ride.

He likely gave up this hobby because it got too expensive with subsequent children (aka "me"). Instead of the newest model of his beloved Mercury, just like David Pearson drove on the NASCAR circuit, he got a lanky buck-toothed son with unruly hair and no idea how to "pop the hood."

Anyway, Linda drove us home. Mama immediately sized up Daddy and did what people in Jamestown did in 1971. She called Dr. Fortney.

"Nancy, it sounds like he's having a heart attack." He told her to call 911.

Dr. Fortney beat the ambulance to our house. Much later in life I would learn that the Guilford County EMS was well ahead of its time and that skilled and expedited response likely saved my father's life. Still, Dr. Fortney was there first.

I tended to brush the entire thing off. My father was stronger than time or nature. Of course he would get better. He came home after a couple of weeks, ate better, sat in his chair and took up birding. He told us about cardinals, blue jays (aggressive!), doves and robins. He saw five yellow tanagers in one day, apparently a birding milestone. He told us more about birding than we wanted to know.

By that November, six months later, he was back at work, doing odd jobs that paid and favors for friends and church that did not. And carping about Carolina basketball. We knew we had Dr. Fortney to thank for this.

So Patsy Willard, the glue of Dr. Fortney's office and almost as well-known as the doctor himself, already holds a special place in our esteem. Dave's father brings his own cachet, a community pillar known for expertise on small engines, coaching Little League baseball and Protestant work ethic. And the Willards love the Tar Heels.

One quirk remains, as always in a typical Southern family. Dave's older brother by two years, Lee, is about 350 pounds, dismissive of sports, a star in community theater and... quite obviously gay. This is not discussed.

Nonetheless, Lee doesn't exactly hide it. Dave gives him the nickname "Peedee," referring to a forgotten comic strip character, and I decide it doesn't encompass the true magnitude of his girth. For the rest of his life, I will greet him with a thunderous "Peeeee-hee-hee-hee-hee-hee-hee-hee-heed," prompting him to perform the theatrical bow of a Broadway diva. He loves me for this.

Do we snark a little about his lifestyle behind his back? Well, yes. We're not quite yet where we need to be on this issue. But I'm way ahead of the game here because Peedee is not my first encounter with homosexuality.

That belongs to Billy. A close friend of my older sister, he has come to embody what "gay" means to us. The message is less about sexuality and more about, well, unconditional love.

Billy was buddies with Sandy and they were quite a pair in the late 1960s. Sandy wore men's clothes and leather jackets with fringes. Loud and husky, she had ravenous appetites for men, food and, I discovered later, smoking pot. And laughing. So hard that she had to bang her fists and stomp her feet to try to express it all.

The two of them befriended my sister, Linda, also wrestling with awkward teen years. She didn't smoke pot, she was straight and she was square. But Sandy and Billy loved her spirit, and she loved them back. They found acceptance in each other and knew better than to quibble about differences.

The concept of Sandy and Billy brought parents to a crossroads. They were freaks by 1969 standards. Art Sullivan, our neighbor and assistant principal at Ragsdale whose daughter was roughly the same age, took a conventional route and forbade Sandy from visiting.

My father read the same New Testament and came to a different conclusion. He no doubt held the common views about authority, drugs and homosexuality as his generational peers, but when he saw Sandy and Billy, he didn't see counterculture war-hating hippies and queers. He saw Sandy and Billy. They were friends of his daughter, so they were friends of his.

When they came over, Daddy talked to them. He didn't put on airs, he just was. They thought his stories were hilarious, though I didn't fully understand until later exactly *why* they found them so funny. My mother made over them. They teased Linda about her middle name, calling her "Linda Jane," and soon came to refer to my parents and "Daddy Jane" and "Mama Jane."

One evening I was in my bedroom, listening to them laugh and carry on in the family room. My mother was making a homemade coconut cake—the kind where you start with the Whisnant Family Nail Set that pierces the actual coconut. Sandy and Billy were hanging around for it to come out of the oven. Of course they were.

My mother brought the cake to the table to be cut, but then stumbled. The cake, still with wisps of smoky heat rising, was face down in the floor. Mama went to get the broom and trash can—she would have made another—and I walked down the hall to see what had caused the commotion.

And there were Daddy, Sandy, Billy and Linda, on their hands and knees, eating cake off the floor. A stoned hippie, a gay friend, a straight girl and a loving father, eating together without pretense. With a horrified mother trying vainly to get them to stop.

So Pee-Heed isn't a surprise to me. The Willards and their deeper connection to Jamestown give me somewhere to fit in. Dave and I, with generous help from his father, mow and rake yards for money and play hoops with his friends, now my friends.

We join forces on a Junior League basketball team, for him a diversion between football and baseball and for me about as far as I'm going athletically. We're way better than the other teams, so much so that when Dave makes a farce of one game by pretending to "dunk" (and barely pinning the ball on the bottom of the backboard), the league officials threaten to shut down the league.

Meanwhile, Carolina in 1976 has one of the best teams in its history. No one remembers this, for a soon-to-be-obvious reason. The Tar Heels are 24-2, ranked fourth, and looking like a top threat to undefeated Indiana nationally as they approach the ACC Tournament.

The Celtics are also undefeated in the Jamestown Junior League as we approach that tournament. Maybe this is the year I taste personal and Tar Heel championship glory.

When suddenly I can't eat anymore. I have a fever, chills and am so, so very tired. Dr. Fortney says it's mononucleosis. Someone calls it the "kissing disease," which is cruel because anyone could tell at this point I haven't kissed anybody.

Standing at 6-foot-4, 144 pounds, I proceed to lose 16 precious pounds in nine days. I miss a week of school. The only benefit is that I get to stay home to watch the first round of the ACC Tournament, this year in Landover, MD., rather than in Greensboro, as God intended. Lefty Driesell, the Maryland coach, has claimed the tournament is unwinnable when played in North Carolina, and the league has taken him up on his dare.

This brings us to Virginia. In the jungle that is the Atlantic Coast Conference, Virginia is the zebra, fearfully hiding from historical predators such as lions (Carolina), tigers (N.C. State), jackals (Duke) and, lately, cheetahs (Maryland) until one of them gets hungry enough and chases an easy meal. Virginia's main goal is not to outrun all of these, but to outrun fellow zebra Clemson, which they usually do. But their grisly death is inevitable.

This year doesn't appear to be different. The Cavaliers finish 4-8 in the league, good for next-to-last place. Having said that, looking back at the scores, you can't help but notice that six of Virginia's eight losses are to the top three teams: UNC, N.C. State and Maryland, and four of those are by three points or less. So maybe Virginia had some reason for optimism.

Eating chocolate-covered graham cookies, the only thing that will go down, I laugh along as the Cavaliers beat 17th-ranked N.C. State fairly badly, their first win over the 'Pack in four years. Then Maryland, ranked 9th, drowns in its own hubris against Virginia in the semifinal, proving the Terps can lose ACC Tournaments anywhere. The Cavs' Wally Walker, overlooked for the all-ACC team, is playing out of his mind.

The zebras are rebelling against jungle law. It's Virginia's first trip to the ACC Final since... ever. Even Clemson had played in one by then.

Their opponent will be the now 25-2 Tar Heels. And they will play the same night as the Celtics, who, without their 130-pound center, have uncharacteristically struggled to reach their final.

Carlos Lopez, our good friend just one year older who coaches us, comes to the house to beg my mama to let me play. I beg. Dave begs. I can't let Dave and the guys down. My health is turning a corner (no evidence of this). I'm not contagious (ha!).

Mama wilts just enough. I'm allowed to dress out and see if I am needed. Which I am. The Toros are on fire. Ricky Morris, who we uncharitably refer to as Rigor Mortis, plays out of his mind. We fall behind 12 points.

Carlos gives me the signal. I pull off my warmup and make like Willis Reed versus the Lakers.[1] The ball finds me, I fire... and miss the entire goal by a good two feet.

However, I do hit a shot or two, Dave and our mates shut down the raging Toros and we climb to within two with the ball. During a timeout, Carlos tries to run a play for me, but I demur. I'm exhausted. Dave gets off a good look, which misses in my direction, but I can no more hunt that rebound than do a back flip.

My body has betrayed me. We lose by two.

Daddy takes me home and we have enough time to watch the second half of Carolina's stalking of Virginia, only to discover Virginia is ahead. I watch the 12-inch black and white in my bedroom, partly because I feel like crap and mostly because Daddy is raising holy hell in the front room.

Wally Walker is too much and Virginia wins. I go to bed trying to process this, our own team's loss and still having mono that will knock me out of school the next Monday and Tuesday. It's a lot.

Carolina gets an "at large" bid to the NCAAs and is sent to the Mideast Regional to play Alabama as a precursor to a second-round match with Indiana that should have been a national title game.

Tell that to Alabama. The Crimson Tide hammers a listless Carolina. Mention the name "Leon Douglas" to a Carolina fan of a certain age and wait for the involuntary shudder. A third-team All-American, he guards Mitch Kupchak, our second-team All-American and ACC Player of the Year.

The boxscore shows Kupchak: 3-for-11, 8 points, 12 rebounds. Douglas: 16-for-23, 35 points, 17 rebounds. It looked that bad in real

---

1   Reed, a Hall of Fame center and the Knicks emotional leader, tore a thigh muscle in Game 5 of the 1970 finals and was ruled out. But for Game 7 in Madison Square Garden, he emerged from the tunnel in uniform, to thunderous approval from the crowd. He started and made two jump shots, then mostly watched as the Knicks pounded LA for the title.

time, too. This is also the game after Phil Ford, another second-team All-American, decided to play pick-up basketball back home in Rocky Mount the week before and hurt his knee. He scored two points versus Alabama.

A 25-3 season peters out to a dreary end. I'm starting to believe I can't have nice things.

6

FIRST LOVE

February 9, 1977

North Carolina 97, Maryland 70

Every three weeks or so, one of my parents has to take off work to drive me to the UNC School of Dentistry, first to pull innocent back-row teeth so my front teeth have room to rejoin the remaining ones, then to monitor the retainer, the braces and the rest of the tools of shame. The mouth is making progress but it's still a long way from knowing how to talk to girls.

We are regulars in Chapel Hill. The conversations during the one-hour drive from Jamestown help me understand my parents as people for perhaps the first time. Today when my friends gripe about having to shuttle young children like some sort of indentured Uber, I warn them how they'll miss this when their kids get their driver's licenses. Because inside the car is a gift that is priceless: They will actually talk to you. Or at least you can pick up their conversations with each other.

Daddy and I drive around campus and marvel at the industry the students seem to possess as they move about.

"When you're a student here, you can just walk across campus to your appointments," he says. We laugh. I mean, I know my teeth are moving slow, but 10 years as an orthodontic test patient?

We listen to WCHL, the local Chapel Hill radio station, and always seem to hit the Marty Robbins classic *El Paso* ("Out in the West Texas town of El Paso, I fell in love with a Mexican girl ..."). At one point in the song, the hero goes to fetch a ride where the horses are tied and manages to hold the "tied" note about 22 seconds.

"Those horses are really tied tight," Daddy says, and that kills every time.

My father is a music lover, though very few know about it. He sings Nat King Cole or Conway Twitty songs on rare occasions when he slows enough to work jigsaw puzzles at home. Sometimes he'll start the hymn *It Is Well With My Soul,* which sparks an impromptu duet with my mother in the quiet of the car. But he doesn't talk much about music, other than to offer his infamous review of Laura T., his older first cousin and a fiddler from way back whose middle initial concealed a name no one knew.

"She could play *Cat Shit and Honey* so plain you had to raise the windows to let the stench out," he would say.

For that matter, he rarely says much of anything about his past. Although he was a veteran of World War II who saw active duty, he didn't discuss it. Until the day we visited the *USS North Carolina*, docked at the Cape Fear River in coastal Wilmington, N.C., in the early 1970s. This was on a sweltering summer day during a beach trip he paid for by doing handy work for someone who owned a crummy cottage nearby. He practically led a tour of the battleship, unable to be pried from the cabins below deck where it was a good 20 degrees hotter, until he had described every nook of the ship and its purpose.

He also witnessed the worst of the Depression and had precious little to say about this as well. We barely scraped together details such as his family having survived two house fires and clothes often coming from neighbors or church people. At one point, he and his older brother shared "the one pair of good shoes," as he called them.

He did tell one story from when he was around age 10. He walked to Stamey's general store in his hometown of Polkville and witnessed a one-legged black child begging the store owner for something to eat. The owner would have none of it, shooing the child away as if he were a dog. Daddy told us if he had only had a dime, nickel or anything to eat, he

would have given it to this child. But he didn't. He cried when he told it, and it probably did more to inform his social views than anything Jim Crow could muster.

He was more comfortable with the story about how he and my mother started dating. The Scotts lived in the parsonage the Methodist church across the street provided for its pastor, my grandfather. He lived there with Bertha, a schoolteacher before she gave birth to six children, the youngest my mother. Next to them lived an alcoholic whose wife held things together working in the fields, taking in sewing

Bob Whisnant, U.S. Navy. He would look at photos of his wry smile and say, "Looks like I caught a whiff of something."

and being the rock for five boys finding their way.

They could not have been more different, but the Scotts learned not to underestimate their neighbors, especially Lucille Whisnant.

One day the Whisnant family cow got loose and wandered into the Scotts' yard. Rev. Scott retrieved the cow and returned it next door, not leaving until he lectured Lucille on her carelessness with her livestock. She would have to do better.

Within a few days, the Scott cow got loose in the Whisnant yard. My grandfather Scott looked into his backyard and was humbled to see Lucille quietly walking the cow back to the barn without saying a word.

My chastened grandfather had enough self-awareness to recognize Christian grace when he saw it. He preached on this anecdote the following Sunday and used it many times over the rest of his career.

The families came to appreciate each other in their own way and grew very close. The Scotts were especially fond of the third Whisnant son, the one with a work ethic and a sense of humor. Bob would drive the preacher around Cleveland County to visit his flock, at home and in the hospital. They were fast friends.

Mama was 11 when Bob went off to war and 15 when she began to notice the lanky red-headed neighbor boy who had come home. In return, he noticed the neighbor girl was growing up. Our Daddy would go next door to "borrow" a cup of sugar, then return it an hour later—both times to get a glimpse of young Nancy. For her 15th birthday, he brought her a cake from a bakery.

One day Bob was loading hay onto the back of a truck, and young Nancy kept throwing the hay back at him.

"If you do that again, I'm going to kiss you," he told her.

"Well, what happened next?" I asked.

"She threw it all over me."

This was an unusually bold move by Nancy Whisnant, regardless of age. Our mother was meek to a fault, but kind and possessing a sneaky sense of humor. My father could not have known the jackpot he hit when the girl next door threw hay all over him.

The Scott family passed for royalty in Polkville but started from the humblest of roots. William Scott, my grandfather, grew up the youngest of 10 children raised by his widowed mother, Emeline, who fed the family by selling herbs she gathered on their Ashe County mountain and fishing in the New River.

When Bill became the first student to enroll at Appalachian State University, she sent him

Nancy Scott

off to school with a quarter. When he graduated, he walked his diploma over to his mother and said, "This belongs to you." Years later, she died in her tracks on the mountain, wearing the only dress she owned clasped together at a buttonhole with a small nail.

Bill became a school principal, then a minister. He and Bertha raised six children in the same tradition of humble dignity as his mother. On the rare occasions they had a chicken to fry, Bertha took the neckbone, claiming it was the best and let the children have the rest.

The children seemed destined for greatness—the first female to be named North Carolina's Principal of the Year, a nuclear engineer, a writer, a lawyer, and a Christian educator. This family from modest beginnings had no shortage of self-esteem.

Except for my Mama. Nancy was the baby of the family and was treated and adored as such. At the age of 3, she ran into the street and was hit by a car. Mama's older brother, Bill Jr., then 14, drove her to the hospital. She survived a coma lasting two weeks.

She had to re-learn how to talk, walk, just about everything. In her mind, and in her mind only, she fell hopelessly behind her more accomplished siblings.

My parents as a dashing young couple, now that my mother is old enough to date.

She and my father courted after the hay incident, staying together even when Nancy went to college because her parents so valued it. But she dropped out at age 20, unable to put off marrying Bob Whisnant any longer. Then the children came and she made up for her perceived shortcomings with a very real work ethic and a sweetness profound enough to dwarf even the prolific accomplishments of her siblings.

I ponder this as we cruise Interstate 85, somewhere between Haw River and Mebane. How could a 22-year-old so openly court the 15-year-old preacher's daughter? If that happened today, it would prompt a scandal. But this was rural Cleveland County in 1946. Mama's parents approved. And it lasted 45 years.

These nuggets make the Chapel Hill trips special. We talk about Carolina basketball, but not about watching it, which is better left unsaid. By now, I have adopted a trick when it comes to watching the Tar Heels. My friends are turning 16, so it's no trouble to get rides and watch at their homes, which usually means the Willard house. If this bothers my parents, they never complain.

So I'm at Dave's house the night Carolina destroys a good Maryland team by 27 points. Coach Smith will later write it's one of the best games a team of his ever played. Carolina looks like a favorite to win the national championship.

At the next practice, senior center Tommy LaGarde, likely on his way to an All-American selection, injures his knee and never plays in college again. From here, the center position belongs to three freshmen: the eternally goofy Rich Yonakor, the wooden Steve Krafcisin and equally immobile Jeff Wolf.

But the Tar Heels keep winning. Ten in a row and 24-4 heading into the ACC Tournament final against—wait, is this a joke?

March 5, 1977
North Carolina 75, Virginia 69
ACC Tournament Final

Virginia is straining credulity. Now without Wally Walker, they finish 2-10 in the league. Carolina clubs them by 24, and Duke beats them twice for the Blue Devils' only two ACC wins. The league's only team with a losing record, the Cavaliers have reached the ACC final again, beating a Wake Forest team that finishes in the Top 10 and a ranked Clemson team.

They again draw the Tar Heels, this time the day after Walter Davis breaks his finger. He plays but he's severely limited. It's looking grim again when Phil Ford fouls out with 5:45 left and Virginia ahead by three.

John Kuester, the other Tar Heel guard, takes over the offense, along with a wondrous freshman named Mike O'Koren who looks like he was born to play on a Dean Smith team.

The Tar Heels inch ahead, go to Four Corners and prevail behind Kuester's clutch free throws. Something about this team. The most unlikely guys keep stepping up. We're far from the best team heading into the NCAA tournament in this condition, but you just gotta love 'em.

March 17, 1977
North Carolina 79, Notre Dame 77
NCAA Tournament Sweet 16

The first game is a near-debacle against Purdue. Davis has surgery on his finger and doesn't play. The Tar Heels trail at halftime. Only Ford's 27 points and a questionable traveling call on Purdue saves Carolina.

Now they play the Irish, ranked 10th, on St. Patrick's Day. This seems to matter to Notre Dame, as the Irish take a 14-point lead in the second half. Davis is bricking his way through a 4-for-12, and a Notre Dame freshman is eating Ford up alive.

Then Carolina becomes Carolina, forcing turnovers, hitting shots, and Ford awakens. With a minute to go in a tie game, he hyperextends his elbow on his shooting arm during a scrum in the lane. Still he hits two free throws to put Carolina ahead, but Notre Dame ties it. Carolina winds down the clock, Ford gets fouled with two seconds left, and by now we know what's next. Swish and swish. The Tar Heels live to fight another day.

March 19, 1977

North Carolina 79, Kentucky 72

NCAA Tournament East Regional Final

Third-ranked Kentucky, fearsomely big and strong, is the Tar Heels reward in the regional final. Ford's injury and second-half foul trouble render him practically useless (two points, 15 minutes). Davis is coming around, but still hobbled. Tommy LaGarde is in street clothes.

The Tar Heels somehow pull off a 53-41 halftime lead, but as Kentucky quickly surges, it's back to Four Corners the final 15 minutes, an absurd length of time. With Ford on the bench icing his elbow.

All the lumbering Wildcats can do is foul. Kuester makes 13 of 14. Krafcisin, the nobody freshman who transfers the following year, is sent to the line for a one-and-one with Carolina's lead down to one and less than a half minute left. He makes both, part of an 8-for-8 at the line for a 63% foul shooter. Carolina finishes 33 of 36 from the foul line and hangs on to reach the Final Four.

We're pulling games out of our ass. This is beyond the Piss Factor. This is destiny.

March 26, 1977

North Carolina 84, UNLV 83

NCAA Tournament Final Four

Watching the first half of this game with a group at Dave's house, we wonder how Carolina could ever have been expected to keep up with the Running Rebels. At 28-2, they can run, shoot, rebound and defend like crazy. They average 107 points a game—still a record - and this is before the three-pointer and the shot clock. Their opponents *average* 26 turnovers a game. Carolina is on its way to turning it over 27 times in this one.

Ford and Davis are healthier, but still not 100%. We're behind just six at the half, an act of mercy in and of itself, when our group decides to shoot some hoops in Dave's driveway during halftime.

Pee-Heed brings us the news. The second half has started, and the lead has grown to 10. Uh oh. Then another update: Carolina is rallying. Well now we can't go back inside. We have to keep doing what we're doing for fear of breaking the spell.

I can no longer stand it. Concluding I can help the Tar Heels more in the Willards' living room, I return just in time to see Carolina go into Four Corners with about 15 minutes left. Billy Packer is criticizing this move as a momentum killer, but he barely finishes his thought before Ford, now rejuvenated, splits the Vegas defense for a lay-up.

This may be one of Coach Smith's finest moments. A zone defense and the Four Corners slow Vegas down. Vegas fires off 80 shots, but Carolina takes 56 better ones, hitting 70 percent in the second half. Walter Davis and his broken finger go 7-for-7 and Mike O'Koren achieves cult hero status with 31 points.

The opponent in the final is one we think we can beat. It's "just" Marquette, losers of seven games during the year but winners of a wacky 51-49 semifinal over UNC Charlotte, ending that school's 15 minutes of college basketball fame.

March 28, 1977
Marquette 67, North Carolina 59
NCAA Tournament Final

Maybe we undersell Marquette. The Warriors (their 1977 nickname, later repurposed to "Golden Eagles" to meet modern criteria) are ranked No. 2 at the end of the 1976 season and are preseason No. 2 for this season. They have a second-team All-American (Butch Lee) and third-team (Bo Ellis). They are ranked seventh going into this tournament, just two spots behind North Carolina.

Why everyone thinks this is the breather Carolina has been waiting for is, in retrospect, a mystery. All we know is we never see Marquette on TV and their coach, Al McGuire, is retiring after the season at a young age. As if that matters.

It apparently does to the Marquette players. I decide to usher in the long-awaited championship at the Willard home and we're all slack-jawed as Marquette is tougher, meaner and just better while taking a 12-point halftime lead. Butch Lee is embarrassing Phil Ford. It's hard to watch.

But... this is Carolina, right? The Tar Heels rally behind O'Koren, even briefly taking the lead. When Marquette ties it, Coach Smith calls for Four Corners with more than 12 minutes left. This time the national media will howl in hindsight, blaming this move for killing the Tar Heels' momentum—the most persistent criticism Coach Smith will ever face.

Four Corners starts while O'Koren is at the scorer's table, waiting to return to the game at the next dead ball. In his place is Bruce Buckley, a thorn to Carolina fans throughout the year.

Buckley's senior season has gone so badly - clumsy missed shots, turnovers, defensive lapses - that Carolina fans boo him. They call him "The Blade," in deference to his prominent schnoz, and in the Willard living room, as well as thousands of others, he is mocked by his own fan base. Coach Smith has to take up for him during his weekly basketball show.

"If you're not a fan of Bruce Buckley, then you're not a fan of Carolina basketball," he says.

I'm a 15-year-old high school sophomore now and fairly certain I can parse the difference. Buckley is toxic. Carolina holds the ball and Marquette is content to let us stall, unlike Vegas two days ago which pressured the Four Corners and wound up watching an O'Koren layup drill.

Coach Smith could call time out and sub in O'Koren, at this point the team's best player. But would he do that to Buckley, a senior who had given him and the program four years? No, he would not. Buckley remains.

Carolina is waiting for an open layup. Buckley gets the ball down low and somehow believes he sees one. He glides in to put up a shot from the left side, and Bo Ellis slaps it off the backboard.

Marquette recovers, takes the lead and the game slips away.

Pee-Heed drives me home, using a route only he would use while managing to coax the sturdy light blue LTD to 80 mph. He's not mad or animated, but this is just Pee-Heed expressing himself. He lives large.

We discuss how this is the first game we should have won throughout this entire run. Any doubt on this point is amplified to an exponential power by my father. His assessment is that Carolina didn't try. Instead of processing grief, I have to defend the Tar Heels the rest of the evening.

The next day the strangest thing happens at school. One of our black classmates who I find particularly angry and intimidating is holding up that day's paper, walking the halls shouting "Carolina gets stuck by eight. Read all about it!"

I notice a fair number of black students seem to enjoy Carolina losing. What's going on here? Yes, we had that racial incident back in junior high school when a fight over a girl turned into a black vs. white brawl by the school buses, enough to make the local news and bring cops to the school for the rest of the year. But that's not who we are. Is it?

Carolina is the school that gave us Charlie Scott. Isn't that enough for racial street cred? The '77 team starts two black players from North Carolina (Ford and Davis, who likely came to Carolina because of Charlie Scott, as did so many black players from North Carolina).[1]

But Marquette seems to represent something else. The almost all-black team wears their shirttails out, openly bickers with each other on the court, plays a more improvised, less constricted style and seems to have a more "urban" vibe. To say they play a playground style is to not give them credit for the team they are, but they're not pointing at each other after every assist.

Meanwhile Carolina is the establishment. *Sports Illustrated* will describe the program a few years later as the "toast of the champagne set." Is this why black kids at Ragsdale High School take perverse pleasure in Carolina going down? Can it be that Carolina's team ethic—no individuals,

---

1   Joining Ford and Davis on this list would be Bob McAdoo, James Worthy, Michael Jordan and Antwan Jamison. First-round draft picks all.

blind authority to rules, give yourself over to the system - doesn't appeal to those for whom the "system" hasn't delivered? Can it be that the Carolina I see doesn't represent the same thing for others? Or more to the point, does it represent something else to my classmates of color?

I've got some work to do. Way more than I can possibly realize. As the newspaper headline waves past me in the Ragsdale hallway, I just know it hurts. Carolina finished second in the nation, dammit. How is that a point of ridicule?

My 15-year-old emotions are somewhere else. For me, the 1975 team that vanquished David Thompson and the 1977 Tar Heels represent a new dimension of fandom.

The 1967-72 Tar Heels, before my 10th birthday, were a default proposition. I loved them because that's all I knew. It's not unlike children who grow up going to church because that's where their parents are.

As a teenager, I am now able to choose what I believe. Like the newly converted accepting the altar call at a Billy Graham crusade, I choose these Tar Heel teams. The '77 team won games it shouldn't have because of how it played, how it was coached and how it stood up to pressure. They win me over in a new way, just as I am.

Future Carolina fans will fall the same way for the '97-'98 teams, or the Tyler Hansbrough teams, the Marcus Paige '16 team or even the '22 team of Hubert Davis' first year. You never forget a first love. And you never forget that Tar Heel team that fully crystallizes why we pull for the Heels.

It's as if the 1977 team threw hay all over my 15-year-old self. My heart still breaks for them, and over them.

7

JACKASSES

March 27, 1978

Kentucky 94, Duke 88

NCAA Tournament Final

The 1978 team isn't quite what it should have been. Top-ranked in preseason, Carolina loses to William & Mary and Furman. Behind Phil Ford, and his senior farewell home game for the ages against Duke, the Tar Heels win the regular season, but lose their first ACC and NCAA tournament games to quietly end Ford's career. Still the best Tar Heel ever, though.

No, this year is more about Duke springing back to life after finishing last in the league four consecutive years. The Blue Devils are fun, interesting and so new to this current success that their fan base hasn't had time to emit a mephitic stew of white privilege, self-congratulatory cleverness and "We win because we're better people." Give that some time.

On this day they play long-hated Kentucky in a national final after having eliminated equally hated Notre Dame in the semifinal. We are actually rooting for the Blue Devils as part of some misguided belief it will elevate the entire ACC.

By this time in my junior year, I have found my tribe, full bore teenagers all. On this Monday, we have the school day off, so Dave invites five of us to join him on a day trip to Carowinds, the amusement park outside Charlotte an hour and a half away. His parents, recognizing his responsible adherence to their rules, his overall character and his discerning ability to select friends of equal character, allow him to take the family LTD to shuttle all six of us.

They have made a grievous miscalculation.

We're not 20 minutes down the road when we pass a car with two young, attractive girls in the front seat. The one in the passenger seat smiles a little as we pass, a polite gesture undeserving of the response it draws. Which is for us to fall back, then pass them again, this time with three bare asses pressed against the windows, a mooning of the highest order.

We are pleased with ourselves, and we relive the moment when we mooned the pretty girls in the next lane. Dave is driving between 80 and 100 mph, so we get way ahead of them. The moment passes, and we pull off for gas or food or something.

When we merge back on the highway, there are those girls again!! Really, what choice do we have? The re-mooning is more powerful and meaningful than the first.

Oh we have a big time at Carowinds, no doubt reducing the pleasure of countless others who just wanted to ride some rollercoasters. On the way back, we terrorize other motorists, throwing ice at some, and carouse in a way that defies death and common sense. We are immortal. We are teenagers.

Back at the Willard home, we all prepare to help ourselves to whatever Patsy has baked, settle into a semi-circle in front of the couch, relegate some to the seats behind the couch (otherwise known as the "upper deck") and watch the Duke game. Dave's father greets us at the door.

"Did you boys have a good time?" Mr. Willard asks.

An unusually solicitous question for him, but we all say "Oh yes. Great time. Great rides. Thanks for asking."

"Anything unusual happen?"

Ok. That question has an agenda. We shake our heads and wordlessly elect Dave as our spokesperson.

"No, Pop. What do you mean?"

Then it comes.

"Well, the North Carolina Highway Patrol didn't call Richard Pittman Willard out of the CLEAR BLUE SKY for NOTHING. You all went up there and acted like a bunch of JACKASSES."

Moon a girl once, shame on her. Moon her twice, and she calls the cops.

Four of Dave's friends suddenly remember they have to be home for the evening. School in the morning! As for me, I have to do some quick calculus. If I get home early, I have to explain why and I don't think this story will play well in our home either. Also, if I leave, things will only get worse for Dave.

Such is my affection for this family and their comfort level with me that I decide to stick it out and watch Goose Givens torture Duke with 41 points in a Kentucky win, while "Pittman," as he will forever be known among our friends, grouses no more. My gambit on this front has worked.

I'm also reasonably certain it's the last time I will be sorry to see Duke lose.

Jan. 17, 1979
North Carolina 70, N.C. State 69

Senior year. Where shall I go to college? Hmmm.

I don't even have a second or third choice. I end up sending my piddling SAT scores to Clemson, the ACC's zebras who never hurt me, and, for unknown reasons, Southern Cal. I was never going there.

By today's standards, Carolina's Admissions Office would laugh long and hard at my application, but I guess the incoming class of 1983 wouldn't be complete without me. I am still making regular visits to the School of Dentistry to monitor my teeth, and my father's prediction will soon come true: In less than a year, I will be walking across campus to my orthodontics appointments.

On this night, I'm doing what I always do when Carolina plays—hanging out in the Willard living room. We're ranked second in the first year post-Phil Ford, and State is slumping but still ranked 14th. To me, the game at State is still the biggest one of the regular season, Duke's recent nonsense notwithstanding.

Cropping a photo for the high school yearbook. Could high school girls resist this specimen of early manhood? Yes. Yes, they could.

And we blow State out for one half. Rich Yonaker, a pale, blond and gangly lightning rod who Carolina fans call "Chick" and haters call "Chickie," fires in a jumper at the halftime buzzer to give Carolina a 40-19 lead. It's one thing to be ahead 21 points at the half, but that score just made it look so much worse. 40-19 on our biggest rivals' court.

State plays a good bit better in the second half, and with Carolina's momentum gone, Coach Smith calls for Four Corners with about 15 minutes to play. And the team then proceeds to set Tar Heel basketball back by a generation or two.

Ask any State, or really any non-Carolina ACC fan, about their most delicious fantasy for beating Carolina and the answer would have to do with Carolina botching Four Corners, losing composure and blowing a big lead that can be blamed on Coach Smith.

This is what we have here. The crowd is so loud it's hard to hear the announcers. Carolina mucks up a free throw situation, fouling while blocking out, which leads to a "deadball" technical foul and suddenly the Wolfpack is shooting a bunch of free throws. When it's over, State is down one with the ball and about 45 seconds left.

Kenny Matthews, red hot throughout the half, tries another long jumper. Of course it goes in. State by one. Dave and I have slumped back into the couch, horrified it has come to this.

Carolina's Dudley Bradley, renowned for his defense but not a shooter, tries a long jumper. Was this the best shot we could get? State's Tiny Pender rebounds. Does State really refer to its 6-foot-7 forward as "Tiny." Yes. Yes they do.

He gives it to Clyde Austin, State's slick ball handler. Carolina tries to give a foul, but the referee ignores it, apparently taking the position that it's too late to bail the Tar Heels out by giving in to their strategy.

So Austin dribbles up court. State fans have lost it. Later, friends of mine at the game will tell me many fans were deliriously hugging each other, not really paying attention as Austin dribbles out the clock.

It's too bad they are preoccupied. As Austin reverses his dribble, Bradley reaches in and flicks the ball away. He's on a breakaway to the rim. Dave and I are inches from the TV screen, screaming with glee. My hope is that Bradley calmly lays it in, rather than risking something more athletic.

Bradley slams it home. Viciously. State gets off a decent shot from Matthews, but it's not happening. Carolina players run off the court, the crowd now in stone silence. As endless rewatches on YouTube later reveal, the ball is still bouncing around the court as Carolina leaves, winners by one point.

Driving back home, I listen to the post-game. Coach Smith is gracious toward State but manages to add in his nasal monotone, "we deserved to win the game."

Point of View:

Kevin Parker, N.C. State fan

For any NCSU fan of a certain age, this is absolutely a "top 5" bad loss. And though I've had plenty of options, this is the only "cry myself to sleep" finish of my life.

When you're a fifth-grader in 1970s North Carolina, your day in school was greatly influenced by the outcome of games like this. I was surely headed for a long day if I couldn't pull off the old thermometer-against-the-light-bulb trick.

Watching alone in my Wilson, N.C., bedroom, I honestly don't remember the comeback because of the finish. It's like my brain watched about 10 seconds of footage and decided to just reclaim two previous hours' worth of memory for future considerations.

Luckily for the sadists among us, the author of this work has made sure to fill me in on any random details that might provide more color to this dark and dreadful night when the No. 2-ranked team in the nation barely held on from blowing a 20+ point lead without a shot clock against the team that would finish second-to-last in the ACC.

And speaking of the author, I find it hard to believe he ever found another that could make him as happy as Dudley Bradley. For that matter, I'm honestly scared to ask who means more to him in front of his wife. I don't want that on my conscience. We all three know the answer. There's no need to go there, especially because children are now involved.

I'm starting to understand why non-UNC fans reserve specific vitriol for our coach.

Once home, I'm full of "did you see that" excitement. My father wants to gripe that it never should have come to this. Why, he asks, did we go into the Sorry Game Plan?

February 24, 1979

Duke 47, North Carolina 40

I have a new job this year. The Greensboro Coliseum needs ushers who will work for minimum wage showing patrons to their seats. Greensboro at that time was the logical stopping point between D.C. and Atlanta, so our reward is watching amazing concerts, staged wrestling matches - one female fan offered me "private time" in the ushers' coat closet if I could get her backstage, which I declined, not out of moral virtue, but utter fear - and college basketball. Some of the best college basketball.

In one week, I will attend my first ACC Tournament this way. But this job has provided something else: A new crop of girls my age who don't attend Ragsdale.

Allison thinks I'm funny—well, some of my school peers do, too, but I'm still relegated to Friend Zone—and we seek each other's company each time we work. Finally, someone takes me seriously as a member of the opposite sex. The only problem here is her 24-year-old fiancé, which I find borderline perverted, even though that's the same age gap as my parents. That's different.

On this Saturday night, I'm working a forgotten wrestling match, where 5,000 fans make more noise than when the building is full. For a fake outcome. For this, I am missing the first half of the Duke-Carolina game in Durham.

Based on last year's success, Duke is top-ranked the first month of the season, and the inclination to become obnoxious has proven to be too much for its fan base. It willfully succumbs during a win over Carolina in the Big Four Tournament in Greensboro, with me paid to usher many of these bastards to their seats.

Carolina wins the rematch in Chapel Hill, and now a season-ender in Durham. Carolina will win first place outright with a win.

I get the wrestling fans situated for the Ric Flair cage match and leave as soon as I can, slightly more depressed about humanity than when

I started a few hours before. In the car, I turn to Woody Durham, our trusted friend, to call the game.

Woody is talking about Gene Banks, Duke's talented forward who, in 1977, became the first black player to start at Duke. Read that sentence aloud. One of many reasons we hate Duke.

For some reason, Banks is "showboating" with the ball, in Woody's opinion. He talks about what a shame it is for someone with this much talent acting this way. Damn, Woody. What exactly are you trying to say?

I soon figure out why Woody is so animated. Duke is playing around because, as the half nears its close, the Blue Devils lead 7-0. That's right. Dean Smith opens the game in Four Corners to draw the slower Blue Devils from the basket. Duke doesn't bite. So Carolina holds the ball for an agonizing length of time, only for Yonaker to settle for a five-foot baseline shot, which he fires a good seven feet, sparking one of the original "air ball" chants.

The halftime score of 7-0 is embarrassing. The Tar Heels play "normal" in the second half and battle Duke to a 40-40 draw. Which means they lose by seven. My father is not off base in wondering out loud how the game might have been had Carolina played the entire time.

The ACC Tournament ought to be tense.

February 24, 1979
North Carolina 71, Duke 63
ACC Tournament Final

This is just one of those games Carolina has to win because we are Carolina. Unlike the two previous rounds of this tournament, the wrought-up fans are in their seats 15 minutes before the start. Fifth-ranked Duke and seventh-ranked Carolina.

Dudley Bradley wreaks havoc on the Devils on defense, and when Carolina goes to Four Corners again to seal it, Bradley drives the lane and dunks on Mike Gminski, a moment that becomes a famous Sports Illustrated cover ("Dudley Bradley dunks Duke"). And I'm there to watch it, live for the first time, from the entrance to Section 118, with my buddy Allison.

The NCAA has set the East Regionals in Greensboro for the following weekend. Then they do something sly. They pit Duke and Carolina in the same regional, a showdown just seven days later, for a Final Four berth - all but a certainty. All both teams have to do is beat some eastern teams we've never heard of.

March 11, 1979
Pennsylvania 72, North Carolina 71
St. John's 80, Duke 78
NCAA Tournament Second Round

Such is my lack of concern for this Sunday afternoon game that I allow myself to watch it at home. Pennsylvania? Unranked? The game is in Raleigh, for goodness' sake.

Carolina proceeds to stink it up. My father is convinced they don't care. This might have been one of the ones where he would have forfeited in shame at halftime. Tony Price takes his place in anti-Carolina lore with 25 points. Somehow we lose. Two of the longest hours of my adolescence.

Duke then takes the court and apparently catches a whiff of what Carolina left behind. Unranked St. John's, which finished 3-3 in something called the "New Jersey New York Seven Conference," is too much for the Blue Devils as well. It would have been hilarious if not for Carolina's opening act.

Instead, the day will forever be known in ACC land as "Black Sunday." The following weekend at the Coliseum, the regional brings Penn, St. John's, Rutgers and Syracuse to Greensboro. The culture shock is palpable. They don't even know Stamey's Barbecue across the street serves hot peach cobbler to die for.

I, of course, had signed up to work both nights, thinking I would see Round 5 of one of the more interesting and underrated years of the Duke-Carolina rivalry. Instead, I am mocked for my accent, for my insistence that fans sit in their assigned seats and for my allegiance to Carolina. Yankees!! The only redeeming factor is that most of them tip, apparently buying them the right to distribute verbal abuse.

When it's over, my uninspired usher crew fails in stopping Penn fans from storming the court after their Final Four berth, which will end with the Quakers getting hammered, 101-67, by Magic Johnson and Michigan State in a game that really won't even be that close. Carolina had beaten Michigan State earlier in the year. The Penn flop just makes the end of the season feel that much worse.

The East Regional has left a mark. By now I understand that 1) Dean Smith is not worshipped regularly in other parts and 2) I need to learn something about people other than myself. Because this won't be my last encounter with Yankees.

8

COLLEGE BOY

November 10, 1979

White 92, Blue 86

I'm about to turn 18 and I'm not ready for college. I don't know how the washing machine works and can't turn on the stove. I can put gas in a car, but I don't own one. I haven't been on so much as a date. I'm a bit inexperienced.

My buddy Allison is here for me. We work a concert at the Coliseum the night of July 24, 1979, then go to a bar in Greensboro past midnight, which turns the calendar to the 25th, which means I'm officially 18. I have to beg the wait staff to card me. Which sums up the state of underage drinking in 1979.

Anyway, I arrive sober and a boy and leave the parking lot, um, drunk and a man. A special Carolina assist point goes to the Greensboro police officer who drives by at an inopportune time and leaves with a story to tell at the next precinct meeting.

Nothing quite like driving home at 4 a.m. and finding every light in the house is on. It's my father who lies awake, waiting for me to get there.

And he's the one who had called Allison's mom at 3 a.m., wondering if maybe she had any idea where we were. How he had the wherewithal to find her number remains a mystery.

I don't get speeches or grounding or anything demeaning like that. I'm a man now, after all. All I get is genuine concern. Which I find endearing.

Less than a month later, my parents are standing with me outside Teague Dorm, across the street from Kenan Stadium on the south side of the campus of the University of North Carolina at Chapel Hill, where I will make something of myself by studying journalism with the goal of a sportswriting career that lands at *Sports Illustrated*.

My parents have already dropped off two older girls at college so they know the routine. But they went to Pfeiffer and Guilford, both religious schools. Chapel Hill is a relative den of iniquity. There's talk in the halls of a keg party. Within my dorm room, if my parents are offended by the giant painting of an Old Milwaukee beer can on the wall beside my bed, they manage to hide it.

A pickup basketball game at the goal behind the dorm fights for my attention. Still, I'm the only boy who's ever been born, or so says my mother. We're having a moment. I shuffle nervously in the parking lot, already having removed my shoes, waiting to get my sneakers on and call next game.

My father solemnly approaches. He shakes my hand and slips a $20 spot against my palm. Then he says what he has to say.

"Wear shoes son. You'll get worms in your feet."

With that, I move from home for the first time to live at the school of my dreams.

I quickly discover that Carmichael Auditorium, the hallowed home of the Tar Heels, is right through the woods behind my dorm, less than a five-minute walk. I also discover that tickets to the game are "free." You don't actually pay for them. You just go pick them up somehow.

Right about here, every parent of a Carolina student is saying "Free, my ass." We all pay "athletic fees" as part of tuition, so you pay for these games whether you attend or not.

I don't know how any of this works. A very kind senior named Quincy, the younger sister of one of my older sister's friends, does the sort of thing I wouldn't think to do. She reaches out to a lost, shy, away-from-home freshman and invites him to the Blue-White game, the varsity scrimmage before every UNC season.

Carmichael Auditorium feels like home, awash in light blue with the banners celebrating prior greatness, the flip-the-number scoreboard on the baseline and the student bleachers that roll out for games, just like every high school gym. Quincy and I sit here as we take in Mike O'Koren, Al Wood, James Worthy and the rest of the gang, now fellow students, up close. Worthy scores 22 points. He has potential.

I cannot for the life of me figure out if I'm supposed to ask Quincy out. Dating anyone would feel daunting enough, but she's three years older. God, I'm awkward.

February 3, 1981
Virginia 80, North Carolina 79 (OT)

The summer after my freshman year leads to another passage into manhood: the real summer job. Somehow I fall into the second shift at Thomas Built Buses. All my friends get first-shift jobs making miserly hourly wages. The company literally lost my application and when I called them about it, they offered me a job working until midnight replacing the guy who makes bus doors for the assembly line.

What a riot this is. The son of a man who could master any tool to do any job can barely hit a nail with a hammer. I learn to use all kinds of drill bits, run a lathe and cut rubber to fit, although I damn near cut off my left index finger. I can make 8-inch, 10-inch and 12-inch doors with ease, and my specialty becomes the jackknife doors that fold together. That's my artwork.

I am paid per door, which is about three times what my friends are making and likely twice what the lifers are making on the other parts of the assembly line. Oddly, this makes me the object of their scorn. They think long and hard on a nickname for me and come up with one.

"College boy," one of them sneers at me. It has a nice ring.

It will be 20 years before I make this much money again. And oh how I hate it. Whatever doubts I have about the utility of college are resolved. I will take Music Appreciation, Deviant Behavior and Old Testament courses, and I will like it. I will learn to think. And I resolve to never have a job where you do the same thing every day.

My sophomore year I move into an apartment, across the hall from three girls bawdier than anything I'm used to. They become my friends, my mentors, my drink mates. They all have boyfriends, so they counsel me in this area as well.

My go-to move at this point is to attend a university-sponsored keg party each Thursday night, get toe up, and ask a girl to dance.

You are reading this correctly. When the drinking age was still 18, UNC Administration took the position that it would be better for the students to just drink on campus, walking to various dorms instead of driving to bars. So taxpayers paid for our beer. As in, as much as we could drink of it. Anyone under the age of about 55 still has trouble believing this.

One night at the mixer in our own Teague dorm I gather the courage to ask out a girl named Constance, who says yes. She had lived the previous year in my friends' dorm, so I seek a scouting report.

"She puts out," Brenda says.

"Yeah, she'll fuck you," Toni says.

Eloquence is not their strong suit. Turns out that all Constance did to warrant this preview was to have a steady boyfriend named Earl. Much like they had steady boyfriends. In retrospect, I'm not sure their motives are all that pure.

Constance and I go out for several months. My idea of a "date" is to ask her to wait in line with me for tickets to the Virginia game. As in "top-ranked undefeated" Virginia, long past the days when they would finish last and then try to win the ACC Tournament.

This version has 7-foot-4 Ralph Sampson, subject of the most intense recruiting battle ever to that date. Carolina and Coach Smith wanted him badly yet didn't even finish in Ralph's top two. That helps fuel a rivalry that is, during my four years, far more intense than anything a fading N.C. State or an again-struggling Duke can muster. We hate Virginia.

My buddy and former Junior League coach Carlos, now a football player at Virginia, got the Jamestown pals tickets to the first Carolina-Virginia game in January. Carolina led by 13 points, went into Four Corners and frittered every bit of it away. I sat in the Virginia student section and absorbed every bit of vitriol as though it were mine to bear.

Now Constance and I are at the rematch in Chapel Hill. Wine and cheese crowd? Not this day. We bring it from well before the game, throughout taking a 16-point lead and into Four Corners, when we proceed to blow it again. Sampson is just too much. The game goes into overtime, Carolina falls behind by three, we score at the buzzer and Matt Doherty churlishly tries to foul, damn near starting a fight.

We lose by one. The fans leave angry, mad and ready to tear something down. I take Constance to Troll's, a classic college dive bar that becomes a second home, and we play Pac-Man and Space Invaders. I am quite a romantic.

March 28, 1981
North Carolina 78, Virginia 65
NCAA Tournament Final Four

A little more than a decade into my passion for Carolina basketball, I have lived to see this date. This may be the biggest Carolina game of my lifetime—a third match against Sampson and Virginia in the Final Four—and I will be 10 rows up in the student section end zone.

Not quite a year and a half from being dragged from a shy stupor to watch the Blue-White game, I have arranged free lodging and a free ride to Philadelphia for the sport's premier event. I lose the student lottery for tickets, but a classmate who won says he can't go. So I pose as him, a red-headed chubby guy with a beard. I memorize his middle name, his social security number, his astrological sign, anything about him. If I were ushering this game in the Greensboro Coliseum, I would have a hard time getting this ruse past me. In the Spectrum in 1980s Philadelphia, I'm convinced I could have carried a spiked ball on a chain. Red-haired Douglas Wilson? Sure, kid, come on in.

Final Four basketball is taut, with fans intensely cheering but also paying attention and not giving in to foolishness. No time for that. We hiss as the Virginia players walk past us during the first game, and they can hear us. We are making a difference.

The game is tied at halftime, then Al Wood goes off. Way off. Our senior sharpshooter scores from everywhere, anywhere, at any time. While Ralph Sampson is struggling to hit double figures, Wood is pouring in 39 points, still a semifinal record. We spend most of the game standing on our chairs, jumping in pure joy and stating "This is better than sex," regardless of how puny the sample size may be. I later meet one of these revelers at a beer truck party on one of the athletic fields and ask her on a date, which I botch by thinking that she wanted to go to Dime Beer Night at some bar and get very drunk.

I've never felt more connected to Carolina basketball. We have won a game we absolutely had to win to re-establish our Carolina-ness. We're finally going to win it all two nights from now. A childhood of tears cried in pillows, games watched through towels, thrown mops and *Sports Illustrated* covers taped to the wall, wishing the headline read "North Carolina" instead of "UCLA," will finally lead to the end goal I've wanted all along—a national championship.

And I will see it in person.

March 30, 1981
Indiana 63, North Carolina 50
NCAA Tournament Final

A couple of issues get in the way. President Reagan gets shot that Monday and apparently some discussion is held about whether the game should be played. It turns out he recovers just enough to give Indiana, our second problem, permission to beat us senseless in the second half and send us home losers.

I come home to look for Constance, who stayed behind while I got "silly in Philly." Rob, my roommate, gives me the news. He spotted her at a party the day before. She's back with Earl.

My personal life and UNC's title dreams seem to be synched, a mutual bridge leading to nowhere.

9

WHO TO CALL?

March 7, 1982

North Carolina 47, Virginia 45

ACC Tournament Final

It's 4 a.m. in the High Point City Jail and I know what I have to do.

By now, I've found my college tribe, just as I had in high school. We know how to drink, party and waste time. My drinking show has gone on the road, back to my hometown, for toddies with some pals in downtown High Point, Furniture Capital of the World to outsiders and the World's Armpit to those of us who grew up there.

My 1970 Camaro is not reliable under these circumstances. It's not like I had a sudden burst of coolness and bought one of the generation's iconic cars. A high school friend needed to sell his so he could get a grown-up car, and the asking price of $700 was too little to resist, especially with me flush with Thomas Built Buses door-making money. Well, add another $100 for the stereo system he put in that would make your ears bleed.

So as a junior in college I finally have my own car. I present it to my parents for inspection before buying it. My mother is horrified by the pea green color. My father looks under the hood, checks some wiring and says, "it's going to cost you $200 a month to maintain," a prediction that never does come true, even three years later when I'm having to stop every hour and pour in more motor oil.

One of the few remaining photos of the pea-green Camaro. I can't explain the fleeting "porn star" look. The woman I have my arm around? Stop it. That's my sister.

It's a man's car, and on this November 1981 night I am a drunken boy. Breathing alcohol at 0.11, I can't keep it from wobbling, and N.C. Highway Patrolman Baxter can't help but notice. My field sobriety test needs work, and no opportunity exists for extra credit. To my everlasting shock, my privileged white ass is going to jail.

It's true what they say. They give you one phone call.

Who to call at this hour? The list is short and it's really not even a debate. You call your best friends in the world, who will love and support you no matter how disappointing you can be.

My father answers. I explain that he can't come right now but can pick me up at 8 a.m. Does he know his way to the jail?

No lecture. No condemnation. No asking what I was thinking. He says he'll be there and he will be.

Such is the essence of Daddy. To his friends, he was a raconteur of the highest order, framing a story and timing it just right for maximum comedy, mixing in phrases like "salts through a widow woman" or the choir member's mouth being "big enough to stack three eggs end to end," and other memorable quips that came from a combination of Polkville, the Navy and God-given talent.

To his community, he was the one who could, and would, fix anything, from a broken car, to wiring a house, laying brick or roofing. Anything, often for no charge when the cause was right, as was usually the case.

To his family, he was all those things, but also the example of stability, common sense (by the bushel!) and living by example. Well, there was this temper thing. He had the ability to flash it at the smallest of things. Like pointing a flashlight at a spot not exactly where he was working or losing at card games. And, of course, Carolina basketball.

But on the big things, oh my God. He came through in the calmest, most non-judgmental way possible, while at the same time letting it be known that whatever it was, it was not ok.

As I hang up the phone, the punishment I feel is that I disappointed him. And it's like he knows that and, for now, that's enough.

Now I can turn my wrath on the staff at the High Point City Jail. I notice that my toilet tank has no lid, so if you keep flushing, the water keeps rising. I decide to flood my cell. Yeah, that makes them sorry they arrested me.

The only disgust my father will show is when we pick up the Camaro, shamefully herded to a nearby grocery store/strip center parking lot, smack in the middle of Jamestown, to sleep it off. When I open the car door to drive it home, he shakes his head and says it still smells like booze. Which it does. I could die right there in front of Edmunds Drug Store.

I self-impose three months of abstinence to ensure this drinking is not uncontrollable. Also, it just seems wrong to go back to hardcore college drinking while your father is working after-hours odd jobs for sympathetic friends to raise money for a lawyer. The lawyer he ends up hiring pays Daddy to install a clothesline. It's not like my parents would ever know what I was up to, but Chapel Hill is just an hour away from home and the guilt can travel that far without losing steam. Maybe I can cool my jets a little.

During this time, I take in a lesson few have the opportunity to learn: The reason people drink at parties is because drunk people at parties are assholes. Drinking is the only way to absorb them. If you're not drinking, they pester you and then become downright angry you won't join their misery. Thank you, Patrolman Baxter, for this insight.

And maybe another Carolina assist point to the judge. Such was the level of regard others held for my father that he had produced two of the best reference letters possible for the court, one from our high school principal, T.G. Madison, and another from Doug Carroll, a respected Chemistry teacher who wrote that Bob Whisnant possessed the "honesty of Diogenes." It's ok at this point to allege white privilege in my life. We didn't have money, but that's not how privilege works. I don't think my peers of color had so many escape hatches in Jamestown in the 1980s.

The judge considered this support, and my purported desire to be a "journalist," and ordered me to find five groups of 10 or more kids to warn them of the perils of drinking and driving. He would sentence me only after that was completed.

In retrospect, it was a clever way to share the message that drunken driving ends badly. And an involuntary way for me to launch my public speaking career. At one church youth group, we met in the leader's living room while I gave my spiel to the bewildered teens. Then they broke out the new video camera and panned the room, pausing on each teen.

On the replay, they laughed and clapped as they watched themselves on video, one by one. Until the camera panned to me. Dead silence. They didn't know what to make of me. A few days of jail wouldn't have seemed so bad in comparison.

I wound up with a "Prayer for Judgment Continued," which basically meant I was never sentenced. That was unheard of even in 1982.

I watch the first few months of the next season sober, and these Tar Heels are a sight to behold. Top-ranked from the start, they outclass No. 2 Kentucky and grind the rest of the schedule to dust, losing only at Virginia, still with Ralph Sampson, and a home game to Wake Forest when Sam Perkins has the flu.

James Worthy, my classmate (along with about 5,000 others), is having an All-American year, Perkins is historically good and the freshman Michael Jordan looks like maybe he can play. I resume my drinking ways, but I will never again get behind the wheel drunk. Maybe after a drink

Point of View:

Judy Whisnant
Sister

When it comes to declaring independence in our family, Scott should try being a girl.

Those of us who established the clan in the days before the "only boy who's ever been born" was born had a tradition of playing Canasta, which also involved a basket, since canasta means "basket" in Spanish. If basketball was chariot racing, Canasta was mortal combat.

I was 20, home from college, probably at Christmas. To know our family is to know that I was the only one who could endure being Daddy's partner, and I always was. Guilty of the mortal sin of not counting cards carefully enough and not intuiting what my sister had in her hand, I "gave away the deck," an act akin to dropping the ball on your toe and punting it to Grayson Allen under the basket.

Our precious Daddy was strong and kind and humble, but he was not a patient man. So, when he berated and humiliated me with that childish temper that dads should never show, I flew into a rage (imagine!) and lifted up my side of the table so all 108 cards went scattering onto the floor!

This did not play well on Route 7, to put it mildly, but it did put a mark between "childhood" and "grown" like nothing else.

or two, but not drunk. The Tar Heels cruise to the ACC Final against Virginia. The game between the nation's first- and third-ranked teams will settle this once and for all.

And I will be in the Greensboro Coliseum, still cribbing off my usher job from high school. They need "extra" ushers for sellout basketball games, and I solemnly agree to serve my home city. I have a servant's heart.

The game is an all-time classic—for 33 minutes. Not just three Hall-of-Fame players, but the greatest who ever played at any level (Jordan), one of the five greatest college players ever (Sampson), and a top 50 all-time NBA player and top pick in his draft (Worthy). Carolina leads by one, carried early by Worthy and in the second half by a red-hot Jordan, scoring at will over the Cavaliers' man-to-man.

Then Coach Smith goes next level. With the ball and a one-point lead, he decides to drag Sampson away from the basket by holding the ball. We're in Four Corners.

Virginia is not having it. They likely watched tape from the Kentucky game. The Wildcats chased the stall and before it was over they damn near had to get new rims from Worthy dunking so hard over them. Virginia is not stupid.

We have the embodiment of a basketball stalemate. Sampson stays in the lane, so the Tar Heels always have Perkins open near midcourt. They hold it for more than seven minutes, down to the 28-second mark when Virginia finally fouls enough to send Matt Doherty to the line. Fans are booing with disgust, and the national media will soon join in.

"Imagine the final 12 minutes of Hamlet if the cast started reciting the Congressional Record," the *Washington Post's* Ken Denlinger will write in the next day's paper.

Doherty makes one of two. Virginia turns it over and Doherty makes two more. Carolina wins it by two. Coach Smith is forced to defend the debacle in the media room, pointing out that Terry Holland, Virginia's coach, could have chosen to chase the Heels. He says he'll vote for a 30-second shot clock and gladly be the first to do so, but he's not attacking Sampson more than he has to. The media reports he is very uncomfortable.

Holland says it takes two to play this way, and he didn't start it. This is the coach who famously named his dog "Dean" because it whined a lot. That's how well those two got along.

It's a matter of time before college basketball gets a shot clock, and this game will be the reason. Turns out, I have a front row seat to history in the making.

Controversy aside, I'm perfectly delighted with how this played out. Because we hate Virginia that much. But it does plant some questions. Am I not seeing something because of unflagging belief in Coach Smith and Carolina basketball? Or is the "objective" national media seeing something else?

10

NICE SHOT

March 13, 1982

North Carolina 52, James Madison 50

NCAA Tournament First Round

The first NCAA tournament game is in Charlotte and Pete, my roommate, and I decide we have to go. We're playing lowly James Madison. Well, maybe not that "lowly." An utterly listless performance (Dean Smith "holds" Michael Jordan to six points) keeps the game in doubt far too long, and only a questionable charging call that goes Carolina's way preserves a two-point win.

On the way back, Pete and I do what we often did - we get massively stoned (I'm not driving!). We're listening to jazz radio a little too intently and wondering if oncoming headlights are destined to hit us head on. We have overshot the mark and need to come down a little. Our best bet is to stop at my parents' house, just off the highway between High Point and Greensboro, and hope for homemade food to settle things down. We're hoping for a lot of it.

I don't recommend this. Mama does in fact have a deep reservoir of homemade goods from which to feed us. But dammit we're so stoned and it's weird to be around them. T.G. Madison, our high school principal and longtime family friend who had vouched for my drunken character six months earlier, stops by and brings his son, John, about three years younger than us. John pulls us aside and asks, "What the hell is wrong with you?" We put him up to doing all the talking until we can gracefully leave.

Before we go, we check in with Tyrone, a constant and everlasting friend from my childhood.

He's the beagle who was my present for my 12th birthday. Our Uncle Charles, who lived a mile down the road, often sheltered wayward dogs, though if this were a passion of his, he never explained it. All he ever expressed was unsubstantiated worry. His finest hour came when his son James was called up by the National Guard during the Vietnam War.

Certain James would see front-line combat, Uncle Charles told my father, "His life's not worth a plug nickel."

The National Guard was calling him to Greenville, North Carolina, not to the Tet Offensive. But Uncle Charles could still worry.

Uncle Charles fostered Tyrone until my parents agreed we could adopt him. As a family, we were uniquely ill-suited to take in a beagle. Our parents would not allow a dog in the house, which meant Tyrone was free to roam past our yard, past moderately busy Vickrey Chapel Road and even onto Interstate 85, one of the primary north-south highways in the United States.

Tyrone was historically lazy, rolling over on his side, hiking up his hind leg and offering his belly to family, stranger, burglar. But he also was a wanderer, and he took us up on the freedoms we offered. The odds were against him. You could say his chances of survival weren't worth a plug nickel.

His daily rounds were legendary. He visited Mae Jones, the widow across the street. He flirted with Ginger, the Spaniel mix next door, eagerly awaiting her next bout of heat. He went to the neighborhood cul-de-sac, taunting Bo, the mean collie mix, and onto the other cul-de-sac. He crossed Vickrey Chapel and visited inside one home at the same time for months, watching *As The World Turns* with this family until a story arc passed.

His strangest ritual was a morning romp onto the median of I-85, crossing two lanes of highway traffic each way. Daddy would pass him on the way to work, taking a mental picture each time. He was sure he wouldn't see this dog alive again. But when Daddy got home around 5:30, there was Tyrone, paws up on his thighs, telling him he was hungry.

So here he is, still among us and unconcerned that we're stoned, hungry and not fit for public viewing. We rub Tyrone's belly on the way out, a calming presence without judgment. It's enough to help us make it back to Chapel Hill.

Tyrone, as always, teaching non-violent anti-establishmentarianism as a guiding philosophy. Had a burglar approached our house, he would have assumed the same pose.

It's not like he wanted to come with us. By this time, Tyrone's bond with my parents had become unshakeable. The house rules were relaxed during thunderstorms, as Tyrone and Mama were both frightened. Tyrone came inside and sat with Mama in her chair until the storm passed and he asked to go back outside and continue his outreach.

During exams later that semester, Mama called me to come home. Tyrone as a physical being had broken down. He made it to Linda Kenner's yard, but after all that wandering, he couldn't make it back. My parents were out of town, so the neighbors called my father's office with Guilford County. His top manager sent a county work crew to pick up Tyrone and take him to the vet. The taxpayers would have to understand.

Point of View:
Tyrone
Family Pet

Some families may have built a fence to curb my wandering, but the Whisnants understood my need to teach about life through the daily flaunting of death.

Life, after all, is less hierarchy and more about close friendships mined each day in person. When oppressors seek power over me, I disarm them by rolling over and lifting my leg high in the air, allowing them a better belly scratch. Genuine connection with others, our greatest gift, is what outlives us.

Much like Christ, I never traveled farther than 35 miles from home. Our best lessons were taught in parables, and we never used violence or power to resolve conflict. We expanded "family" beyond biological bonds - in my case, from the Armfields to Linda Kenner's house. I belonged to all.

Death was but a stage of life, and not to be feared. My dance in the I-85 median was part of a spiritual journey, as was hunger, friendship and Ginger's bouts of heat. Each car could bring the end, or not, but I will always be with you.

So instead of fearing death, why not live life as the gift that it is?

Some saw me as just a lazy beagle, the scales never falling from their eyes. But I took such joy when others "got" me. Scott's college roommate, Pete, once said he "grew through Tyrone."

It's those times when I knew the journey—the long naps, the listless afternoons, the howling at nothing in particular and, yes, the highway romps—was not in vain.

The vet ushered me into a back room, just Tyrone and me. He trembled, unable to move, and looked at me with sad, brown eyes. "It's okay," he seemed to be saying. "It's time to go. It's been a good one."

He seemed sad on my behalf.

A few days later, I received a letter from Mama that should have been saved. The entire page was a tribute to Tyrone that never mentioned him by name. "He" was enough.

"He was a special friend," Mama concluded.

March 19-21, 1982
North Carolina 74, Alabama 69
North Carolina 70, Villanova 60
NCAA Tournament East Regional Final

The East Regional is in Raleigh, home of Pete's parents and just 25 minutes from Chapel Hill. Again, we decide we have to go. This will make eight consecutive Tar Heel post-season games I have seen in person. And to think I once thought the dream of seeing one ACC Tournament game was farfetched.

We visit his parents—sober –then get really stoned on the way to Reynolds Coliseum, N.C. State's old barn of a gym at the tail end of its run as a basketball landmark worthy of hosting a regional. The ACC Tournament started here when it was the best site in the South, but time has moved on.

We enter the building toward the end of the first game between Memphis State (several scandals later, just "Memphis") and Villanova. The assault on the senses is palpable. It's during a timeout, both fan bases are riled and both pep bands are playing. Even fans of the other two schools are nervous.

This I do recommend. Nothing quite like watching NCAA Tournament games among 12,400 invested fans, with two teams playing as hard and as disciplined as they can, trying to play loose but with everything they have worked for the past 12 months riding on every play. Later as a sportswriter, one of my favorite passions will be to watch from press row tournament games that do not involve the team I am covering. It's passion, effort, emotion, and players playing for each other as well as themselves and their schools. It's fan base vs. fan base, right there in the same building, a purity that pro sports fans will just never get. It's why the NCAA Tournament is the best three weeks in sports.

Memphis State does something stupid in overtime and loses. Then we play Alabama, and whatever ailed the Tar Heels the weekend before in Charlotte has been cured. All five starters score between 11 and 16 points, and the Tar Heels make free throws down the stretch and win a five-point game that, while intense on every possession, is never really in doubt.

Two days later, they pull the same trick against Villanova, all five starters hitting between 11 and 15 points and the Tar Heels shooting 57% from the floor, assisting on 21 of 25 field goals and making 83% from the line. The national media is still howling about the stall at the end of the Virginia game, but these two games are as Dean Smith as Carolina basketball under Dean Smith can get.

On the way out, Pete and I speculate on whether we have won more games this year on State's home court (three, counting the 20-point beatdown of the Wolfpack in January) than N.C. State did. Not because it's true, but because we are assholes.

We're certain we've heard the last from N.C. State.

March 27, 1982
North Carolina 68, Houston 63
NCAA Tournament Final Four

Back to the Final Four, but I've had my fill of chasing the Tar Heels around the country. Last year's Final Four filled that dream, and after the win over Virginia, the students—including all my friends—unveiled a new tradition: storming Franklin Street. Oh, how I heard about drunks climbing trees, setting fires and painting themselves blue. It sounded like the stage of human development just before the invention of the wheel, but everyone agreed it was not to be missed if it ever happened again.

I expected it to happen. After six Final Fours resulted in no championships for Coach Smith, I have elevated this Final Four to "we have to win this because we're Carolina" status, just as I have various inter-conference games of my childhood against State, Duke and even Virginia. We can't go on having the best program in the nation and not win one of these.

The Final Four is in New Orleans, where I don't know anyone or have any way to get there. They tell me it's a 17-hour drive. My Camaro can't do four hours. Sign me up to get painted blue on Franklin Street.

Well, the *Daily Tar Heel* does describe a different way of distributing tickets this time. Some 450 student seats will be given out. To get one, you sign sheets of 25 names. If your sheet is one of 18 picked, you get to go.

And the kicker is this—the first four sheets picked will get 100 courtside seats.

I know enough about the Louisiana Superdome to know I would never sit in the upper deck. The court at that point would be about the size of a postage stamp, and you would spend the game watching the overhead TV screen. I can watch TV at home and then get painted blue on Franklin Street.

But four chances for a courtside seat? I owe it to the process to at least sign up. I find myself signing sheet number "6." Why that number? I still cannot say.

The *DTH* reports that the first sheet picked is... 6. Some of the guys I sat with last year in Philadelphia are going and need a fourth to help pay for gas. One of them has a girlfriend in law school at Tulane and her apartment floor is open to us. Events have conspired against getting painted blue.

For someone who can't figure out how to register to vote, I have somehow arranged courtside tickets, free lodging, and a small share of gas costs while someone else drives. What else can I do? The universe is taking me to New Orleans.

I eat my first raw oyster (my lifetime total still stands at one). We go to Bourbon Street before it's a boobs-for-beads exchange. We hear jazz in clubs. And now we're sitting in the fifth row on the baseline in the biggest building known to man, the cavernous Superdome.

We're up 14-0 on Houston, with relative no-names such as "Clyde Drexler" and "Akeem Olajuwan."[1] Houston runs its offense through Rob Williams, who goes 0-for-8 from the field and scores two points.

Still, the game is closer than it should be, considering we shoot almost 60 percent. But we're looking like the best team in college basketball. We settle in to watch Georgetown slog past Louisville in what commentators today refer to as a "rock fight." We can't lose at this level again, can we?

March 29, 1982
North Carolina 63, Georgetown 62
NCAA Tournament Final

During the off day in between games, I find time to call my parents. It turns out that WFMY, their local TV station, sent a reporter to capture the "scene" at New Orleans and I was interviewed. I think back to the interview and, yes, it was outside Pat O'Brien's, but I'm relieved to recall I was sober.

My father seems almost proud that I have found my way back to the Final Four. They sense I am resourceful. UNC basketball is forcing me to grow up.

As the teams gather for the opening tip, I have that feeling that you can only have so many times in a lifetime: There is nowhere else on planet Earth to be. This is where it is happening.

Then it starts. Georgetown has a frightful 7-foot freshman named Patrick Ewing who sends our first four shots, and soon after a fifth, screaming back at the shooters who offered them. All five are obvious goaltending calls, but it's clear that Georgetown will not take any shit off North Carolina.

Nor will we take any of theirs. James Worthy is having his best game as a Tar Heel, spinning, driving and dunking his way to keep us in the

1   Later "Hakeem." Both these guys would later easily be selected to basketball's Hall of Fame. In all fairness, at this point Olajuwan is a freshman still learning the game.

game. We're down one at the half, and later down four—the biggest lead of the second half—when Worthy gets loose on a breakaway and slams it over Sleepy Floyd, also from Gastonia, N.C., and draws the foul.

We eventually go ahead by a point and here comes Four Corners. Will this doom us again in a big game? We twice hit both ends of a one-and-one, but Georgetown won't go away. With about three minutes left, Jordan sees an opening and decides to try a flying left-handed layup over Ewing. Which goes in.

Down three, Georgetown works it around and finds Ewing, whose shot hits the rim about 18 times before dropping. Now it's one again, and Georgetown readily seizes on a chance to foul Matt Doherty with a little more than a minute to go.

Doherty is 20 years away from returning to UNC as head coach and damn near shipwrecking the program beyond recognition. So, we don't yet have antipathy for him, but he's not our first choice at the foul line.

He looks nervous, antsy and as if he may have a dry cleaning problem. Anywhere but at this foul line, his body language says. And he bricks. Georgetown comes down and scores, and we sag. Carolina, now behind one, looks lost at its end—our end of the court—and Coach Smith calls timeout. Thirty-two seconds remain.

For the first time, I'm entertaining the thought of the 17-hour drive back, trying to process this loss, and making up for lost class time. The national media, hounding Coach Smith as an ultimate loser, will never live this down. The Tar Heels have a chance to finally win one while I am a student and in attendance, only to come this close.

Reorganized, Carolina swings it around, looking for a shot. The ball finds Jordan, and he queues up a 17-foot jump shot.

History has played this moment so many times, and Jordan's eventual greatness makes the outcome seem inevitable. Ask any Carolina fan at the game what raced through their mind and I'm betting you'll get something like this: How dare *you*, of all people, with James Worthy and Sam Perkins on this team, take this shot? You better hit that.

After endless review of this game, Jordan's shot is all the more startling given that it's one of three shots from that distance the Tar Heels attempt the entire game. Worthy hits from near the top of the key during his torrid stretch in the first half, and Jimmy Black misses from the same spot. Jordan's shot in that context in that game is indeed startling. We would learn much later that Coach Smith essentially called the play for Jordan to shoot it.

When it goes in, we celebrate by jumping on the tops of our seats, but quickly settle down because Georgetown is racing up court and... did that just happen?

I would love to see a photo of our individual faces the moment Georgetown's Fred Brown threw the ball directly to Worthy. It wouldn't be glee but pure befuddlement. You never see teams do that. It's the most improbable turnover at the most improbable time, and it's the most glorious thing a 20-year-old college junior can fathom.

Right after it's over, as our group is back on Bourbon Street, we're exhausted. A little-known fact about intense fandom: the big games take everything out of you. Some Louisville fans begin castigating us for not "partying," saying we don't know how to win, an encounter that defines Louisville fans for me for life.

Because we're just getting started. Back at Pat O'Brien's, the hurricanes flow like wine. I'm ahead of my skis. Some members of Cornell's wrestling

National Champs

UNC Students Cheer The Tar Heels On To Victory Monday N
. (from left) Greg Lumsford, Nancy Dorer

Squeaks Past Georgetow

© Charlotte Observer

Here's proof that I attended the Georgetown game, as captured by the Charlotte Observer's next-day front page. That's my 150-pound frame in a dark sweater and beanie, struggling to lift a pom-pom.

team find me amusing and throw me into the iconic bar's fountain. Good times.

The next morning, or maybe afternoon, we groggily come to life on the apartment floor. Our host tells us she can tell we went at it hard based on the snoring. We're wondering why she has to talk this early.

One of my new friends looks at me and says, "Hey man, we saw Jordan last night."

Well of course we did. He took a shot we all knew he could make and...

"No, we saw him at Pat O'Brien's."

"We did?"

"You don't remember?"

"Umm. No. Not even close. We saw Jordan?"

"Yeah, you spoke to him."

Oh dear God. What on earth did I say to our special freshman who took the most special shot that we all wanted him to take?

"What did I say to him?" I ask, wincing. I'm bracing for anything.

"You shook his hand and said, 'Nice shot.'"

Dignity in hand, I exhale. Indeed it was. It was a very nice shot.

11

RONNIE MO WOULD

February 10, 1983

North Carolina 64, Virginia 63

Seeing as how I'm a senior in college, I figure I may as well start thinking about a career. My journalism classes are going well enough, though my friends don't really respect it as a major. My business major friends coerce me into taking a "Marketing" class and laugh uproariously when I drown in statistical minutia and beg the professor to let me drop it. They still laugh to this day.

I can't deny I have it easier than my Pre-Med or Business major friends. Exam time finds me perfecting my jump shot at Woolen Gym. I deduce stressing about exams won't help, and I think history has borne me out on this.

None of it will help me get hired. If I am going to be a sportswriter, I need to sports write. My current career is delivering pizzas for Pizza Transit Authority, a job I take out of guilt from the DWI incident. If I'm making some money, I won't have to ask my parents for as much.

I'm quite good at it but getting tipped with bong hits will only take me so far. I take the "Practicum" journalism class under the vaunted Jim Shoemaker, the cantankerous professor so idolized that he inspired the comic strip "Shoe."

"Practicum" means the school, through Shoe's numerous contacts, places you somewhere to work in an actual newsroom. He finds the *Durham Morning Herald* will tolerate me for a semester, so I spend my Friday and Saturday nights there. For the entire semester, I never meet Shoe. He calls me once toward the end to ask me what grade I should get, and finds that I think I deserve an "A."

And I probably do. My time at the *Morning Herald* coincides with a time when newspapers still mattered but readers were beginning to watch most games on TV. Recounting the play-by-play is no longer enough. Now reporters must tell readers something they wouldn't know from just watching TV.

The staff makes merciless fun of me being a Carolina guy, mocking Dean Smith and the program's rituals. (One of the more strident mockers will later take a job as sideline reporter for the Carolina radio network, as sycophantic as a job can get). Everybody, it turns out, does a Dean Smith imitation.

But they let me learn. I cover high school football and basketball games on deadline. When coaches are rude about my questions (The worst, by far, is a former Duke basketball player. I'm just sayin'), I whine to Keith Drum, the editor who, unbeknownst to me, is a legend. He soothes me and tells me these grown men have lost lots of games and will lose more. They need to learn to take it, and so do I.

I start to see what it takes to be a professional. The guy who covers high school sports keeps his own spiral notebook with box scores from every prep game in the region. While one writer insists on recounting the blow-by-blow for every game, even blowouts, I'm drawn to guys like Ron Morris, or Ronnie Mo, who instantly recognizes trends, themes, history and comedy while the games are unfolding. I want to be like Ronnie Mo.

Friday night is chaos at the sports desk, as football or basketball high school games from about a dozen counties pour in. We cover some of them and take dictation from clueless teenage "stringers" for the others. One night, Drum hands me the phone to take dictation from Ronnie Mo. His portable computer is not working.

Ronnie Mo proceeds to read me a flawless game story on deadline, complete with illuminating quotes. It makes the paper. I ask Drum how he found time to write this out and read it to me, and Drum tells me he didn't. Ronnie Mo was writing a game story in real time in his head.

With that standard in mind, I cover a game a week or so later that goes into overtime and runs late. I call Drum and explain I cannot get the game into the region's first edition but will have it for the city edition.

"I understand," he says. "Just get it in when you can."

I apologize. The clock says what it says. I don't see how anybody could beat it.

"Ronnie Mo would," he says.

That game got in first edition. I'm starting to look like a sportswriter.

Just one more brutal lesson. My primary job is the "agate" page, or the small type for box scores, standings, and scores from other minor sports. The schools would often fax over tennis or golf match results, for example, and I would write them up for the agate page.

Drum calls me into his office one evening before I start my shift. I prepare for praise, as the staff has come to rely on me to cover even meaningful prep games.

"I got a call from Carolina about the golf scores," he said. "The score for 'Davis Love' was written as 'David Lowe.'"

I start to giggle. David Lowe is a punter on the UNC football team. Most everybody knows this. Davis Love is an unknown golfer. At that time. He's had a near-Hall of Fame worthy career as a PGA golfer since, but how am I to know this? Anybody could have made this error, right?

"I'm not going to fire you," Drum says, as though he seriously considered it. "But that won't happen again."

That sobered me up. After my semester, Drum hires me for the second semester, with more hours. I'll have to leave my pizza delivery career in mid-bloom. My boss at Pizza Transit Authority sits me down and advises me against it. I have a career in pizza delivery, a franchise manager job surely in my future. Don't get carried away by the prospect of school.

Wow. What a decision before me. After about 1.8 seconds, I declare for journalism.

All this work stuff interferes with my Carolina game watching, as I miss some Saturday games to serve the *Durham Morning Herald*. But I manage to make the games that matter.

I've become friends with two girls in our apartment building who are from Pennsylvania and Maine. Yankee women fascinate me. They are direct, bawdy and not the least bit passive aggressive. Their frustration/befuddlement over Southern men is hilarious.

Stephanie, the one from Maine, is a linguistics major and I discover, deep into her final semester at UNC, she has never been to a basketball game. But of course she's been paying for it all four years, so she might as well go to one.

Pete and I arrange to get her a ticket to the Virginia game, Ralph Sampson's last in Chapel Hill. We explain to Stephanie who Sampson is. Such was the state of ACC basketball in the early 1980s that we could casually bring along a neophyte to watch the top-ranked and third-ranked teams in the nation. Just something to do on a Thursday night.

Being stoned will be part of this experience, but where to take flight? If we do it in our apartment, we face the logistics of driving onto campus, and logistics are not our long suit even on our soberest day. Instead, we come up with a novel idea to celebrate Stephanie's wonkiness.

We go into Wilson Library, the graduate library, where scholarship is taken seriously, with nary a word spoken above a whisper. It's next to the undergrad library, where a dull roar worthy of a diesel generator prevails. People serious about the education side go to Wilson.

It's also less than a one-minute walk from Carmichael Auditorium. On the top floor, we've been told a pulldown staircase leads to an attic. And there it is! We climb up the stairs as though we belong there and proceed to do something that would likely have gotten us expelled—three months from graduation—if discovered. We know we can't laugh out loud, which makes it that much harder to keep from laughing.

We climb back down, somehow without discovery, and enter the cauldron that is Carmichael. Our seats are in a corner, behind the pep band, whose loud, clanging music has the effect you may expect. Our senses are overwhelmed.

And this game is a dud. We're starting to come down, it's so bad. Stephanie is not getting the impact of a typical Carolina game. The Tar Heels are flat. Virginia leads by 16 at one point and by 10 with three minutes left.

Then Michael Jordan does his best impersonation of Michael Jordan. As the rally builds, the noise rises and the buzz returns. It's down to seven, then five, then three. Jordan tips in a miss to cut it to one with less than a minute left. We can't even hear each other at this point.

Poor Rick Carlyle dribbles upcourt for Virginia. Jordan hounds him then just takes it from him as though Carlyle had just been promoted from an intramural game. Jordan soars in for a dunk to put Carolina ahead. The building has never been louder. Stephanie, reserved and not knowing exactly how to cheer, is jumping up and down and singing the fight song.

When Virginia misses and Jordan outjumps Sampson for the rebound, the game is Carolina's. I doubt Stephanie has watched a Carolina game since. She probably thinks they're all like this.

March 27, 1983
Georgia 82, North Carolina 77
East Regional final

Before the NCAA Tournament, the *Morning Herald* conducts the least interesting tournament pool possible for its employees. All 52 teams are put into a hat, and you draw one. That's it. You're as likely to draw Lamar as North Carolina or Virginia.

Nancy, a tired woman beat down by press room wages, asks our high school reporter if she can pick N.C. State, the team she loves. No, he tells her, that's not how it works. You just draw a team.

So she draws one and picks … N.C. State. She's delighted, like she pulled one over on the system. We smirk behind Nancy's back rather than rub her nose in the fact that the 'Pack has no shot. One of her chief mockers, an editor, draws Houston, and boy is he pissed about that later.

N.C. State is already played out, anyway. Beating Carolina again in the ACC Tournament was mildly frustrating but turning around and beating Virginia was downright comical. Ralph Sampson will graduate without having won an ACC Tournament.

The real tournament begins now. We're certain State is done against Pepperdine, down six with less than a minute to go. Then Pepperdine's best foul shooter misses two one-and-ones. Derek Whittenburg has a chance to tie the game from the line in the final seconds but misses. Only to have Cozell McQueen (a South Carolina native who once said he attended N.C. State because he wanted to go "up north") rebound and tie the game with his only points of the game.

State wins in overtime. We laugh. We laugh a little harder two days later when, the day after UNLV's best player says Thurl Bailey hasn't "shown him much," Bailey leads a comeback and scores at the buzzer to cap another win. This State thing is quaint.

Meanwhile, Carolina has serious title aspirations. The East Regional is in Syracuse, N.Y., near my roommate's wretched hometown of Elmira. It's our last year. Why not watch another Final Four run?

We cruise past Ohio State, then watch on TV as N.C. State, now in the West Regional final, draws Virginia and, tee-hee, ends Sampson's career. State is in the Final Four. If we beat Georgia, the year after their best player ever, Dominique Wilkins, turns pro, we will play State when everything really counts. It's all just too delicious.

Except we can't beat Georgia. Jordan gets his 26, so it's not on him. Perkins looks so lost we wonder what he did the night before. I'm stunned as my last game as a Carolina student quickly comes to an end. After two Final Four trips, we just assumed another one.

That's not the way college basketball works.

April 4, 1983
N.C. State 54, Houston 52
NCAA Tournament Final

It doesn't work this way, either, but 1983 was a little different.

Back home, we're fully invested in the runaway karma train that is N.C. State. The Wolfpack can do what it wants, as we know it will return to its rightful mediocrity as soon as this is over.[1] And so, when Lorenzo Charles slams home the errant Whittenburg miss at the buzzer, we're in the floor howling with laughter. Nancy has won her jackpot.

We must go to Raleigh to see the celebration, though it takes until past midnight before we find a ride for our drunken selves. When we get there, State fans are burning couches, drinking hedonistically and hugging one another. One co-ed asks us if we have a joint and says she would screw us, but she's just too tired. It's the thought that counts, so we offer what we have. A great moment in inter-collegiate détente.

College basketball will never be this silly again. It's time to get a real job.

---

1 Not exactly true at first. State wins ACC tournament and regular season titles and plays in two regional finals over the next seven years. But since 1990, coinciding with the school running off Jim Valvano, yes, you can laugh at N.C.

12

OUCH

January 18, 1984

North Carolina 69, Virginia 66

My success at the *Durham Morning Herald* notwithstanding, I graduate from the University of North Carolina on May 15, 1983, with no job prospects, no interviews and basically no plan. I just know I'm supposed to get a job. Because that's what people do.

On Monday, May 16, I get a long overdue haircut, and it's all I can handle.

The following day, I report to Howell Hall, home of the Journalism School, and look at jobs posted on the hallway wall. The *Rocky Mount Telegram* needs an entry level sportswriter. Well, gotta start somewhere. All I know about Rocky Mount is that it is in North Carolina and it's Phil Ford's hometown.

Two days later, I meet the editor. Along with some clips, I have gathered my academic transcript in a neat folder, duly impressed with my own 3.2 grade point average. Somehow, I leave the folder on the secretary's desk. The editor never asks to see it and no one has in the 40 years since.

It's a life lesson I will repeat often, usually to undergraduates who are a threat to obsess over that extra tenth of a GPA point at the expense of experiencing college. It's so much more than classroom achievement. These four years are the exhibition season of your life, where you try out some ideas about who you are, where you stand and how you'll interact with the world. You fail, but the regular season hasn't started yet. No one is counting this against your record (absent outright crime or boneheaded social media posts that haunt forever) and everyone starts life, the real season, 0-and-0. Yes, some are more prepared than others, or "favored" to win right away. But we're all 0-and-0 when we start.

My first game in life's regular season is in this editor's office. I win the job not because of my Hemingway-esque clips or knowledge of zone defenses, but because I ask if I would have to wear a tie to work. My editor is charmed.

Thus begins a seven-month "learning opportunity" in a fading town in Eastern North Carolina. As part of a two-person sports department, we produce an afternoon paper on six days and a morning paper on Sunday. That means on Saturdays we put out two papers, one in the morning and one a few hours later. On football Friday nights, with high school games raining in from all over, my editor and I sleep on the desktops more than once so we can get up in the morning early to work on the next paper.

Nothing in college prepared me for Rocky Mount. Downtown, where the office is located, looks like the deserted set of a movie about small forgotten towns. The Tarrytown Mall sells T-shirts that say "Will the last person leaving Rocky Mount, N.C., please turn out the lights?" Civic pride! The locals call the paper the *Tell-A-Lie*, unaware that we are too overworked and inexperienced to know any better.

As a local sports reporter, I am a bit of a celebrity, so I am asked to take part on a panel predicting winners for upcoming high school football games. Tarboro has some decent returning talent, prompting me to speculate they will upend the Rocky Mount Gryphons. Then I have to cover the game. When Rocky Mount prevails, the Gryphon coach tells me he had planned to never speak to me again. Because the Rocky Mount reporter should always pick Rocky Mount to win.

They don't cover this in Journalism 553. I thank God nightly the Atlanta Braves are on WTBS every night. I hope for every game to go into extra innings, so that I might have more to do in Rocky Mount, North Carolina.

The opportunity to work at *The Chapel Hill Newspaper* can't come fast enough. I return to my college town, even move in with my old roommate, and discover another hard lesson: At age 23 and working full-time, I have nothing in common with 22-year-old students who haven't yet figured out they are living in life's exhibition season.

But I am back in town in time to cover North Carolina basketball. The *Chapel Hill Newspaper* is not exactly an independent voice, but we're not connected to the university in any way. I have to look at Carolina basketball objectively for the first time.

My editor, Elliot Warnock, and the other reporter on that team, Draggan Mihailovich, decide they need to find out if they have an "ACC reporter" in me. Draggan, a Chapel Hill native, is my age but already a journalism veteran, having served as Woody Durham's football color commentator at age 19. He guides me to the rickety press box, above the Carmichael court.

I'm assigned to do the "sidebar," or a feature story related to the game against Virginia. A vastly superior Carolina team squanders a huge lead to the plucky Cavaliers. After the tragic Rick Carlyle rims out a short baseline shot that would have tied it in the closing seconds, Carolina hangs on.

The sidebar will be about whether undefeated top-ranked Carolina is getting a little bored being this much better than everyone else, perhaps the genesis of the late-game collapse. Brad Daugherty, the sophomore center who will be the top NBA pick in two years, gives the money quote. He says he was already planning to take Carlyle's shot out of the net, assuming the game was tied and wondering if Carolina could pull it back together in overtime.

Years later, YouTube proves Daugherty otherwise. The ball slowly rolls off and Daugherty jumps for the rebound like everybody else. Maybe he was merely thinking it would go in. No matter. The quote makes the sidebar sing, and Draggan declares we have an ACC reporter.

I learn that Daugherty and his teammate, Matt Doherty, are quote machines. Doherty especially seems to understand exactly what angle you are taking and how to supply just the right quote. ("Don't tell coach, but I find myself watching Michael, too"). Jordan and Perkins will interview, but they just want it to be over with.

However, the players on other teams, and their coaches, are just as interesting, if not more so. In fact, the N.C. State locker room, with Ernie Myers, is hilarious, and, forgive me, but the Duke players are engaging. A light flickers, not quite ready to come on.

January 21, 1984
North Carolina 78, Duke 73

I'm not enough of a reporter to be trusted with this one. It's my job to put together Sunday's paper back in the office, and this game, best I can tell, is not on TV. I don't hear about it until well after it's over—the last time that will happen with a UNC-Duke game.

The game will become known as the one where Coach Smith literally re-arranges the score. Duke, just 11-17 the year before and with many in its fanbase ready to fire its no-name coach, has grown enough to play the top-ranked undefeated Tar Heels, the rock stars of college basketball, as equals. Duke has rising stars in its sophomore class and, on this night, its crowd has perhaps its cleverest moment, albeit unduplicated since.

Duke's crowd in these days is not made up of "crazies." They don't yet dress up, paint their faces and pine for camera time like the studio audience for *Let's Make a Deal*. But they are loud, obnoxious and bad to delve into performance art. When N.C. State and Clyde Austin, who had issues about "borrowing" a car, come to play, they wave car keys. When Lorenzo Charles, also with N.C. State, visits just after an unfortunate encounter with a pizza delivery driver, they fling pizza boxes. When Chris Washburn of N.C. State (hmmm, do we have a trend?) appears after stealing a stereo, they toss albums like frisbees onto the court, causing them to smash. One wag reporter writes that it's a rare chance to actually watch records broken on the court. Ok, the wag was me.

At the home game before this one with Carolina, they sink to a new low. Maryland's Herman Veal had been accused of sexual misconduct, if not outright rape. The episode is made much worse when Maryland Coach Lefty Driesell calls the victim to "discuss" the case. Not that he was pressuring her to drop it.

The Duke fans throw condoms and women's panties onto the court and serenade Veal with chants of "Spermin' Herman." Duke loses. Veal scores 12 and grabs 10 rebounds.

The school president, Terry Sanford, sends a famous "Uncle Terry" letter to each student, expressing his disappointment in each one's behavior. Duke University, he says, has to be better than this.

For the Carolina game, they are. Fans present a bouquet of roses to Coach Smith and hold up signs that say "Welcome, honored guests." Instead of waving arms behind the backboard to distract foul shooters, there's just one sign: "Please Miss." Instead of the vulgar "bullshit" chant, they disagree with the ref's calls with "we beg to differ."

In other words, a perfect night for Coach Smith to show his ass. Irate that game management staff cannot properly buzz in one of his players to sub into the game, he becomes so animated that he bangs on the scorer's table, nailing the device that's keeping score and, ironically I suppose, adding 20 points to Carolina's total.

I'm reading about this hours after it happened. Network and cable television will never make the mistake of not televising a Duke-Carolina game again. But even I, despite the indoctrination of my 23 years on this earth, can tell this behavior deserves a technical foul.

Coach Smith doesn't get one. Carolina wins. Mike Krzyzewski, the rising young Duke coach, then returns the favor by showing his ass after the game. Complaining that it wasn't Duke students or Duke coaches banging their fists on the scorer's table, he concludes with this zinger:

"So, let's get some things straight around here and quit the double standard that exists in this league."

Double standard? On a night when the Duke crowd is memorably well-behaved, the coaches lower the bar themselves. Double standard? Both schools howl to the ACC Commissioner, and Director of Officials Fred Barakat literally has to review previous UNC-Duke games to see if a "double standard" exists in favor of UNC. His conclusion? It does not.

The comment implies—well, not even implies but explicitly says—that Carolina's success the past 20 years is not earned but given. Everybody is in on it. Coach Smith intimidates the referees. The media all went to the UNC Journalism School. It's patently ridiculous.

Duke fans forever love Coach K for this, as he gaslights a fantasy that has been playing in the heads of ACC opponents basically since 1967, when Larry Miller enrolled and Coach Smith went to his first Final Four. Before the week is out, Duke will have given its coach a five-year extension.

Fans have historically complained that the refs, or the league, or the media, are against them. But in almost 60 years of my tracking ACC history, there remains only one coach, athletic director or school official who has directly alleged an organized conspiracy against his team. And that is Mike Krzyzewski.

Still, I'm starting to see how the rest of the world perceives my program and coach. As I slide deeper into a media persona, they're not even "mine" anymore. I'm losing my Carolina virginity.

March 3, 1984
North Carolina 96, Duke 83 (2 OT)

It's quite a year for the rivalry. On Senior Night in Chapel Hill, Duke basically outplays Carolina again, taking a two-point lead in the final minute and rebounding a Carolina miss. The Heels foul Danny Meagher, sending a 65% shooter to the line with nine seconds left.

If you think this is going in, you haven't been paying attention. Meagher's attempt does everything but drop. Carolina sets up a play, but Duke foils it. All that's left is for Matt Doherty to dribble up court with dwindling options.

This is Doherty's last home game. For the better part of four years, he's been a steady ballhandling and defensive presence on some really good teams, but his incessant pump-faking on 15-foot shots that I'm certain I would take and make, and his general uncertainty on the court have made this a long, tenuous relationship. On a team with Michael Jordan and three other players who will be chosen among the first six picks in their NBA drafts, this can't be the first choice.

As Jay Bilas, the excellent commentator who gets a good view of this play as Duke's center, will say later, "Matt Doherty hits a shot out of his ass."

On press row, I don't wildly cheer. That would be inappropriate times 10. I just laugh. So do most of my fellow reporters. Carolina piss factor at work.

The Tar Heels' win, though it takes double overtime, is all but inevitable.

March 10, 1984

Duke 77, North Carolina 75

ACC Tournament Semifinal

I get this cheeky idea for a column at the ACC Tournament. Who talks the most, and best, shit on the court? That's something you don't hear about on TV, and it's something we all do at all levels of basketball.

I create an all-ACC trash talking team, interviewing provocative players after tournament games who I know will give this some thought. Maryland's Lenny Bias is the best, giving a nuanced rundown of the league's leading talkers (Jordan excels in this area, too), not mentioning himself.

When I ask him for the team's MVP, he pauses and says "Myself. I can't lie." His grin is warm and infectious.

I try to catch someone from every team. For Carolina, it's my go-to, Matt Doherty. He'll get this concept and rise to the occasion.

"I don't think that's appropriate to talk about," he snaps.

Maybe I shouldn't have approached him right after the 27-1 Tar Heels, top-ranked and undefeated in ACC play, finally lose a close one to Duke, which, despite two close losses to Carolina, had finished seven games behind the Tar Heels in the ACC standings.

With Duke's ascension, you can't help but think that something is changing. This isn't N.C. State winning games with smoke and mirrors for three weeks. This one has the air of permanence.

March 22, 1984

Indiana 72, North Carolina 68

NCAA Tournament Second Round

Only two of us can cover this game in Atlanta, and I'm third on the three-man team. So Pete and I are hosting a viewing party in our apartment for the perfunctory win over a seemingly average Indiana team. Despite the loss to Duke, Carolina still has one of the best teams in its history, rivaling the '82 team that won the championship. Jordan is by far the best in college basketball and ready to take it to the next level. Whereas in '82 he lived in James Worthy's world, this is his team.

Someone forgets to tell Indiana this. The Hoosiers take it right to Carolina, outrunning them, thwarting the double team traps and doing all the fundamental stuff right. Jordan picks up two cheap fouls, sits a good part of the first half and winds up scoring just 13 points—a fact Coach Smith will never live down. He "held" Jordan below 20 points.

Carolina rallies late, but the game is a full-on debacle. The mood in our room is sour and I'm doing everything I can to not sound like my father. This sort of thing doesn't happen to North Carolina.

Draggon tells me later he and Elliott debate on the lead for the game story. Objective as we are, he says, we are still homers.

"Ouch," says the one-word lead.

Ouch indeed. The Jordan era closes, and I turn a corner in my career and my orientation toward North Carolina basketball.

"Ouch" describes where I am personally as well. The town is full of students with whom I have nothing in common. Nor are the professor types my thing. No prospects for dating, either. I can't hang out in college bars forever and getting stoned four or five nights a week has its limits.

Though it's been just seven months, I have to get out of here before it gets to where I can never leave. The newspaper in Wilmington is looking for a sportswriter, and I figure maybe I can live at the beach. I turn to my mentor, Keith Drum, for advice.

"Wilmington?" he says.

"Yes. Is that a good place for me?"

"You can get laid in Wilmington."

This is what I need from a mentor. I get together my clips and interview. They really like the all-trash talking team column. So, kiss my ass, Matt Doherty. The *Wilmington Morning Star* hires its next sportswriter.

13

GUYS IN SHORT PANTS

January 9, 1985
North Carolina 75, Maryland 74

For a group that is supposedly in Dean Smith's pocket, sportswriters sure are hateful about him. They mock his accent, his smoking habit and the smug air that seems to hover about the program. They make fun of the clichés and blandness that comes from him and the players. They dare to impugn the "Carolina Way."

I'm becoming one of them. Years of sustained excellence have created a different sort of vibe at Carolina and it's not all good. The Sports Information Department is wonderful, but it's hard to get interviews with Coach Smith or the players. Or if you do get interviews, it's hard to get them to say anything worthwhile. It's as if the players are coached to keep it vanilla.

It's not that Coach Smith doesn't care about the media. Oh, he does. He does indeed. It's a well-known secret that he keeps a file on every sportswriter and publication, basically creating a "naughty" and "nice" list. I start to wonder, in my nascent career in Wilmington, writing a column twice a week with my name and photo on it and regular attendance at ACC games, if I have a file.

The difference between Carolina and the other Triangle-area programs within easy driving range of Wilmington is stark. Mike Krzyzewski at Duke lectures the *Durham Morning Herald* in 1984 about not positively covering the Blue Devils during the struggling years, claiming his ninth-grade daughter is having to defend Duke at school. But he basically makes himself available because he still needs media goodwill. And his players are insightful and even funny.

Jay Bilas is an especially good interview, although I once heard him give a thoughtful interview to *Sports Illustrated's* Curry Kirkpatrick and followed up with a question of my own, only to have him snap at me. So, there may be an element of Duke whoring themselves to influential national outlets while having little patience for the *Wilmington Morning Stars* that cover them every day. Or maybe I just asked a dumb question.

Then there's Jim Valvano at N.C. State. He definitely seeks publicity but doesn't have an ounce of guile about him. Just a few months after his 1983 national championship, he fulfills a contractual obligation and appears at a Rocky Mount pizza joint while I'm still at the *Telegram*. The only reporters are a local TV guy and me.

The TV guy asks a question about next year and whether State can repeat with this lineup. Valvano patiently answers, then as soon as the lights go off lectures the reporter on the fact that his top three starters are graduating and repeating is not likely with this lineup.

"Do your homework," he barks, and the guy deserves it.

He seems relieved to talk to a print guy who actually knows something about college basketball. We settle into a booth, I turn on my tape recorder and we order a round of beers. I cannot believe I'm talking to the reigning coach of the national champions, having just completed one of the most storied runs in history, just four months after watching couches burn in the after-party on State's campus.

Six beers later, I have two cassettes full of Valvano recounting every game in that tournament, how every decision he made worked and how it felt to run around the court looking to hug Dereck Whittenburg after the final dunk. The tapes themselves would be worth something - if I still had them.

During the next season, Lorenzo Charles is performing like an All-American the year after his championship moment—much as Michael Jordan did the year after his. I decide to write a story comparing the impact this success had on each of them. The interview with Jordan is a walk-and-talk after a game on his way to his car—a really nice one for a college junior, but what do I know? Jordan is polite and answers the questions, but this is the only way to get him.

To interview Charles, I visit a State practice in Reynolds Coliseum. Valvano is sitting in the stands, talking to some friends. The players are shooting jumpers, balls flying everywhere. I ask the Sports Information staffer if he can grab Lorenzo for me, and he says, "he's right there." So, I pull Lorenzo off the court and ask him about life after his famous dunk.

I'm not suggesting State didn't have organized practices, or that Valvano didn't coach them. I am suggesting that Dean Smith didn't sit down with a reporter he didn't know and talk about the '82 championship over six beers, or that anyone wandered into a Carolina practice and pulled a starting forward off the court for an interview.

It was just different at the other schools. And I am starting to appreciate that different isn't necessarily worse. For my professional purposes, it is actually much better.

But old habits die hard. Maryland comes to Chapel Hill in early January and has the Tar Heels all but beaten. If they can just make some free throws. They can't. Adrian Branch, the most experienced of the Terps, misses a crucial one-and-one, UNC's Dave Popson hits from the top of the key, and Carolina wins by one.

In the locker room, I can't resist asking Branch about the delay before his foul shot, orchestrated by Coach Smith by taking his time replacing his player who had just fouled out. Did this gamesmanship by Coach Smith "freeze" Branch and have anything to do with why he missed?

Branch looks at me with well-earned disdain. Must every foible be credited to Coach Smith's wiles? He snorted and said no, he just missed.

March 10, 1985
Georgia Tech 67, North Carolina 62
ACC Tournament Final

Something is off about this Carolina team, the first post-Jordan and Perkins, but it's hard to pinpoint. They're having to get by with just three first-round NBA picks and a handful of other high school All-Americans, and they spend nine weeks in the top 10, finishing at 7th in the polls. This is "off" by Carolina standards under Coach Smith.

This version is hard to explain. Duke comes into Carmichael Auditorium in mid-January and lays a 16-point beatdown on the Tar Heels, their first win in Chapel Hill since 1966. It gets so bad that Coach Smith calls a timeout to correct poor performance, something he rarely does, and a minute or so later calls another timeout. He later explains, candidly for him, that the team didn't do what he told them in the first timeout.

They finish in a three-way tie for first, but during the first round of the ACC Tournament manage to trail pesky Wake Forest late into the second half before Wake's Charlie Thomas hangs on the rim after dunking to keep from crashing onto Warren Martin, UNC's dorky center, who had fallen under the basket. Referee Hank Nichols dutifully calls a technical foul, as the rulebook does not yet have a provision to allow hanging from the rim to protect players from injury.

I'm in a press room in Williamsburg, VA, at the conference tournament where UNC-Wilmington is playing. The TV is on, and the Thomas technical prompts ungodly carping from the gathered reporters. Carolina is getting their way again. A four-point Wake lead becomes three, then one, then Carolina leads. Carolina wins in overtime.

The Carolina backlash continues into the final against Georgia Tech, by contrast a feel-good story led by Coach Bobby Cremins, who threw away the pass that cost South Carolina the 1970 ACC title game and promptly hid in the North Carolina mountains for two weeks afterward.

Georgia Tech has been in the league just six years, losing 27 of its first 28 ACC games. They are scrappy, led by Mark Price, and have already beaten Carolina twice. Everyone seems to be rooting for them.

They win another close one against Carolina, redemption for Cremins. It's easy to be happy for them. I can honestly say I'm neutral on whether Carolina wins or loses.

March 24, 1985
Villanova 56, North Carolina 44
NCAA Tournament Southeast Regional Final

I've become totally enamored with Auburn basketball. The year after Charles Barkley leaves, they finish eighth in their conference, then come out of nowhere to win the SEC Tournament. In the first two NCAA games in South Bend, Indiana, they win by one and then by two over a really good Kansas team. I'm sitting at press row watching because the Tar Heels don't play until the evening session, and I have never seen a team play so hard. I'm convinced I'm watching an N.C. State replay from two years before.

When the Tar Heels drag me to the regional in Birmingham by squeaking past Notre Dame on the Irish home court, I am thrilled to continue to watch the Auburn run—against the Tar Heels. I go to dinner alone and the entire Auburn team, eating like regular human beings, is seated nearby. I'm on the ground floor of something memorable.

It is not to be so. Carolina squeaks past Auburn. I am agitated, and totally blind to who the real upstart team is.

The Heels play Villanova in the final, a team that barely made it into the field and had served as lapdogs for Georgetown, St. John's and the rest of the Big East Conference for a while now. I assume I am headed to the

Final Four the next week in Lexington, Kentucky, and not entirely happy about it, tired of hotels and phony press conferences.

Villanova is accommodating in this regard. The Wildcats simply seem to want it more. The lowlight comes about midway through the second half, when a loose ball heads our way, slowly, toward press row. Carolina's Curtis Hunter watches it bounce, bounce, bounce.

Harold Jensen has time to recognize this, swoop in to pick it up and lay it in at the other end for Villanova. It's a shocking lack of hustle from a Carolina player in a big moment.

After the game, a 56-44 loss, Coach Smith does the most passive aggressive thing. Each coach brings three or four players with him to a NCAA Tournament post-game press conference, and we look up to see Hunter following his coach and Brad Daugherty into the room. That's Curtis Hunter, who played 16 minutes and scored six points. Well, it is two more than Kenny Smith or Joe Wolf, future first-round NBA picks, scored.

Is Dean daring us to ask Hunter about the loose ball? Is this a mind game on Curtis or on us? Is he actively embarrassing one of his players? Let the record show that no, none of us ask Hunter about it.

I stay home, a gift from Villanova, and watch the Wildcats pull off a masterful upset of Georgetown to win it all. I was indeed on the ground floor of greatness, even if it escaped me in the moment.

February 20, 1986
Maryland 77, North Carolina 72 (OT)

My good friend, Blondie, has joined me in the press box for this, the sixth game in the new Dean E. Smith Activities Center, already known as the "Dean Dome." It may come as no surprise that "Blondie" is not her real name, but the derisive nickname my future wife gives her. We can't use her real name because, Lord, she's a wife and mother now.

Blondie is actually more than a friend. I meet her at the tail end of my Chapel Hill days, after I had basically given up on finding a romantic interest. I had gone to a fairly wild house party out in the country at a house condemned to be razed for the expansion of Interstate 40, sporting my MTV sweatshirt and cowboy hat. A golden Labrador comes up to me for some attention, and I figure this will be the best I will do at this party.

"You look like that dog," says a girl, now standing over me.

"Excuse me?"

"That dog. You look like him."

"Look, I don't know... " I start.

"It's a compliment."

So we chat. She's very interested in the cocaine hits going on in the bathroom, and I assume this entire convo was a front for her to crash that.

But she calls me a few weeks later to meet her at a Raleigh hotel bar, where she drags me into the ladies' room. She's crazy, but we connect. Before long, she's the first actual grown-up girlfriend of my life. She teaches me basically how to act like a man, how to wear a grown-up shirt, how to organize a date and how to treat a woman.

Like a ragged team that cuts down on turnovers, shares the ball and coalesces during a season, I'm starting to take on an identity. My apartment on Stone Street at Wrightsville Beach is about 200 yards from high tide. Of my five neighbors in the building, four of them sell drugs, so when their "ship" comes in, all tides in the building rise accordingly.

During the summer I swim all day before my evening shift, achieving all-ocean status riding waves. During football and basketball seasons, I travel to the Triangle area, cover a game and hang out with Blondie until I have to come back on Tuesday afternoon. I am beach sportswriter guy. It's a good gig.

Naturally, then, I dump Blondie. So confident have I become in my viability as a romantic partner, I take up with a friend from college. Then Allison, my old high school flame, comes back for a fling. And so on. It could have something to do with free lodging on summer weekends at Wrightsville Beach, but please let me think otherwise.

The more I learn about women, the more I realize I shouldn't have dumped Blondie. She agrees to go with me to the Maryland game, probably to pull against the 25-1 Tar Heels of 1986, top-ranked all season. She could be disagreeable that way.

Instead of another Carolina romp against an unranked team, we witness greatness in the purest form, now known as "The Len Bias Game." The Maryland forward scores 35, but it feels like more. In the second half, he hits a shot and I look down to make a note of it. Before I can look back up, he's hanging from the rim from a backwards dunk, the result of having stolen the inbounds pass. He is magical.

No one could possibly fathom that in four months, two days after he's the second pick of the NBA draft and headed to Boston to play with Larry Bird, he'd be dead from a cocaine overdose.

Carolina freezes up, backs into overtime and loses for the first time in the Dean Dome. I take Blondie home, knowing I can't keep doing this to her, but thankful for every minute of our time. I'm growing up as a writer, as a basketball observer and as a man. I'm ready to test my act in my childhood home. Or at least I think I am.

March 7, 1986
Maryland 85, North Carolina 75
ACC Tournament First Round

After starting 21-0 and 25-1, the Tar Heels have a rough go of it. They lose three of their last four games and somehow slip into third place heading into the tournament in Greensboro.

As was my custom, I save the *Morning Star* the cost of a hotel room and agree to stay with my parents. I let them know I won't get there until after the last game of the first round, sometime around midnight. And I will have covered four games and written eight stories by then, so I'll probably want to shower and go straight to bed.

As the third-place team, Carolina gets the 9:30 p.m. slot and a rematch with Maryland. You would think Maryland would get an inspired Carolina team bent on revenge, but for whatever reason, you would be wrong. The late-season malaise continues. A team that has been top-ranked 13 weeks and in the top 5 all season looks mentally tired. Maryland is just the better team, and the Terps send Carolina home with extra time to get ready for the NCAA Tournament. That's about all I read into it.

The family Whisnant near my beach apartment, around the time of the "guys in short pants" episode with my father. As soon as the camera flashed, all five of us began adding pounds. Relentlessly.

Surprisingly, Mama and Daddy are both up when I get home, Daddy in his recliner and Mama on the couch. The fire is still going, so I stand in front to warm up.

"Have you ever seen anything so sorry in your life?" my father asks.

I was expecting a question about living alone at the beach. How is work? What do I eat? Do I grocery shop? Have I met anyone? Do I have hopes, fears or aspirations?

No. We're going to do this and we're going to do it now.

"Well, they weren't very good tonight." I'm trying to deflect, but I fear it's coming.

And it does. If he were coach, he would have forfeited at halftime and resigned. The players don't care. They are an embarrassment to the university. They executed the sorry plan.

It's been a long day, I'm tired and I decide I just won't take it tonight.

"They don't owe you anything," I said. "They're putting a lot more into it than you are. They're more disappointed by losing than you could ever be."

It comes off as an affront to his manhood and his dominion over the home. Other than that, it does not go over well at all.

Daddy says he puts his heart and soul into every game, so the players should, too. He is owed more than this. Don't I care about it?

"No, actually I don't. I'm a sportswriter now," I tell him. "I see it objectively for what it is. They don't define who I am by whether they win or lose, and they shouldn't define it for you, either."

"If you don't care, what's the point of watching the game?" He's shouting now. "You have to care about it or why bother?"

My poor mother doesn't know whose side to take. She remains silent.

"It's just a game. They're just guys running around in short pants. They tried tonight and it didn't work. They'll try again next week. But I can't put all my self-worth into it."

"That job has done something to you," he says. And on that note, we retire to our rooms.

Sleep doesn't come easy. I have two stinking semifinal games to cover tomorrow, and it's another grind. How can a man who gets the big things so right get so hung up on this? Where does this sense of entitlement come from? My father is not outwardly obnoxious about Carolina basketball. He's not that guy who didn't go to school there but acts like every victory is an invitation to feel superior.

It's hard to say what he gets out of it. He wrestled life to the ground through the Depression, World War II, working multiple jobs to support a family, and holding a mundane job with Guilford County long enough to literally retire with the gold watch, putting his whole self into all those endeavors. And that doesn't stop when he's playing canasta or ping-pong or watching his two sports passions—the Washington Redskins and the North Carolina Tar Heels. He just really hates losing. He's in it to win.

He doesn't need his grown son challenging him on the concept of fandom and perspective. He's plenty comfortable about where he is on that issue. Still, what must it be like to be so competitive that you wager all your emotion on something you cannot control?

How did I get away with challenging my father like that in his own living room? And what will tomorrow bring?

When I wake up, the first person I see is my father. He says he has thought about our conversation. Yes, they are just college guys in short pants. He *apologizes* for carrying on so and promises to try to gain some perspective.

Whatever was left of my boyhood has just evaporated. My father apologized to me. I am fully a man.

14

THE SWALLOWS
OF CAPISTRANO

March 31, 1986

Louisville 72, Duke 69

NCAA Tournament Final

The 1986 ACC Tournament is not a total personal bust. The *Morning Star* sends its top lifestyle reporter to cover the final game, to uncover a fluffy feature on the atmosphere of the ACC Tournament.

I am thrilled to see her, as she has become my best friend, listening raptly to stories about locker room antics, the players' "credentials" in that space and other stuff no one else I know would seem to care about, especially not my female friends. We laugh at the same things, mostly at ourselves, and talk easily about so many subjects.

Jerry Hooks, my editor, rolls his eyes. The sportswriter he hired before me ran off with a lifestyle reporter just a year ago, and he had been married at the time. He's having a sense of déjà vu he doesn't like.

Because, as it turns out, Celia is married, too.

Nonetheless, decorum rules the day. Celia heads for the nosebleeds to interview fans who can barely see anything but are thrilled nonetheless, files her story and I don't see her for the rest of the weekend. Duke wins the tournament in a nailbiter and starts a march through the NCAA Tournament. I am enamored with the Duke locker room. The players are quotable, thoughtful and accessible. They each have their own personality and give nuanced responses to questions. They are part of a freshman class that almost saw Mike Krzyzewski get fired, then progressed to foil UNC, and now on to national greatness.

They lose to Carolina in the first game in the new Dean Dome and their next one to Georgia Tech. Then the Devils rip off 21 in a row to make the national final against Louisville as the top-ranked team. The *Morning Star* has me covering every step in this journey, and, contrary to my life's ethic today, I am in total harmony with the Duke vibe. They love their coach. They sleep over at his house. The senior class has this incredible shared bond of having overcome adversity. Sign me up.

Then "it" happens. On the day between the semifinals and final, the NCAA holds a press conference with each team. The coaches bring as many players as they see fit, and Krzyzewski brings his entire starting five.

They are charming, funny and spontaneous. The national media openly swoons.

It quickly becomes revolting. The media, from New York and other normally cynical outposts, ask the players their major, their impression of Duke academics, and their grade point average. They all decline that last one, except Jay Bilas, who says his GPA is the same as his per-game scoring average. The media laughs as one.

I should mention that two Duke starters are white. This will become relevant.

Louisville comes in, brings in just two players, both black, and gives the standard press conference fare. One player makes the mistake of mentioning that, with all the travel, they have barely been to class this semester and have had to do their classwork on the road. I cannot recall anyone asking them their major or GPA.

Apparently, Duke has become the standard bearer of the "student-athlete," the program that does everything the "right" way, where kids go to learn and just happen to play basketball as well.

Louisville represents everything else. And White America has some problems with what they fear "everything else" is becoming.

At this point, you can start filling in some cultural blanks. I am offended not only on the barely concealed racial profiling, but I suddenly remember I'm a Carolina fan and alumnus. We've been doing things the "right" way for about 20 years (don't worry, a commentary on the AfAm scandal of the 1990s-2000s is coming) and the media now discovers a Duke University program that didn't start a black player until less than 10 years before, a private, elitist university that has hardly been, to anyone who grew up in North Carolina, a symbol for diversity, equality or anything other than faux Ivy League wannabe status.

Carolina, primarily through Dean Smith, practically integrated college basketball in the South, and its black players have represented the university, the academics and the "collegiate" experience every bit as well as these Duke guys are doing now. Why is the national media, quickly aligning with each other like a middle school clique, just now falling for this?

Could it be the large number of white guys, here today and including top reserves like Danny Ferry, and the exceptionally well-spoken, non-threatening black starters? Hmmmm.

The media's sadness after Louisville prevails in a close game, making the heady, scrappy plays that typically... oh never mind... is palpable. Here's some of what Dave Anderson, an award-winning venerated sports columnist with the *New York Times*, wrote the next day under the headline "Duke won, too":

"Duke didn't score the most points in the title game, but its players scored the most points in the Final Four's oral exam, the annual Sunday news conference."

For perspective on this, he offered:

"Through the years, the Final Four has often reflected the academic atmosphere surrounding the team, if not the players' development as college students. Moments after Georgetown won the 1984 title, two players were virtually incoherent in a network television interview. Several players from Kentucky's 1978 championship team sat stiffly behind a long table on an elevated stage at the Sunday news conference, without a smile, without any apparent sense of enjoying what they had accomplished..."

Anyone care to guess the race of those Georgetown and Kentucky players?

He goes on. Duke had the "guts" to bring all five of their starters, all but saying they didn't hide their ignorant ones.

"Quickly it was apparent that these five players were not representing Renegade State, where slam-dunking is considered a major."

Not sure I have a team photo of Renegade State, but I can only imagine.

Duke can't exactly be blamed for this. They didn't set the media agenda, but just showed up and cleverly answered some questions. But instead of self-awareness on how absurd this is, they eagerly fed the narrative.

"At their Sunday news conference, the five Blue Devil starters were the epitome of what college basketball players should be," Anderson wrote. "Mature but humorous, clever but disciplined. In their quiet, pleasant manner, they realized who and what they were."

"'I think we've set new standards as far as academics and basketball are concerned," Johnny Dawkins said. "This team shows they can go hand in hand.'"

Yes, no team had previously tried academics and basketball at the same time.

The *New York Times* is not alone in this take. The *Chicago Tribune* writes in its day-after edition that "Funk wins, scholarship loses. So much for literacy. Drape all the campus libraries in black."[1] This exercise is no doubt repeated wherever white people publish newspapers.

Even my own paper gets caught up in it. In my column reviewing the Sunday press conference, I try to highlight how ridiculous the perception was that Duke had suddenly discovered academics in college basketball. But apparently I pull some punches, so my copy editor doesn't quite get where I'm going and puts the headline of "Athletes vs. Academics" on my column, with my photo on it. I pray to God no one digs that up.

I'll never look at Duke the same, safe to say. In fact, I'm losing my ability to look at the media or college basketball in general the same. Working the games, dreading going to the locker room to pry quotes from reluctant college kids who just want to get dressed and hoping against hope that this great game doesn't go into overtime so I can make deadline are not what I had in mind when I dreamed of *Sports Illustrated*.

Keith Drum, the mentor who also gave me tons of practical work-related advice, had told me to expect this. Sportswriters, at about the two- or three-year mark, have to decide if this is really for them, or if it's time to get a grown-up job. Most of them leave. I'm three years in and starting to wonder.

After the season, a group of graduating seniors from ACC teams band together for a "barnstorming" tour throughout the state, giving the locals not fortunate enough to see their games in person a chance to gawk at them. The players get some actual cash, which had been denied them while carrying the banner for their schools.

---

1   This gem was dug up by Bomani Jones in his HBO show Game Theory with Bomani Jones. A segment in his first show, which aired March 13, 2022, brilliantly explained how racially polarizing the early Krzyzewski Duke teams, based on many white stars, were to a nation that wasn't ready to give college basketball over to Black America. It includes a promo from CBS in advance of a 1991 Michigan-Duke game saying "Fab Five against America's Finest, coming up next!" Yup. America's Finest. Versus the thugs from Michigan wearing black socks and long shorts. Any questions on why Duke became the darlings of racist America and the scourge of everyone else?

Organizers have historically struggled with exactly how to structure these games. The ACC players aren't playing so they can be challenged athletically or struggle to win. They are past that. But who to enlist as the opponent?

In 1978, an ACC group came to High Point Central's dilapidated high school gym to play, and organizers rounded up a group of local small college stars as the opponent. This proved to be a mistake. A High Point College stalwart named Pearlee Shaw, still on the school's top 10 scorers list, got free and dunked on the famous ACC group, and he let them know about it.

Two possessions later, UNC's Geoff Crompton, 6-11 and generously listed at 280 pounds though 325 would easily have been believed, got a breakaway at midcourt. He dribbled in with purpose, organizing his steps while Shaw chased. It was a bad idea. Crompton dunked over Shaw, the backboard shattering, the rim ripping away and leaving us stunned. The silence in the gym was broken only by the laughter of Mike O'Koren, then a college sophomore who came down to watch his teammates.

Lesson learned. When this ACC group comes to Leland, birthplace of Charlie Daniels but an otherwise undistinguished suburb of Wilmington, they are playing high school kids who know better. It's the best piddle going in April, so I cover it, hoping that maybe these guys, freed of their college affiliations, will give some real quotes on what playing in the ACC has been like.

Instead, I learn that my weariness is mutual. They are weary of sportswriters, and that includes me. David Henderson, one of those charming, mature, clever and disciplined Duke Blue Devils at the Final Four press conference, blows me off in the rudest way possible.

Len Bias, the carefree guy who two years before had been the star of my all-ACC trash talking team, glares at me behind sunglasses—we're in a locker room—and just says "No!"

I will give credit—Johnny Dawkins gives me a pregame interview and is fairly gracious about it. The rest of them are done with me. I'm about done with this scene, too.

Later that hot summer, I cram in one more act of disillusionment. The local Carolina Alumni Club hosts an event at a posh Wrightsville Beach club, with Coach Dean Smith the featured speaker. We arrange a brief interview with Coach Smith before the event, my first one-on-one with the legend of my childhood.

These events are for the committed followers, or I should say "donors." They can be as dry, or as entertaining, as the coaches' personalities allow. I once attended Jim Valvano speaking to the N.C. State club, and he not only gave me great insight on what it was like to actually be *expected* to win (recruiting had picked up post-1983) but allowed me to hear his speech if I understood he would be making anti-Carolina jokes he didn't want repeated.

That may have been the hardest I've laughed. Example: Valvano said he had the month of August off that year, so his wife said she wanted to make love 31 times that month.

"That's great. Put me down for two," he told her. Yeah, State lost a good bit of its soul when they ran him off, or, perhaps more accurately, allowed the media to run him off.

Chief among the pitchfork-carrying journalists was Peter Golenbock, whose book *Personal Fouls: The Broken Promises and Shattered Dreams of Big Money Basketball at Jim Valvano's North Carolina State* might have been the worst example of for-profit gotcha journalism in history. Almost all of it was based on a disgruntled team manager. Misspelled names. Placing State in the wrong NCAA regional. A claim that Muggsy Bogues dunked "several times" in a game—Bogues stands 5-foot-3.

My personal favorite: The assertion the Dean Dome was so hostile to opposing teams' fans the Carolina crowd would pick offenders up and hoist them, row by row, to the top of the arena "until he is no longer able to be heard." That doesn't happen anywhere, and especially not in the home of "wine and cheese" fans.

Yes, the Wolfpack program had relaxed some standards by the late 80s, and Valvano was distracted by the idea of being Jim Valvano. And his players sold comp tickets and shoes (as did players everywhere). But Valvano and the program didn't deserve the shafting it got.

UNC media plays it closer to the vest. They make it clear I will not be attending the actual speech by Coach Smith. I am given 15 minutes to explore issues with him. I'm nervous beyond belief, but come up with what I think is a provocative line of questioning: Would you rather be in national contention every year even if you don't win it very often (ahem, Carolina hasn't won an ACC Tournament or Final Four berth since 1982 and this gap is becoming uncomfortable), or win it all every now and then but suffer through truly down years in between? Like, say, Indiana— an inference the Hoosiers don't exactly deserve, as they were pretty good every year, even if the year before included the infamous Bobby Knight's chair-throwing incident.

"Ah, not Indiana," he replied. "Bob Knight is a friend."

Non-sequitur, but ok. How about Louisville (19-18 in 1985, national champs in 1986)?

Now we get an answer. He values a program that competes for a national title every year, etc. etc. The real takeaway here is that he obviously doesn't consider Louisville Coach Denny Crum a friend.

I can't shake the feeling this interview is a contest I am losing. Suddenly the famously punctual Coach Smith conspicuously looks at his watch. We're 15 minutes in. This interview is over.

March 8, 1987
N.C. State 68, North Carolina 67
ACC Tournament Final

The thing about Celia and me is that, owing to her marital status, we started as friends. There was no pressure to "date" or figure out how to ask someone out. Had there been, I surely would have flunked this, as my childhood had provided no experience in this domain. I blame my teeth.

We hang out in the newsroom and at staff parties. But the pressure to do something about this becomes too much. The husband, also a *Morning Star* employee, takes up with yet another newspaper person, someone I had just dated two weeks before ("dated" would be a generous term). Celia and I then out ourselves as a couple, the entire development tawdry even by newsroom standards. But we own it.

In fact, it soon becomes so serious that I introduce her to my parents. I'm apprehensive how they will react, their 25-year-old son never having done this before and certainly not with a formerly married, older woman.

We meet at a barbecue restaurant near the beach, as my parents happen to be traveling to a spot in nearby South Carolina. Celia charms my father right there in the parking lot with her passionate description of her love of fresh butterbeans. It would never have occurred to me to try this tactic on future in-laws, but it's brilliant in its originality and execution. My parents now understand their son is grown, likely relieving them of substantial worry.

During the 1987 season, I decide to write a column lampooning the coaches' silly weekly TV shows, which are basically a few highlights wrapped around a bunch of commercials. In the pre-Internet era before thousands of ESPN outlets, this was often the only way to see pieces of the previous week's games.

All the area programs had these shows. Valvano's was hilarious—he didn't even need a host. Krzyzewski's was informative. The East Carolina program's theme song was *Funeral for a Friend*, which summed that one up. But I poked the most fun at the Carolina show, mocking the length of Coach Smith's tie and comparing the "review" of the week's games to *Pravda*. I think I'm on Coach Smith's naughty list.

UNC in 1987 manages to have the most uninspiring 32-4 season possible. The Tar Heels spend the entire season in the top five nationally, roll through the ACC undefeated yet look vulnerable heading into the

ACC final against a 19-13 N.C. State team that finished sixth in the eight-team league and won two overtime games to reach the final.

The Wolfpack's opener against Duke highlights an untold story that some reporters were trying to find a way to print, that Mike Krzyzewski and Jim Valvano do not like each other. Or, more accurately, K hates losing to Valvano. The two faced off several times when K was at Army and Valvano at Iona, and of course twice a year, at least, at Duke and State.

The theory went that, to Krzyzewski, State comes off as undisciplined, with shirttails out, jawing at each other and their opponents and led by Valvano's seat-of-pants style. It went against his Army upbringing.

Years later, after Krzyzewski and Valvano truly did become good friends as Valvano was dying from cancer, this "rivalry" became more widely reported. At the time, it was something we strongly suspected. By the time Krzyzewski had so much as coached an NCAA Tournament game, Valvano had already won an ACC and NCAA title.

Overall, Valvano won 17 out of 28 games against Krzyzewski, often when Duke had superior talent. And you just know that every one of those 17 galled Mike Krzyzewski.

One writer friend even tells me that in the UNC-State final, Mickie Krzyzewski, the bete noire of the Duke fan base and presumably the mood ring of her husband's true affections, openly roots for North Carolina.

The Tar Heels absolutely squander this game to a lesser team. In fact, Jim Valvano dragging this sixth-place team to an ACC title is likely a better coaching accomplishment than taking a talented, though under-appreciated, team to the 1983 national title.

The image Carolina fans probably have of this game, if they choose to remember it at all, is State forward Bennie Bolton helping his 7-year-old child with his homework on the court after the game. Well, it might have been a toddler. An infant? My memory is hazy on this. We just weren't used to college basketball players sharing post-game celebrations with their children. This wouldn't happen at Duke.

March 21, 1987

Syracuse 79, North Carolina 75

NCAA Tournament East Regional Final

Why this game is considered an embarrassment to North Carolina is unclear, but it is. Yes, Carolina is 32-3 and top-seeded, but Syracuse is top 10, plays in the rugged Big East Conference and has three players— Sherman Douglas, Rony Seikaly and Derrick Coleman—who would play more NBA games than this Carolina roster combined (some stat games here. This is true if you subtract the games Scott Williams would play, but he was but a freshman that year and played 12 minutes without a point or rebound in this game).

It's no accident that Syracuse goes on to the national final and loses by one point to Indiana, once again very good, on a last-second shot.

Nonetheless, the sportswriter room is merciless toward Carolina when this is over. Since the 1982 title, Carolina has twice gone undefeated in ACC play, yet failed to win the ACC Tournament or a regional final, squandering the rest of Michael Jordan's career as well as those of Brad Daugherty and Kenny Smith.

We try to out-do each other on how to put this into perspective. The winner, in my estimation, is my friend Country Dan Collins of the *Winston-Salem Journal*.

"How's this?" he asks me, then quoting his lead. "Just like the swallows of Capistrano[2], the North Carolina Tar Heels are returning home right on time."

I love it, except for one part. I am not familiar with these swallows. I tell him I thought "Capistrano" was a type of coffee. Poor Dan has wasted greatness on me.

After these tournament games, a reporter can either go to the press conference where the coaches, and some players, are, or work the locker

---

2   Each spring, cliff swallows migrate from Argentina and, since the early 1800s, a large number find the Mission of San Juan Capistrano at a time so predictable—March 19 - it became a local celebration. Thank you, Internet.

rooms and pick up quotes from the presser later. Kenny Smith is one of the players at the press conference, so when he returns to the locker room to take off his Carolina uniform for the last time, a handful of reporters, including me, ask him questions, or more accurately, aggravate him one last time.

"What's the point doing the press conference if I have to answer the same fucking questions in here?" he shouts to no one in particular.

He has a point. We wish we had seen that kind of candor from him and his teammates during his four years at North Carolina.

Sportswriting and Carolina basketball have become almost adversarial. It's time for me to return home to my roots, perhaps for a timely cup of Capistrano.

15

MELT LIKE BUTTER

March 13, 1988
Duke 65, North Carolina 61
ACC Tournament Final

Working nights is a blessing for a single bodysurfer dude who lives within earshot of a breaking wave. I can get in a good three-to-four hours of wave-riding, beach walking and general goofing off until it is time to go to work. Getting off work around 1 a.m. isn't a problem, as this is a time to hang with the coke-headed restaurant staff in my apartment building who work the same hours. Throw in getting to see some quality ACC football and basketball games, and it's quite the gig.

But now, I'm a boyfriend. Working Friday and Saturday nights is not the way to nurture a relationship. I am completely out of step with normal society, working crappy hours. There's high school football. Boys and girls basketball. Lots of prep basketball. I have seen enough of those games to last a lifetime. Watching high-caliber ACC games is not enough to make up for this. I think I'm the only sportswriter on the ACC circuit who spends the previous night covering a godforsaken prep game.

The issue is seldom the game itself but, when on the road, finding a place to write it up and, finally, a standard telephone with a receiver that fits the hard rubber "couplers" so I can transmit the story on the portable computer. It's 1988, after all.

These computers are prickly. At a baseball game in Hallsboro, I drop it and the screen smashes. So I call up the office and dictate from the home of Dan Biser, my friend at the *Whiteville News Reporter* who looks after his own kind. In my best Ron Morris imitation, I write in my head in real time. Readers would never know the difference, which either says something about organizing my ideas on deadline or the standard fare they are accustomed to from me.

The low moment in this regard comes when I cover a Whiteville High School football playoff game in Fuquay Varina, every bit as rural, remote and backward as the name suggests. They watch *Andy Griffith* reruns for a glimpse of the future.

On this night, it snowed to beat the band. Now, truth be told, the stadium had a press box that kept me warm and dry, with hot beverages. Celia, who joins me as we have plans to go to the Triangle later that night, freezes in the stands, a lump of snow by the third quarter. No, they wouldn't let her in the press box.

After it's over and Whiteville wins big, I start to write in the Fuquay-Varina coach's office. But he's butthurt. He wants to go home and runs me out, apparently unconcerned with whether the *Morning Star's* readers find out the next morning what happened.

Now I'm faced with finding an open business, with an available telephone that's shaped correctly, in Fuquay-Varina around 10 p.m. on a Friday night. No one tells you about this when you're dreaming of writing for *Sports Illustrated*. The only building that's open is the police station, and, after a few pointed questions, they graciously allow me to record this game for history.

It should come as no surprise to anyone when I decide I've had it. Yet it does. I walk into the *Morning Star* newsroom early in 1988 and demand a career change, seeking a role as a news reporter and its 9-5 (sort of) hours, Monday-Friday.

You would have thought I had asked permission to cover the White House.

"But you're a sportswriter, not a reporter," they all but say.

Yes, it's offensive. The newsroom loves to brag about how it covers an election every year or so, with results pouring in from multiple counties and requiring a network of remote "stringers" feeding numbers, quotes and sometimes even analysis—all against deadline, the real kind where if you don't get done in time, it doesn't go in the paper. In other words, just like every Friday night during football and basketball season in the sports department. I think I can handle this.

They acquiesce, probably out of curiosity more than recognition of my skills. For all I know, there's a pool on how long I will last.

They give me a beat where I can do the least harm—Columbus County, a rural, corrupt county that has not kept up as time marched forward. In some of its towns, you would swear you drove through a fog upon entering and, when it cleared, realized you were in 1955.

Without daily newspapers to report on them, fraud and grift run rampant in provincial counties like these. As one reporter tells me, in Columbus County you don't even dig for corruption—you just blow off the dust. The *Whiteville News Reporter* staff writer gives me stories too polarizing for her paper to print. But lest anyone castigate that newspaper, it did win the Pulitzer Prize in the 1950s for standing up to the Ku Klux Klan. That's one more Pulitzer than I have.

My first story? A pit bull has bitten the ear off a 2-year-old in Delco. The boy is brought to Wilmington, home of the nearest hospital. The plastic surgeon asks for the ear so that he might reattach it. No one can find it. The surgeon sighs.

"Bring me the dog," he says.

The dog is brought to Wilmington and put down. Well, the editors make me use the word "killed." Have editors never owned dogs?

The surgeon opens the stomach and—voila!—there is the ear. He reattaches it.

This never happens in high school football. The story makes the front page. The *National Enquirer* picks it up and writes a shockingly accurate version, crediting my work.

So, yeah, a sportswriter can become a news reporter. Ten years later, as a more established reporter, I return to the home of this child with our favorite photographer to do a "10 years after" story. Sadly, the reattached ear did not stick and the young man has to go without. He earnestly tells me how his schoolmates ridicule him. I'm hoping Gray is getting photos of this youngster's anguish.

"What names do they call you?" I ask.

Without pausing he blurts "one-eared fool."

A little on the nose, but that does sum it up. Over the next 15-20 minutes, the child may have told me the meaning of life. But all I can think is "don't look at Gray," or otherwise we will both burst into church giggles.

In seven months on the Columbus County beat, the hits keep coming. There's the sheriff accused of making deputies, in lieu of solving crimes, place his campaign re-election signs in yards across the county, and of kissing a horrified 15-year-old girl. That poor child has to testify in open court, and no one there will forget her one-word answer to describe the sheriff's kiss.

"Slobbery," she says.

And exploding pigs. Someone in the heat of summer dumps pig carcasses in the middle of the Green Swamp and it's so hot their innards swell up and explode. This is actually a case of illegal dumping, so I ride into the middle of the "swamp" with Sheriff's detectives and take their photo wearing gas masks.

And I'm back in the *National Enquirer*.

The *Morning Star* (now *Star News)* no longer covers this county daily. The naked, bare corruption didn't stop after I left the beat later in 1988. A subsequent sheriff was caught on tape castigating his black officers in the most racial of terms. There was sexual impropriety as well. The District Attorney removed him from office. The guy promptly ran for re-election that November—and won. This was in 2022.

Two practical outcomes result from the career change. I am able to join Celia for proper date nights and I make a conscious decision to return to college basketball fandom.

That last part is a byproduct of the overall goal—to rejoin society's mainstream and conduct a reasonable relationship—but it's not to be overlooked, either. I missed fandom. My father kinda had a point by the fireplace two years ago after that disastrous Maryland game. Sports are way more fun when you have a rooting interest, when the outcome of the game *matters* to you in some way.

The greatest hobby of my lifetime has been Carolina basketball. Nothing else—ping-pong, pick-up hoops, obsession over issues that ultimately don't add up to much—marks the passage of time or the milestones of life like the ever-changing yet consistently excellent Tar Heels. It's like finding a treasured, well-worn book you had misplaced and picking up on the page where you had left off.

But I'm not going back to the fan I was. No more mop-throwing, theologically questioning sycophantic devotion. I've come to believe that much of what is said about Coach Smith—that he cares for his players as family, counseling them about things bigger than basketball and sending them and their families encouraging cards at meaningful times; that he meticulously remembers the names of people he meets, as well as their children; that he's one of the game's few true innovators—is spot on and true. It's true to some degree of many coaches.

It's also true he has his faults, that's he's competitive and protective of his program almost to the point of obsession, and even that he smokes. Also true of many coaches.

I think I see the players for what they are as well. They have given over their lives, to this point, to the game, and nothing I have done compares.

No, I cannot make shots that Matt Doherty will not take. In no scenario can I do anything he could as a UNC player. He would win every game of H-O-R-S-E we ever played. And Kenny Smith should be able to take off his Carolina jersey for the last time without answering questions about the Syracuse zone or whether this team had "chemistry problems."

No more of this foolishness.

Oh sure, Carolina players do the same dumb things all players do. They sell their shoes and their extra tickets. Some of them are for sale. Let's not kid ourselves. I was never an everyday ACC reporter like those at the larger newspapers, but I was around enough to know that kids are kids, they all want to win, and the more skilled ones see college as a pathway to the NBA, not as a time to serve as knights in a Holy War to suit their fans.

I would like to think I had gained perspective, not entry level but the 400-level kind where you have to have a base of general courses just to get in. There's no going back.

My first act as a newly minted fan? Celia and I go to the ACC Tournament in Greensboro. For someone from North Carolina, especially Greensboro, it's the world's best sporting event.

Eight schools, all rivals, living out their one dream of winning the league as a step toward playing for a national championship. Just 15,000 tickets. Nothing but students and season-ticket holders. The status of being seen at these games. Nothing is like the ACC Tournament. Sure, after the NCAA opened up its tournament and the ACCs were no longer a winner-take-all, it lost some luster. But in 1988, this is still a very big deal.[1]

We show up for the semifinal round, a harder ticket than the finals. By the time the final rolls around, two semifinal fan bases are utterly pissed and likely to dump their tickets to the two last teams. But here we have four teams that have just won a game and have hope. Maybe momentum is on their side.

1   Unlike today, with 18 teams, mega-domes, half the teams making the NCAAs and fanbases that just don't care. The Boston College-Pittsburgh matchup, among many others, just doesn't do it for most of us. We know why the ACC expanded (football, no, make that "greed") but the irrelevance of the ACC Tournament was a steep price.

This semifinal round includes North Carolina, Duke and N.C. State —all about 70 miles from Greensboro. So it's possibly the worst scenario for a buyer's market. The best price we get is $120 for the round, an absurdly high figure in 1988. We are but humble newspaper reporters, still maintaining separate living quarters. We literally don't have that much on us, and we also had hoped to have enough for the final round.

We could use some B.J. Newell right now.

A kindly retired postal service worker, B.J. stood a little more than 5 feet, a little bit pudgy, always with a ball cap. He looked like he was auditioning for the part of rumpled little old man who needed a life partner to help him dress. The *Morning Star* used him as a "stringer" to cover games they couldn't get to, maybe when an ACC team was on the road or when there were too many games to staff. You could expect B.J. to deliver a straightforward, though far from flashy, game story done on time.

But B.J.'s passion was scalping his way into athletic events. All and any of them. He went to Super Bowls, Final Fours, World Series games. He went to World Cup events and the Ali-Frazier fight in 1971, the Forrest Gump of late 1900s sports history.

His hallmark: He never paid more than face value. Never. This was as true of a Carolina road game at The Citadel as it was of a Super Bowl or that Ali-Frazier fight at Madison Square Garden. He waited. He waited until the game started.

Someone was always about to eat a ticket and decide to recover the sunk cost. And B.J., this milquetoast diminutive retiree, would be there. Maybe they felt selling (and sometimes even *giving*—as was the case at that famous Ali-Frazier fight) to this grandfatherly man was their way of doing something good in the world.

If only we could get B.J. to write about this otherworldly skill. He refused. He barely talked about it. He often rode with me to games where I reported and he would scalp, long interstate rides where, make no mistake, he would talk. Yes he would. But about post office work.

At first, you would try to change the subject. He'd talk about bulk mail some more. You would gladly chew off a finger if he would stop. He loved the post office.

We could use some of his ticket magic now. But there was one B.J. could not get at face value—and often not at all. He made it inside some ACC Tournaments, but walked away from many others, the only event that defeated him. And the ones in Greensboro were the most challenging. According to B.J., these were the hardest tickets in sports.

We try and try. We're mocked. Suddenly, the "free game" aspect of sportswriting looks a little different. We're sobered.

But I once ushered in this building. Why not walk around the perimeter, to the back side, and see what's over there? Maybe someone is selling tickets as a charity, and that "charity" can be us?

Celia scowls. This will require a good bit of walking. But we do it. No one is over there. Not a soul. I walk to a door leading to the backside of the concourse of the Greensboro Coliseum.

I push on the door. Oh my god. It opens. The concourse is filled with people milling about, getting ready to take their seats. There doesn't seem to be any security.

Celia and I step inside.

"Melt like butter," I tell her.

The trick is to act like you've been there before, like every football coach tells players who score a touchdown. We fall in line, milling about as though we're looking for the perfect pretzel with brown mustard.

We have just broken into the ACC Tournament semifinals.

Where to sit? Unlike the modern-day Dean Dome, empty seats won't be available in every section. It's the ACC Tournament. Carolina is about to play Maryland, then Duke against State. And we have schmucked our way in to see it.

Suddenly I channel a Zen moment.

"The question is not where we can sit. It's where we can be."

Right. Let's go where no one sits. The student section next to the UNC pep band. Two more standing down there won't be noticed. They'll think we're sociology majors who took a gap year. Or 10.

It just so happens that these seats are courtside, in the end zone, among the best in the building. If you're going to schmuck, go all in. Celia even finds a discarded ticket stub in a restroom, to show any prying usher who may ask what we're doing. She's proving to be useful.

Carolina, and then Duke, prevail. Oh sure, State could have beaten Duke, but they are auditioning for their 35 years of ensuing futility. With the game on the line, they give a virtuoso performance on how not to win, a rare opportunity Valvano misses to stick it to Coach K.

With our newspaper IDs showing, we arrange to go into the pressroom between semifinal games and eat pizza and snacks meant for working reporters, as at this point we have no shame. Celia rubs elbows with Lefty Driesell, fired two years before as Maryland's coach, and realizes he is 1) large and 2) mostly unintelligible.

So what to do about the final? By now we've gone full felony. The *Morning Star* somehow has an extra press pass for someone who didn't make the game. Celia bootlegs the press pass and presents it as though she were a working reporter. Then she "forgets" something in her car, and discreetly shoves the pass under my coat as I wait outside a fence. Then I become a reporter!

We resume our place next to the Carolina band—and they greet us from yesterday. Yes, classes are going fine. So glad I took that time in Europe...

As for the game, I revert to a younger phase of my fandom, my pious claims of "growth" notwithstanding. Duke has beaten Carolina twice this year, even though Carolina, the regular season champion, may be the better team. This can't happen a third time. Surely this is a game Carolina will win, because "we" (it feels good to say it again) win games like this.

The game is taut, tense and nerve wracking. At one point, Carolina's Rick Fox slams a ball in disgust, and it gets away from him, bounding high into the air. Coach K calls for a technical. The referees just want everyone to chill.

The television cameras pan to a crowd reaction. They find a Carolina "student," holding her palms out in the universal "calm down" sign, the correct response by intelligent UNC fans. That face belongs to Celia, a Ferris Buehler moment caught on camera. The biggest schmuck in the building, who has not only broken into the last two rounds but gorged on media food during halftimes, has set the proper tone for the final 10 minutes of this game. Let's get on with it.

And yet Carolina loses. The Tar Heels blow a 2-on-1 fast break in the final minute that would have put them ahead. They fail to rebound a missed Duke free throw. They don't do the things that "Carolina" teams of my youth did, seemingly because they wear light blue.

My re-introduction to fandom is complete. Carolina will not win games just because they are Carolina.

16

WHY AREN'T WE THERE?

March 12, 1989
North Carolina 77, Duke 74
ACC Tournament Final

We're standing around the TV in the *Morning Star* newsroom watching the first round of the ACC Tournament played in Atlanta's Omni, site of the 1977 loss to Marquette and a college basketball jewel that will be demolished eight years later. News may be breaking right and left throughout our region, but the Carolina game is on. Show some respect.

We're playing a pretty good Georgia Tech team that beat us nine days earlier in one of the dumber endings of the Dean Smith era. Carolina led by three in the final seconds and Tech scored to cut it to one with less than five seconds to play. Dennis Scott stole an inbounds pass and had enough time to turn and fire in a three-pointer. It's a humiliating loss.

Then Carolina turned around and lost to Duke on "Senior Night" at home, ending up 9-5 in the league in a three-way tie with Duke and Virginia behind N.C. State, our regular season winner. Drink that in because you won't hear it again.

We're adequately worried about Georgia Tech, but Duke is on our mind. We're tired of them. The Final Four run in 1986, lauded by the white media, was almost quaint. Losing Danny Ferry, a recruit seemingly made for the Coach Smith system, to Duke was insulting. Losing three times to them in 1988 was gross. Then watching a better-than-average, but hardly great, Duke team march to the Final Four, with the media falling in line with the "program" Coach K was amassing (two Final Fours in three years!!) was borderline pornography.

Meanwhile, Carolina has zero ACC titles or Final Fours since 1982. When will this stop? Yet, this is not the subject everyone is talking about in advance of a possible rematch with Duke.

That would be, of course, SAT scores.

Earlier that season, on Jan. 18, 1989, Carolina marched onto top-ranked Duke's floor and mopped them with it, 91-71, a night when everything went right in that building for UNC. Except Coach Smith took exception to one sour note. A Duke fan, part of college basketball's most storied fan base in terms of passion and cleverness, held up a sign addressing Carolina's best player.

The sign said "J.R. Can't Reid."

Get it? The hulking 6-foot-9 black guy with a flattop and built like a linebacker, attending the public school eight miles down the road, must be dumb. Isn't this funny? Never mind that J.R. Reid, the son of two public schoolteachers, so valued his education that, after leaving UNC one year early, came back to graduate. He had done or said nothing to warrant this slur.

Coach Smith saw it for what it was—not-so-subtle racism from the most privileged fan base in the conference, if not the nation. No one had done anything to stop it or said anything about it. Other fan bases, stooping to Duke's lowest common denominator, picked up the "chant."

So Coach Smith stewed. For a while. After Duke beat Carolina a week before the Tournament, writers asked if Reid would be turning pro after the season.

Now it would turn out that Reid would go pro—with Coach Smith's blessing. He was drafted fifth in the first round, which was why Coach Smith encouraged him to leave. This was a time when it was assumed players who left early were selfish, didn't love their school, or something. Again, this perception was most exemplified at Duke, where players for some reason stayed all four years (now tell me who's selfish). Boy, would this perception change.

The question hit Coach Smith wrong. Why are these questions asked only about black players, he wondered aloud in an interview. Why aren't they asked about white players?

Then he threw in a zinger for the ages. He had recruited Ferry and Christian Laettner, Duke's star white players, so he had access to their SAT scores in high school. In the greatest of Smithsonian ways, he made the point that the combined SAT scores of Laettner and Ferry were lower than those of Reid and fellow black frontcourt teammate Scott Williams.

What? Who talks about college kids' grades and test scores? Well, Dean Smith does. In his own opaque way. When he believes a great injustice is at stake.

At face value, the comment is inappropriate. Upon deconstruction, it's brilliant. There's no way of knowing who made what score. Ferry could have been sky high and Laettner low, or vice versa. The same with Williams and Reid. It's close to infringing on student privacy, but not quite.

To Smith, the risk to privacy didn't measure up to the reality of students parading racist signs in Reid's face, just a little more than 20 years since Charlie Scott had basically integrated ACC basketball.[1]

This went over with the Duke power structure exactly like you would imagine, with shock and revulsion. Ferry and Laettner wondered what they did to deserve being dragged into this, a reasonable question. The

---

1   Scott was the first starter and significant black player in ACC history. The first black player was Billy Jones, who debuted at Maryland in December 1965. Props to him. And let's mention one more time: Duke didn't start a black player until the 1977-78 season, about a decade before its fans were chiding black players on whether they could "reid."

only answer: You chose to go to Duke. You knew what that fanbase would be like and you knew you were joining the darlings of "white America." But, otherwise, they had a point.

So, unlike any other ACC Tournament, this exercise of first-round games was just an exercise to get to a Duke-Carolina rematch.

It's really too bad Atlanta is seven hours away, we have no tickets, no place to stay and the tournament has already started. It's mid-afternoon on Friday. At least by now I have Sundays off and Celia and I can watch this in our home.

"Why aren't we there?" she asks.

Well, I patiently explain, again: No tickets, no place to stay, it's already started.

She may or may not have called me a pussy. I have a cousin who could board us in Atlanta. We're living together so we are a quintessential double-income, no kids couple. Cost should not be a barrier. And if I would quit talking about why we can't go, we could go home, pack and start driving—and get there at midnight. We'll find our way into the semifinals and, of course, the final.

Her logic is impeccable. I'm still 27 years old. When else are we going to act like this? I have found a true partner in Carolina fanhood. We'll be married in two months.

The plan works as forecast. My cousin and his wife welcome us. We get some sleep and legitimately scalp our way into the semifinal. Carolina hammers Maryland, a 1-13 team in ACC play, by 30 points. Why is a Maryland team this bad in the semifinal? Oh, that's right. The Terps beat first-place N.C. State by 22 points in the first round.

Duke scraps past Virginia in its game. Had they lost, I would have been fine with that, but at least now we have the match-up we drove to Atlanta to see. The tickets for this final cost us $90, which we believe is steep but worth it.

And was it ever.

In Will Blythe's seminal book, *To Hate Like This is to be Happy Forever*, he points out a reverse ripple effect in the Duke-Carolina rivalry. The closer the ripples, or the closer combatants are to the rivalry, the more respect and less antipathy they have for one another.

The players, those closest of all, typically don't come from North Carolina. They know each other on the recruiting trail and have a healthy respect, sometimes cultivating friendships, while playing at the two schools. As is often reported, they go to the same barber shops.

The coaches, one ring farther out, also have a respect for one another. Other athletic staff, radio broadcast crews, etc. are a little more distant, so more vitriol.

The alumni, toward the ripples' outer rings, can't stand each other's program, but they tend to have experienced the rivalry in such a way that there exists an underlying respect for the anticipation and atmosphere they were allowed to be part of.

The ones who didn't attend either school? The most distant circle of the ripple, their hatred is laboratory-quality purity, beyond what is warranted, really. They are the worst and are often an embarrassment to both teams' fan bases.

Today, that model is not in play. The players just simply hate each other. Danny Ferry has just been selected ACC Player of the Year over J.R. Reid. The racist signs, Reid will later say, did not bother him. Losing this honor to Ferry did.

And the coaches are just outdone with one another. The shit is real this time.

Carolina takes an early lead, but Duke hangs around. The players approach the five personal foul limit as license to commit four felonies. Scott Williams goes through a phase where he's either sprawling on the floor every trip down or elbowing somebody, causing them to sprawl. The referees will call 49 fouls, yet they cannot discourage the violence.

Reid, while guarding Ferry, opens a two-inch cut, causing Ferry to bleed like a tomato can. Later he shoots and misses over Ferry but grabs his own rebound as Ferry falls. Reid scores, then stands over Ferry and talks vulgar trash—you can tell even from our upper-deck end zone seat.

By today's standards, Reid would not only have been given a technical foul and ejected, but would also have spent the rest of the game doing community service, picking up cups in the Omni concourse or something. It was that bad.

Today? Play on.

It's rough out there. Williams hammers Laettner to prevent a lay-up, too hard by a factor of four for this purpose, and Krzyzewski screams for a technical foul.

From where we sit, we can see that he also screams at Williams. This prompts an interchange between the coaches that we can't hear, but later hear about. And the actual dialogue is not surprising.

"Don't you yell at my player, Mike," Coach Smith says.

"Hey Dean, fuck you."

Ladies and Gentlemen, the 1989 ACC Duke-Carolina final. There's not been a game like it before or since.

It's tied late before Carolina's Steve Bucknall, a senior, makes a three-point play to put Carolina ahead, then makes free throws to keep them ahead. King Rice, who missed a free throw to force overtime in the game in Chapel Hill a week before, makes a few, but with Carolina up three with 3 seconds left, he misses.

Ferry has time to rebound and heave a 75-foot shot. From our vantage point, it's terrifyingly on target. It hits the back rim, maybe one-half inch too high to drop through. Instead, it's a program win Carolina had to have. I'm hoarse from screaming. My future wife and I drive the seven hours back talking about it non-stop.

Being a fan is so much better.

17

PAPA BEAR

December 23, 1989
North Carolina 79, Kansas State 63

In my married life, my father has taken on the name "Papa Bear," courtesy of his new daughter-in-law. The name fits this cuddly, affable mountain of a man, but from her it's an endearing reference to our entire family—always ravenous and foraging, sometimes clumsily.

So Papa Bear (and Mama Bear) it is. But the old lion is starting to age. He's retired from Guilford County and he lets on to my older sister that his boss all these years was an "asshole," a remark notable enough to be relayed because we almost never hear him swear (or see him drink).

He's slowing down in so many ways. He's not up on the church roof fixing the flashing, a legacy of his legendary sense of balance. He would walk on a 75-degree pitched roof as though he were walking through a meadow. As a 16-year-old student at Brevard College, he would climb atop buildings, then stand on his head on the chimney, his classmates begging him to get down.

Nor is he helping Uncle Charles deliver furniture from the store he runs. They lived about a mile apart and in their heyday, they had a code when it was time to make a delivery. Uncle Charles would say when Daddy answered, "I got the yo-yo."

"I got the string," Daddy would reply. Then they would hang up, the delivery arranged. In another time and place they would have mastered social media. Or dealing drugs.

Nor is he laying concrete blocks for the high school baseball dugout. Or spending nearly every waking moment either working for the county or working for his family and friends who count on him to do anything and everything.

He's finally found some ways to make things easier for himself, some of them bordering on genius. Take our "electric" ice cream maker. Daddy loved homemade ice cream from a hand-crank freezer but noticed it was getting to be too much work to crank those last dozen or so turns, after the ice cream hardened. He thought about a store-bought electric ice cream maker, but that was expensive and the ice cream lost some of its flavor being churned in those sterile machines.

So he bolted a washing machine motor to a sheet of plywood, then connected the ice cream crank to one end of a pulley, with a larger wheel at the other end. A car's fan belt connected the wheels, powered by that motor he appropriated.

The result? A homemade electric ice cream machine that preserved the integrity of a hand-cranked freezer and made perfect ice cream. When my sister Judy brought home her future husband to meet the parents for the first time, Daddy had this creation humming in the carport, whipping up strawberry ice cream. John Bell almost proposed on the spot.

Daddy's passion has now migrated to restoring furniture he finds by the side of the road. This is his art. We have several dressers and bookcases he refurbished, each one a cry gift when they were revealed. He builds his own shop behind the house and hangs out with his buddy Delbert

Everhart, his partner in this craft. Sometimes Mama walks out there and finds them both asleep in their recliners.

Restoring furniture, making art from someone else's refuse, may have been his calling. But there was no time for that. My father was a practical man whose family ran a corn mill and grew their own food during the Depression. No time for crafty pursuits that may or may not have made money. He had his mother and brothers to support—at age 27, when his father died, he was the only one of the five boys who had money for the funeral. Later he had a wife to support and children to put through college.

No, he worked for an "asshole" at a bureaucratic job beneath his calling. And never, to my ears, did he complain.

Well, he did complain about his knees hurting, and we went behind his back to his doctor to "talk him into" knee replacement surgery.

"He'll know when it's time," the doctor said.

And Daddy did. He got both replaced within six months, an enormous amount of pain to overcome at once, but something he could get through if he was just determined enough. Which he was. Through sheer will, he ground his pain to dust.

We had not talked about Carolina basketball since the blow-up after the 1986 ACC Tournament loss to Maryland. I think he griped a little about the Syracuse game in 1987, but I was living in Wilmington and starting my own life. We managed to talk about other things.

Carolina had not been particularly noteworthy the last few years, anyway. The 1989 debacle over "J.R. Can't Reid" and SAT scores didn't interest him. My father didn't sit around and ponder the racial implications of college basketball. He just wanted to watch the games.

As I look at the 1989-90 UNC schedule, I notice a date two days before Christmas in Charlotte, a nondescript game against a Kansas State team headed for a 17-15 season. I decide to give him tickets to this game as his Christmas present, with me taking him to the game as part of the "gift."

I am quite pleased with my magnanimity, showing my father a piece of my former sportswriter world. I know it's a long walk from the parking lot, so I reach out to then-UNC Sports Information Director Rick Brewer, who offers me the never-forgotten kindness of a parking pass to the game.

The plan is for me to leave Wilmington, then have Celia fly one way the next day, Christmas Eve, to join us for the holiday. As I leave early on the 23rd, some talk is made about the chance of snow in Wilmington, which is hilarious. It almost never snows in Wilmington, and when it does it's usually right at 32 degrees, so the only drama is whether any of it will stick. On this day it's around 17 degrees, way too cold. Snow indeed.

I later find out the snow started the minute I crossed the bridge out of Wilmington. The 17 inches it dumps, referred to today as a "winter hurricane," remains legend. It keeps Celia from leaving our beach apartment all weekend, the heat pump gone and the water pipes burst. We would say dumb things from Greensboro like "why don't you order a pizza," and she would explain that it's cruel to expect a delivery driver to even try in this snowdrift. She survives by opening the oven door to heat the kitchen.

I pick up my father, drive the 1½ hours to Charlotte, show off my handy parking spot, and walk him through the same entrance the players use. We're at courtside, watching the players warm up just a few feet away. I am quite pleased with myself.

Then we get to our section and look up where our row must be. My father stands silent, looking a bit forlorn. So many rows, he doesn't say out loud. So many steps.

Then it hit me. At his age—which is 66 but seems so much older back then—he isn't interested in going to see live Tar Heel games. He could see it better on his TV. He could relax in his recliner and go to bed after it is over. He wouldn't have to walk anywhere.

The Tar Heels win without incident. We exit through the concourse, without those steps, and find the car another way. Not only does my father not complain, he goes out of his way to seem appreciative.

About then, I realize this game is not about what I am doing for him. He's doing it for me.

March 17, 1990
North Carolina 79, Oklahoma 77
NCAA Tournament Second Round

The Tar Heels go on to lose 13 games in 1990, the most of any Dean Smith team in his 36 years. They lose at home to N.C. State, 6-8 in the league. They do manage to beat 8th- and 5th-ranked Duke twice, convincingly each time.

They're out in the first round of the ACC Tournament and have no expectations in the NCAAs as an 8 seed. They win one game over Missouri State and draw top-ranked and top-seeded Oklahoma, the presumptive favorite to win the championship. Oklahoma has the kind of speed, tempo and skill that tends to embarrass lesser opponents, which the Tar Heels certainly are.

All this I can accept. But there's a complication. My parents are in Wilmington this weekend and no graceful way to avoid my father watching the Oklahoma game with us.

I don't believe I have watched a game on TV with him since 1979, 11 years ago when I was a senior in high school. I know the Kansas State game earlier this season went well, but that was in person. He couldn't cut a shine in front of a bunch of strangers. But he damn sure could in front of me and his still new daughter-in-law.

I dread this game for this reason far more than for the inevitable beatdown from Oklahoma. I enlist my mother's help to control Daddy. I warn Celia what may happen, what triggers to watch for and how not to respond. For all my advancements into manhood, in marriage and career, I am back to being 14. This game terrifies me.

Carolina plays well and takes an early lead. I almost fear this more, as it raises expectations. I'm not sure my father truly understands that Oklahoma is waaaaaaay better than Carolina this year. It's a matter of time. But he's behaving quite well. Oklahoma takes the lead, as feared. Papa Bear growls some, but Mama Bear heads it off. He checks himself and, Lord knows, he's trying. He's come into my home and is really trying to keep his angst to himself.

Rick Fox hits a 3 in the final minute and Carolina leads by two. Oklahoma scores, adds a foul shot and retakes the lead by one. Why did they let him do that? Why did they foul? The questions rise but quickly subside. Effort is being made.

Carolina mucks up the final possession, leaving King Rice in such a state that he tries to call timeout. But Oklahoma is called for a foul before the timeout is awarded. We can't believe we're trusting our season to Rice at the foul line, but he makes the first. Tie game.

The second clangs so hard off the rim that Oklahoma has to scrap with Carolina's Pete Chilicutt for it, and it goes out of bounds to Carolina. About 10 seconds left and we can hold for one shot.

Which Carolina does brilliantly. Hubert Davis—yes, the future coach—handles the inbounds pass and shuffles it to Fox, who glides in for a driving bank shot as time expires. Carolina has the upset of the tournament.

In watching replays of this many times, the highlight is the look on Oklahoma Coach Billy Tubbs' face after the horn sounds. Taken down by an inferior team but a better coach. His hatred and God-knows-what kind of skullduggery have come to no good. Pure disgust.

But in live time, what we remember is the "woo-hoooooo" that came from Papa Bear and Mama Bear's couch. Pure joy. Not "why did they wait so long," but pure joy. No conditions. In all the Carolina games I had watched with him, I can't say I had seen that before. Just pure joy.

It was the last Carolina game we would ever watch together.

18

THERE SHOULD BE AN INVESTIGATION

January 19, 1991

Duke 74, North Carolina 60

The *Morning Star* has a press pass to the Duke-Carolina game in Cameron and doesn't use it. Instead they offer it to Celia, a known Carolina fanatic by this point, so she can sit on press row at this event rapidly establishing itself as college basketball's high holy moment. Carolina at Duke. Everyone should go if they have the chance.

I scalp my way in for $60, which seems like a lot at the time, and sit with the fans you don't see on TV.

Here's the thing about Cameron Indoor Stadium. It is iconic by today's standards. Most of the ACC schools once had bandbox gyms that were loud and quirky but *every one of those programs outgrew it*. Duke never did.

When Carolina was rising, N.C. State living off the David Thompson years and Maryland seemingly in the Top 10 every year, Duke was finishing last in the ACC four consecutive years from 1974 -77. Yes, Duke was good in the 1960s, but during the UCLA years, college basketball around here was all about conference pride. It was a foregone conclusion UCLA would win it all, but didn't the ACC have the most competitive league and that charming tournament?

In the 19 seasons between 1967 and 1985, Duke had a cumulative ACC record of 116-132, finishing fourth or lower in 12 of those seasons. During that time, Dean Smith's program rose to national prominence with seven Final Fours and a national title. N.C. State won two titles. The ACC became so dominant the NCAA was basically forced to expand its tournament field beyond one team per league.

At a national level, Houston filled the Astrodome and defeated UCLA, bringing the sport to a national TV audience. Magic Johnson and Larry Bird squared off in the highest-rated final game ever. Villanova played the perfect game to beat Georgetown. The sport got so big the NCAA Tournament expanded multiple times, finally to 64 teams. Any team that was good could get in, and conference pride no longer mattered. The sport developed, evolved, and became a multi-billion dollar industry.

And Duke was around for none of this work, other than an outlier run to the national title game in 1978. They underachieved with good players the next two years before three years of utter mediocrity to begin the Krzyzewski era. When they finally got good in 1986, ESPN was waiting for them, having gone all-in on college basketball and in need of a pet. The sport had blossomed on the backs of others, and Duke picked up just in time to become a national darling for white fans. And was immediately credited for becoming a powerhouse that did things "the right way."

And this—this - is why Carolina and ACC fans of a certain age resent the hell out of Duke University basketball.

With the sport now basically a studio event for TV, with the students as willing props, schools didn't need large domes or modern arenas. Cameron Indoor Stadium could thrive as the quaint stage to televise this national brand, where the students camp out for tickets and paint themselves blue. It's still worth pointing out that Duke does not really have that big of a fan base in North Carolina (let's not count the bandwagon fans who aren't buying tickets to see Duke play). They have trouble selling out Cameron for certain non-conference games or when the Blue Devils are down.

All that said, it is fun to watch a game there. The students on the side you see on television are the only ones acting engaged. They spend a good bit of time you don't see on camera getting the booster club members—known as the "Iron Dukes"—to perk up. Just like in every arena.

Carolina, much better this season and capable of a national title, leads through much of the first half, and Celia and I meet at halftime to remark that Bobby Hurley, the churlish Duke point guard, looks like a little boy out there. But in the second half, it caves in on the Tar Heels.

I'm sitting alone amongst Duke fans, obviously pulling for Carolina but not obnoxiously so. I will not be that fan. I even strike up friendly conversations with my Duke neighbors, reasonable people pulling for their team.

When the outcome is inevitable, a few other Carolina fans in the area get up and leave and I am outdone. This is a violation of the code. We came to represent the University of North Carolina and we'll stay in our seats as long as they are playing. We're not making a show of leaving in disgust ("They have not pleased me!") in front of our rival fans. I mention this to my new Duke friends and I think they register respect.

In the final minute, Celia, a Cameron rookie, doesn't realize that a few hundred blue-painted Yankees are getting ready to crawl over her and rush the court. I will have to violate my own rule, make apologies and rush down to press row to retrieve her.

Just in time to watch the court rush, as I had predicted. This place is a hellhole of a high school gym. They should invest in air conditioning. It's time to leave.

March 30, 1991

Kansas 79, North Carolina 73

NCAA Tournament Final Four

For the first time since 1982, Carolina has made it to the Final Four. We even managed to repay Duke for two losses by routing them by 20 in the ACC Tournament final.

The problem is Duke has also made the Final Four, for the fourth consecutive time. There hasn't been a truly great Duke team in the bunch, but they always manage to draw teams they can beat in the tournament. This only feeds the national perception that Duke has historically been the better program. Our only recourse is to remind everyone they haven't even won a national championship.

Carolina draws Kansas in the first semifinal, or as my anti-Carolina friends derisively refer to it, the "JV game." Kansas, led by former assistant Roy Williams, is just a little better this night. Our star senior, Rick Fox, suffers a 5-for-22 shooting night he doesn't deserve. Coach Smith gets so aggravated he draws a technical foul in the first half and then, in the final minute, baits the same ref again who—horrors!—gives him a second technical, ejecting Smith from the game.

None of us will forget the perp walk our legend of a coach makes past the Kansas bench, shaking hands along the way, enroute to the locker room.

Then Duke plays an undefeated UNLV team threatening to become college basketball's first unbeaten team since Indiana in 1976. This is basically the same UNLV team that clubbed Duke by 30 in the finals the year before.

UNLV, the one time we need them, goes to pieces. Confident players like Larry "Grandmama" Johnson, full of swagger, shrink from the moment, fearful of taking the big shot. Duke wins, then takes the championship two nights later over Kansas.

Let's review this Final Four run: Duke gets one of the biggest wins in NCAA history, wins its first championship and Carolina loses to its former assistant coach with Coach Smith ejected and leaving in disgrace.

College basketball can be so unfair. Yet somehow it's going to get worse.

March 28, 1992
Duke 104, Kentucky 103 (OT)
NCAA Tournament East Regional Final

The success of the Duke team in 1992, on one level, was not as annoying as the championship the year before. Duke really did have the best team in college basketball this year. Carolina rebuilds from the loss of Fox, Chilicutt and others, and we brace for the season the same way dirt poor farmers in Oklahoma in the 1930s would see a dust storm coming on the horizon. Nothing to do but to hunker down and try to outlive it.

The Tar Heels would have another bland year by their standards, losing 10 games. Oh sure, we beat top-ranked and undefeated Duke in Chapel Hill, otherwise known as the "Bloody Montross" game. Our star and exceedingly white center from Indiana, Eric Montross, gets elbowed and hit, likely by the foul Christian Laettner, several times, leaving blood gushing down his face as he shoots free throws, a gallant and brave metaphor for the Tar Heels' fight in this game. And yes, I did just describe Duke's bleeding Danny Ferry as a "tomato can" in a previous chapter.

But on balance, this is a year with only one metric for success: Either Duke does or doesn't win another national championship.

It's not a lofty goal worth my diligent pursuit. During the NCAA Tournament, Carolina having long ago exited, I have the TV on during Duke's regional final against a scrappy but undermanned Kentucky team. I am working on the first draft of a true crime book resulting from a murder case from Fayetteville I covered as a *Morning Star* reporter, the grisly murder of a young mother and her 5- and 3-year-old girls. It's a

Jeffrey MacDonald lookalike case in many respects, and I have an advance and a deadline.

No time for Duke foolishness. I check in on the Blue Devils and they lead by 10. Kentucky hits a three-pointer, steals and hits another one. Now with Kentucky down by four, I figure I can take a well-earned break from writing.

I'm starting to think this is happening. Kentucky has all the energy, and Duke seems mortal. Somewhere in the middle of this, Laettner cries about a non-call at the defensive end of the floor. At the other end, he scores and the Kentucky center—I think his name was Justin Timberlake —falls to the floor. Wait. I looked it up. Aminu Timberlake.

To remind him and everyone else the true content of his character, Laettner lifts his foot and stomps—lightly, but stomps—Timberlake on the chest.

Technical foul, Duke. We're waiting for the subsequent ejection so we can wave Laettner good-bye, perhaps forever.

The ejection never comes. Just a good 'ol technical foul.

The game continues. Laettner hits big shot after big shot. I am secure in my belief that basketball karma will catch up to him. It always does.

We have overtime. The teams go back and forth. In the final seconds, Kentucky trails by one when Sean Woods banks in a prayer of a shot with 2.1 seconds left. How Duke immediately gets a timeout so quickly—this was before the clock automatically stopped after a made basket in the final minute—has always haunted me, but so be it.

I use this timeout to crow to Celia.

"John Wooden always said—lot of teams win one in a row." I say this with great historical insight, as if Jon Meacham suddenly were in the room. We're giddy with delight. Duke will be remembered as just another really good team that won one championship.

Play resumes and Grant Hill starts to inbound. I'm thinking someone should be guarding him. Before I can become indignant about it, Hill has thrown a rocket. Plenty of time for someone to step in and steal or knock it away, but it traces right to Laettner at the foul line.

Prick that he is, only Laettner would think to catch, dribble and turn to shoot as if he had all day. The second it leaves his hand, we know where it's headed.

It may be the hardest loss I've ever absorbed, if that tells you where I am with Duke hatred. I immediately revert to the 6-year-old version of myself, wondering how a loving God can allow the player who openly stomped his opponent on the court to not only win, but to be blessed to hit the winning shot, now college basketball's most famous.

In what world is this fair? If God were a basketball fan, Laettner would air ball a free throw or get arrested for tax fraud in the final minute. Something like that. Alas, God is not.

We sit stunned on our couch. Something needs to be said. Duke's repeat national championship the next week is inevitable, and we all know it. I'm not sure I'm equal to the moment.

"There needs to be an investigation," is all I can mutter.

19

ENOUGH

January 27, 1993

North Carolina 82, Florida State 77

Five years into my re-commitment as a Tar Heel fan, I have witnessed five Duke Final Fours, two Duke national championships and Duke's emergence as college basketball's darlings. Carolina's one Final Four proved to be such an embarrassment that we may have been better off without.

I'm holding fast to my pledge not to become "that fan," the one who's entitled to championship teams because, you know, I put a lot into it. But I've had it with the Duke thing. And I think I can speak for Carolina fans from Murphy to Manteo, as they say in this state, and for those throughout the South and those hitting the "Carolina" bars in every major city in the United States, when I say "Enough."

Enough of this Duke bullshit. We cannot watch nearly 30 years of sustained excellence vanish because Christian Laettner hit a couple of big shots. It's time to make a stand.

Which brings us to the 1993 Tar Heels.

A team without a star, each player fits a greater whole as though Dean Smith locked himself into a laboratory and refused to emerge until he had this group. The Tar Heels play defense, share the ball and find the right shot for the right player.

Duke still has Grant Hill, Bobby Hurley and a few other key scoundrels, and is good enough to be ranked 3rd in preseason and even ascend to No. 1 for five weeks. But Carolina has a better team. The Blue Devils start dropping games on their way to finishing third. But new rivals are emerging. They never will be Duke-level rivals, or even N.C. State back in the day, but a few dogs are having their day.

Like Florida State. The previous season, the Seminoles made their first trip to the Dean Dome as an ACC member, a December game that found a flat crowd and flatter Tar Heels. Florida State won it easily, 86-74, and not even that close. Afterward, a reporter asked Sam Cassell, their skilled and colorful guard, about the crowd in the vaunted Tar Heel home.

"It's more like a cheese and wine crowd, kind of laid back," he said, a devastatingly accurate jab that fit every anti-Carolina fan's attitude about the elite Chapel Hill faithful. And, yes, he said "cheese and wine." The quote was later switched for literary purposes, to maximize the insult's impact. Carolina and its fans have yet to live this down.

The rematch against the '93 team promises to be intense. The Tar Heels need to stand up for their fan base's very soul. "Wine and cheese" cannot stand.

Florida State comes back to the Dean Dome, this time against a team with national championship aspirations, and takes a 21-point lead with a little less than 12 minutes to go. The lead stands at 20 with 9:36 left.

That's when Henrik Rodl, an often-mocked German transfer student who's pale, thin and cartoonishly uncool, hits a three-pointer. It's like Debby Boone striking the first note of a song that evolves into a Beatles reunion.

If Rodl can do this, the crowd seems to realize, then all is possible. Its roar is so loud the "ambient" crowd noise on the Tar Heel Radio Network distorts the overall broadcast, forcing engineers to make adjustments. That's a first.

From here it's just a rich, delectable buffet of Seminole turnovers, Tar Heel three-pointers and Seminole panic. Their coach draws a technical foul. They use all their timeouts. They are rattled.

Finally, the lead down to one, Charlie Ward throws a crosscourt pass that George Lynch intercepts and sails in for a dunk with 1:40 left. Carolina by one and the building further explodes.

When it's over, wine and cheese storms the court. Over beating Florida State. But it's worth it.

March 13, 1993
North Carolina 74, Virginia 56
ACC Tournament Semifinal

Carolina wins the regular season and heads into the ACC Tournament as I am reaching my own professional apex. *Innocent Victims* has been released, and my first major book-signing will be held the same day as the ACC semifinal against Virginia.

I can't wait to have my friends, co-workers, book sources, and others who just love true crime come to Waldenbooks, this being back when bookstores like Waldenbooks were still a thing, and get a glimpse of how I made this come about. I think about the pithy things I will write inside their books, things that will cause them to frame them and pass them down to generations. This event will be a referendum - on me. I'm confident I will pass.

Almost no one comes. Well, a few do, but they scurry out quickly, unaware I have things to say about how to construct a chapter, or how to deal with New York editors. Soon, not

Publicity photo for Innocent Victims during a short-lived period of rakishness.

a soul is there. About then, I look out the window and watch as one of those roadside trailer signs blows across the street as though it were a paper cup.

Yes, I pick the same day as the so-called Storm of the Century, about which movies would be made. About an hour in, we tuck tail and watch the Tar Heels destroy Virginia in the ACC semifinals, a comforting salve to a humbling day.

April 5, 1993
North Carolina 77, Michigan 71
NCAA Tournament Final

Carolina doesn't even win that ACC Tournament, but it's ok. The Tar Heels navigate the only tournament that matters now, and, for what it's worth, Duke loses in the second round. The day Duke loses in the NCAA Tournament has become the best day of the year. I know I'm supposed to say "birthday" or "anniversary" or "Christmas," but Duke losing for good is such an unscheduled burst of joy. Extra points for TV shots panning desolate player faces on the bench, and double points if they work in crowd shots.

The Tar Heels are back in the Final Four in New Orleans and playing Kansas again. No problem this time. It's on to the finals against the darlings of urban hip-hop America, Michigan's Fab Five. Suddenly, Carolina is the square white team.

Michigan is better at almost every position, but, again, Carolina maximizes what it does best and hangs in. Michigan goes up by four with five minutes left, but Donald Williams hits yet another three-pointer to bring the Tar Heels to within one.

The TV we're watching is plenty big, yet nothing will do than for Celia and me to sit on the floor about 18 inches from the screen. And to yell loud enough for the players to hear us. This is why we can't watch games at parties or among guests. We would likely be humiliated - if we were even aware there were others in the room.

George Lynch blocks a shot at the other end and Carolina has a runout. Derrick Phelps lays it up... and the ball hangs on the rim. For a long time. The ball appears to be awaiting direction on what it should do next.

"GO IN!!!!!!!" shouts my wife. In all caps mode, her lungs seemingly hotwired to a booster speaker.

The ball hears her and drops. Carolina by one. Then it becomes three, then five. Michigan cuts it to one and, with 13 seconds left, fouls Pat Sullivan, an undistinguished reserve. And what exactly is Pat Sullivan doing in the game at this moment?

Both of us instinctively recall the sarcastic chant by Duke fans whenever Sullivan enters a game.

"Oh no, not Sullivan," we both say.

But shame on us. He makes one. Then misses the next. Chris Webber rebounds for Michigan and looks to pass to Jalen Rose, but Carolina has him covered. So Webber, confused, drags his pivot foot before he starts a hesitant dribble.

That's traveling, as outlined by Dr. Naismith when he invented the game.

"You have to call that," I say, pounding the floor. The referee apparently does not.

Instead, Webber, freed from prosecution, dribbles up court and into a corner, the worst place for him to go. Carolina has him trapped. If he seeks parole, we have three fouls to give before they shoot free throws. Webber, wily fella that he is, trumps the Carolina trap. He calls time out.

But Michigan doesn't have any. Technical foul.

The first thought is I can't believe we're going to win another national championship on a fluke play, harkening back to Fred Brown throwing the ball directly to James Worthy in 1982. The next thought is that it doesn't matter. We're going to win.

And we do. I'm not sure Coach Smith's career really needs further validation. At the moment Chris Webber signals timeout, Coach Smith's program has been by far the superior one in the league and possibly, given all factors, the nation, for about 25 years. But Duke and N.C. State had won two titles each and Carolina just one under Coach Smith.

So, yeah, he needs the second title.

And so do we. The Duke thing has gone on long enough. During the championship trophy ceremony, Tom Butters, Duke's Athletic Director and Chair of the NCAA Men's Basketball Selection Committee, literally hands the trophy to Coach Smith. I'm not proud of the things that were said in the Whisnant living room at that moment, but the capsule version is that this is proper, that the trophy is back where it belongs.

I'm fairly certain this was repeated from Murphy to Manteo, and beyond.

20

THE LAW THAT NEEDS PASSING

March 12, 1994

North Carolina 86, Wake Forest 84 (OT)

ACC Tournament Semifinal

The day after the Michigan win, while Carolina nation engages in revelry, Coach Smith shows up in Philadelphia at the home of Rasheed Wallace, one of the top high school players in the nation. Rasheed is no match for this pitch. He commits, joining the nation's top incoming freshman class.

Our optimism knows no bounds. I am a published author. Celia is a renowned humor columnist. Save for a couple of entitled cats, we have no other mouths to feed. Carolina is the presumptive favorite to repeat as champions. We feel another golden era coming on, and we can chase the Tar Heels anywhere to watch it.

This starts with the 1994 ACC Tournament in Charlotte. My former sports editor, Jerry Hooks, somehow lines up tickets, so I watch in person as Carolina wins a game it has no business winning. The Deacons of Tim Duncan and Randolph Childress outplay the Tar Heels all afternoon, yet Carolina is close enough at the end for Dante Calabria to rebound a missed free throw and throw up a shot he would be ashamed to try in H-O-R-S-E.

Overtime. Carolina wins in the final seconds. It turns out to be Coach Smith's 800th victory.

That evening, we're hammered at the Longhorn Steakhouse, turning the place into a Carolina rally and counter-rally by the haters. The "it" place to be in Charlotte that night is rocking with drunk ACC fans crunching peanut shells on the floor.

I remind Hooks he got to witness Coach Smith's 800th win. A lifelong N.C. State fan, Hooks recoils. His love of State is easily outpaced by his hatred of Carolina. He pulled for the Russians in the 1976 Olympics, rather than the USA team led by Coach Smith. I later find out he was hardly alone in this.

"Every one of those wins personally hurt me," he says.

It's a telling and useful glimpse of how the other half lives. We find an extra ticket and fly Celia in from Charlotte on a one-way flight. It's worth it because we smell a title, which Carolina wins that afternoon.

March 20, 1994
Boston College 75, North Carolina 72
NCAA Tournament Second Round

Poor Derrick Phelps.

The senior point guard, an underrated hero on the championship team and a steady influence on this one, is sitting on the bench while his top-ranked teammates trail lowly ninth-seeded Boston College. The Eagles, hitting three-pointers at will, lead by an incomprehensible 14 points before Carolina starts a bit of a rally.

Phelps makes a steal at halfcourt and has a breakaway that will cut it to eight. BC's Danya Abrams, whose name is about to live in Carolina infamy, chases Phelps, about 80 pounds lighter. The foul is swift and merciless, a chop to the face that sends Phelps sprawling, head in hands as soon as he lands.

Really? Could he not have just pinned his arms? Of the multiple ways to give fouls, this wasn't one of them. Coach Smith lobbies for Abrams' ejection and says after the game that film study of Abrams predicted this. The energized Tar Heels rally to tie four different times without the concussed Phelps, who can't even look up because the lights make his head throb.

CBS reports the UNC medical staff has asked Phelps to count backward from 100 by seven. Why not "how many fingers am I holding"? They may as well ask him to carry out pi to the 50th decimal. 100 backward by seven?

"I couldn't do that on my best day," Celia says, dead serious.

BC fends off Carolina, leading by three in the final seconds. It falls to Wallace, who has tried two three-pointers all season, to try to tie the game. Way off. BC rebounds and the seconds tick away.

100, 93, 86, and so on. A wasted opportunity. Banners don't come around that often.

January 28, 1995
North Carolina 62, Wake Forest 61

My lawyer thinks I am lying.

We're at a deposition in Fayetteville, a military town of pawn shops, used car lots, Asian restaurants and strip joints, on a Saturday afternoon in late January, a prospect every bit as dreary as it sounds. One of the byproducts of writing a true crime book, or anything involving recent history, is the subjects of your prose will most likely live to read it.

And some of them won't like it. I have been sued twice, once by a key female protagonist who believed she was wrongly portrayed as a sex-hungry drug user. She dropped the suit after she was arrested in a hotel room, accused of trading sex for crack cocaine.

This second lawsuit was filed by a key defense witness who - well, we're not sure about her objection. She claims she never gave me permission to use her name in the book, even though she had testified publicly in the second trial and was quoted in just about every major newspaper in North America. She also doesn't remember one of our conversations taking place, an interview I have on tape.

When her lawyer, a manifestation of sleaze with a taste for ambulance, asks me a poorly worded question, I do exactly what my lawyer had advised me to do. I answer truthfully but briefly.

My lawyer calls a time out. Let's break for lunch.

"You have to tell the truth," says my lawyer, a slick New York guy hired by my publisher.

"Hmmm?" I reply. From our booth in Applebee's, the Carolina-Wake Forest game is on. Yes, this deposition was not only scheduled on my off

This computer didn't have enough memory to download the Internet. Vinnie, our rambunctious cat, walked on the keyboard during bouts of writer's block. I dedicated Innocent Victims to him.

day, but opposite a crucial Tar Heel game on the road.

I can't quite get a view of the screen, but it vies for my attention, nonetheless.

"Oh. I did," I finally reply. The lawyer didn't ask what he thought he did, and so the timeline of events I gave him was actually accurate.

Carolina trails Wake Forest by 10 with a little more than 5 minutes left. Even bad Wake Forest teams manage to beat the Tar Heels in Winston-Salem. This is not a bad team. Ranked 16th at the time, this Deacon team, still featuring the historically great Duncan and Childress, is destined to win the ACC Tournament and gain a top seed in the NCAAs. It's one of the best Wake Forest has ever had.

Trailing by 10 late to this squad seems terminal.

My lawyer is still talking. He's either making fun of his opposing counsel or this Applebee's. He couldn't pick a Tar Heel out of a photo lineup. Some of the customers are making a stir. Are the Tar Heels rallying?

It's doubtful Wake Forest has many fans here in Fayetteville, about four Applebee's from their Winston-Salem home. But when the Deacons play Carolina, they welcome hordes of new fans, freshly minted with green card visas that will last the duration of this particular game. They will root not for Wake Forest to win but for Carolina to lose.

The other half of the room is Carolina's, followers of the People's University. Every North Carolina town is a Carolina town.

I sense Carolina has done something great, but that Wake Forest has responded. The Deacons in fact have blown every bit of the 10-point lead, but Duncan's free throws put Wake up by four with 40 seconds left.

"We need to think about how to wrap your testimony up," my lawyer says as I catch a second-hand whiff of Jerry Stackhouse completing a three-point play, cutting the deficit to one. When Wake turns it over—the mighty Duncan eating the ball for five seconds instead of inbounding it - the Tar Heels have one possession left to steal a win.

One by one, sometimes in groups, the diners leave their riblets and brownie bites and gravitate to the television, much as revelers in Key West drift toward a water sunset. Something beautiful is happening. You can't help but think this scene is being repeated in public places across the South.

Conversational manners must be put on hold. Carolina has the ball down one with time running out.

I leave my lawyer mid-sentence and find the TV. Just in time to catch Donald Williams driving right of the lane and flipping up a runner that goes in with 5.5 seconds left. Wake has time to score, but they don't. Half the room roars.

"Did you guys win?" my lawyer asks.

God help him. He missed a beautiful sunset while thinking about how to outflank a two-bit Fayetteville lawyer.

He gets the lawsuit dismissed at the summary judgment level.

February 2, 1995
North Carolina 102, Duke 100 (2 OT)

At the first read-through, I didn't like the script to this one at all.

This is the famous "back pain" year for Duke and its Coach K. The Blue Devils had been to the national title game the year before, losing in the final minute. Many of those players returned, and they added some really good freshmen, including Trajan Langdon. Krzyzewski recruited them, prepped them in preseason, had them ranked as high as sixth, and standing at 9-2 when Duke entered conference play at home against Clemson, a team headed for a 5-11 conference season.

Clemson won at Duke. Krzyzewski, citing back trouble, excused himself for the rest of the season. Pete Gaudet, his top assistant, took over and the Blue Devils went to pieces. Not sure what it says about the culture over there in Durham, but without their Coach K, Duke - with a roster of future NBA players and high-school All-Americans - has no chance.

Duke is 0-7 in the league when it welcomes second-ranked Carolina to Cameron. The Tar Heels now feature Rasheed Wallace and Jerry Stackhouse and have a truly great team, headed to the Final Four.

This should have been a walkover, even at Duke. Carolina jumps to a 26-9 lead, then clings to life, falling behind by 12 in regulation. That it takes two overtimes to pull this out annoys me to no end. Carolina fritters away a lead in the first overtime and almost again at the end. Only Duke's fecklessness keeps the Blue Devils from regaining the lead or possibly forcing another overtime.

But - watch this game again. It's one of the most remarkable college games you will see. That opening spurt by Carolina, highlighted by a Stackhouse reverse dunk over defenders that brought Carolina to 11-for-14 from the floor, is as good as a team can play for eight minutes.

Then Duke outscores Carolina by *29 points* over the next hour and a half, making shots, playing defense and hustling in a way that renders its final 2-14 league mark as inexcusable.

ESPN airs the game on their ESPN 2 network, a mistake it will never make again. This game sets the rivalry onto a new course.

It's the end of the first overtime we all remember. Carolina leads by eight with just under 20 seconds to play (!!!) but Duke gets six while the Tar Heels miss a free throw. The lead is still three with four seconds left, and Serge Zwikker is at the line for two free throws. Just make one and the game is over.

Clang. Just one goddamned free throw, Serge. Clang again.

Jeff Capel is allowed to dribble unfettered past midcourt when he launches from about 40 feet. It rattles in. Bedlam among the Crazies. This is before they dressed as basketball hoops or bananas or posed for TV. Back then they just cheered for their team.

The shot will be shown over and over, to illustrate that in this rivalry, anything can happen. It comes off as a Duke glory moment.

If I were ever to be elected to any state or federal office, my first act would be to introduce a law mandating that any time a replay of Capel's shot is shown, a crawl across the bottom of the screen must run. And that crawl will say: "You know, Carolina actually won this game. This shot going in only allowed the Blue Devils the opportunity to lose in the next overtime. Which they did."

Or something like that.

March 10, 1995
North Carolina 78, Clemson 62
ACC Tournament First Round

We're back in Greensboro, live at the ACC Tournament, watching a forgettable first-round win over Clemson. Except the most remarkable thing happens during a time out.

Carolina is ahead 16 points with three minutes to go when Clemson's Iker Iturbe fouls the living crap out of Jerry Stackhouse rather than watch Stack score again. This harkens back to both Clemson games during the season, when the Tigers, and their young coach, Rick Barnes, decided the best way to close the talent gap would be to "get physical" with the Tar Heels. In other words, foul, foul, foul.

Coach Smith decides to air his grievance directly with Iturbe. Coaches talking to opposing players is not generally accepted in college basketball, or really at any level. This is the very thing Coach K did to Carolina's Scott Williams in the 1989 ACC final that prompted Smith's objection and the subsequent "Fuck you Dean" comment.

But Iturbe has crossed some sort of line in Coach Smith's mind. "Iturbe" he shouts, his nasal twang piercing the Coliseum. Then he points at the Clemson forward.

This prompts Barnes, a North Carolina native, to confront the coach he's heard about and studied his entire adult life. A "conversation" starts during the time out and the next thing you know, the coaches are shouting and having to be separated from one another.

We've never seen anything like it. Coach Smith is in his mid-60s, an icon and on his way to his 12th Final Four. Clemson is... the Clemson of the league. Their next ACC title will be their first. Barnes is either the most presumptuous bastard the league has known, or the man who finally calls out Coach Smith's imperiousness.

I guess it depends on where you stand. I know where I do.

March 19, 1995
North Carolina 73, Iowa State 51
NCAA Tournament Second Round

I'm not sure what got into us, but we decide to catch the Charlotte Hornets, the novelty of an NBA team in our state still being fresh. We pick a game in March and, sure enough, the Tar Heels are playing an NCAA tournament game the same day.

No worries. It's just Iowa State and we will listen on the way home. Woody Durham, our beloved play-by-play guy, will paint a vivid enough picture for this one.

The Hornets subdue Utah, despite Karl Malone (26 points) and John Stockton (16 points, 16 assists). Rather than reflect on having seen two future Hall-of-Famers, we scramble for the radio dial in the parking lot. We swear a lot—where is the game?—while hunting the streets of Charlotte for the U.S. 74 that will take us home. Finally, the dulcet tones of Woody.

He has us behind by 14 points. I can't focus on traffic and the Tar Heels losing early to a crappy team. Rasheed Wallace, questionable before the game with an ankle sprain, makes a steal and cruises in for a slam. Woody is excited. So are we. Our Ford Taurus, almost acting on its own accord, has pulled off the highway and into a TK Tripps.

We ask the bartender to turn the TV to the game—c'mon Charlotte!— and watch the Tar Heels gain control while devouring meh burgers, lots of fries and some beer. We get home two hours later than planned, but we were needed.

March 25, 1995
North Carolina 74, Kentucky 61
NCAA Southeast Regional Final

It's hard to remember a team as good as the 1995 Carolina team being as disrespected as this. Though having just lost to third-ranked Wake Forest in the ACC final, this fourth-ranked team can play with anybody. But when they draw second-ranked Kentucky in this regional final, it is just assumed, from all corners, that Kentucky will win.

The game is in Birmingham, which is in the heart of Wildcat country. The arena is full of Kentucky fans. Kentucky is big, fast, and coached by Rick Pitino, a rising star in the field. Just three years before, his plucky overachievers were the sons we never had, as they appeared to have knocked Duke off its repugnant perch (before the Laettner nonsense).

Now they are again the smug partisans we knew they were all along, with Pitino seemingly unwilling to be bothered with North Carolina.

Meanwhile, Carolina is starting to seem a little stale, at least from the national perspective. Hell, even seventh-place ACC coaches are challenging Coach Smith to fight.

Early in the game, Rasheed Wallace basically gets in a fight with a Kentucky player, choking him with both hands at one point. It's a gracious mercy from the referee he is not ejected. The tension goes from about 8 to 10 plus.

So when Carolina seems to have wrapped it up, we're shouting at the bedroom TV, now the largest one in the house. When Wallace gets loose for a screaming, thunderous dunk in the last 30 seconds, and the camera pans to the sour Kentucky bench, we're jumping up and down. And when Donald Williams gets one more run-out dunk at the buzzer, we're euphoric, dancing about and hugging one another.

Almost immediately a recent tradition kicks in. The phone is ringing. I pick it up and it's College Friend.

"HOW BOUT DEM HEELS," is all that is said. I hang up and it rings again. College Friend. Some more asking about the Heels.

This goes on for a while. For fans of a certain age, this win ranks high on the most gratifying list. Disrespect Coach Smith? I don't think so.

April 1, 1995
Arkansas 75, North Carolina 68
NCAA Tournament Final Four

Back in the Final Four, starting to look like a birthright. This will be the last run for Rasheed Wallace and Jerry Stackhouse, as they are too talented to return for their junior year. Instead they will be selected 3rd and 4th in the next NBA draft.

We're playing Arkansas, the defending national champions. The first half is back-and-forth, two great teams having at it. Donald Williams starts hitting threes, like he did two years before in that Final Four, and we're up seven with 3 seconds left. It's a strong seven, well-earned through almost 40 minutes of solid, smart play.

Then a foolish inbounds pass from under our basket. It bounces, hits the backboard at the other end and ricochets out to Dwight Stewart, a chubby reserve forward who averages seven points and one three-pointer a game. He has just enough time to fling a 65-footer toward the other end.

Swish. The halftime lead is four, but in the Whisnant home it feels like that basket is worth about 20 points. In the second half, Arkansas takes control, Carolina goes 12 minutes without hitting a shot and the Hogs lead by 11 with 3 1/2 minutes left.

Then comes the most frustrating comeback ever. Carolina cuts it to two with under 50 seconds left and Stackhouse at the line for two. He misses, the third free throw miss in the last three minutes. Then, trailing by just one and more than a half-minute left, Dante Calabria mis-hears a command to "don't foul." He intentionally fouls a good shooter. We look foolish.

One more miss, and it's over. The '93 title still salves us, but we're wasting some really good players here.

January 6, 1996
North Carolina 88, Maryland 86 (OT)

Innocent Victims has been made into a TV movie—a two-part, four-hour "miniseries" actually—and the Fayetteville premiere is on this night. We have shown it privately to the lawyers and to Tim Hennis, the protagonist who is charged, then acquitted, of triple murder. The tension the night before is beyond uncomfortable.

During one scene, the Hennis character—John Corbett, of *Northern Exposure* and *Sex in the City* fame—loses his temper over a court proceeding gone wrong. The last thing the real Tim Hennis needs is a national audience to see him as angry—angry enough to commit a crime.

"That never happened," Hennis says. "I never did that. It's got to come out."

No, the premier is the next night. Everyone we know is coming. ABC will air this in a couple of weeks. It is what it is.

The question then becomes who let this happen. The chat starts to resemble a family meeting for the *Succession* family. Who saw the script and greenlighted this? Who proposed this as a good idea? Who will throw whom under the bus?

The producers step forward. It's their job to be glib and handle moments like this, and they rise to the moment.

"Tim, this was our way of explaining to the audience, in a short amount of time, why you couldn't testify in the first trial," one of them says. "We have to condense a lot of material to make a point."

That hangs in the air a while, but finally we move forward and somehow get through it. It's time for the public premier. The only problem on this night is freezing rain, icing over the roads. Only a fool would try to get to this event in person.

The room is packed. My parents and one of my sisters are here, the other one having spun a 360 on the way from Chapel Hill and opting out. Hennis' lawyers, with whom I worked on this project, are here with their families. People from all of Fayetteville who remember this crime are here.

It goes well. Really well. Right after it's over I meet an older man, standing 6-foot-9. He introduces himself as Joe Quigg, a retired dentist in Fayetteville. He doesn't mention that he was starting center on the 1957 Tar Heel undefeated championship team, but I recognize the name.

It was Quigg who made two foul shots in the final seconds to put Carolina ahead by one in the third overtime against Kansas. And Quigg who knocked away Kansas' last pass to none other than Wilt Chamberlain. Quigg is a Tar Heel treasure.

I am honored, I tell him. And he tells me, with utter sincerity, that it is a greater honor to meet me, author of this story. This night can't get much better.

Then it does. Billy Richardson, one of Hennis' lawyers, enters the room and commands its silence. Either someone has been assassinated or the United States has gone to war.

"I just wanted you to know," Richardson says, his voice cracking with great solemnity, "that Carolina has defeated Maryland on a last-second shot by Dante Calabria."

This can only happen in ACC country.

21

THE WAVE GOOD-BYE

January 25, 1997

Wake Forest 61, Florida State 58

There's no graceful way out the moment Shad mentions it.

My eccentric, crusty neighbor knows good and well I love college basketball. So when he offers me a chance to watch a Wake Forest game in person during his beloved Tim Duncan's senior year in 1997, I can't decline. At 73, he's finally found a team representing his alma mater he can believe in, making the four-hour drive to Winston-Salem for every home game then driving back the same evening.

I have no interest in doing this. It's an eight-hour round trip with the unspoken agreement that I will drive, listening to a man my father's age swear about how much below expectations his Deacons are playing. He swears a lot. Or, as a product of his generation, he'll suddenly describe Maryland's offense in the crudest of racial terms. Or, as a lover of language, he'll start reciting poetry. Or he'll remember growing up in the Depression, or his wife having died three years before, and start crying.

He lays out the Wake Forest schedule so I can pick my medicine. The Carolina game is off the table, which proves to be a relief when the Tar Heels open the ACC season by getting crushed by 24 at Wake. I pick the January 25 date against Florida State, a certain Wake Forest win and therefore a likely more pleasant ride home.

Talking Wake Forest basketball may be a better choice, anyway. Carolina starts the ACC season 0-3, losing by 24, 10 and 12, and damn near make it 0-4 save for an N.C. State meltdown in the final two minutes in Chapel Hill. The Tar Heels, supposedly a national contender, are 2-4 in the league when we head toward Winston.

I am able to exact some terms from Shad. If we are passing this close to Greensboro, then we will eat lunch with my parents. We never want to miss a chance to eat my mother's cooking, often timing our visits to Route 7 so we arrive at meal time. High school buddies, college roommates, nervous girlfriends and later my fiancée all wonder at first why we make this detour. Then they sit down at the table and immediately understand.

Shad is as trapped as I am. No graceful way out. Of course we will meet your parents, he says.

I tell Mama "it's up to you" on what to serve, a bit like asking the King's jeweler to pick any diamond. I do drop a clumsy hint about strawberry cobbler.

Truth be told, it's a cynical ploy bordering on criminal. Of course Mama will make the cobbler. Her work ethic, combined with a willingness to serve, knows no bounds. By now, she is in her 35th year as financial secretary at Jamestown United Methodist Church, a job she first took despite no experience but wrestled to the ground through sheer persistence. Her job was part-time, designed so she would be there when we got home from school, dinner already under way.

On many occasions, my exhausted mother would lie down for a nap and instruct me to wake her in five minutes. After four, she would wake with a start and yell at me for not getting her up. When I told her it was only four minutes, she would accuse me of having no intention of waking her. Which was true.

At 65 and still of cobbler-bearing age, Mama's service heart will be tapped again without shame on my part. Because, strawberry cobbler.

Papa Bear, though, is starting to fade. In recent weeks my sisters have told me he is creaking in the joints and not sleeping well, with allergies flaring and trouble swallowing. He has begun to talk openly about his miseries, so unlike him.

But he has maintained his garrulous sense of humor. A window salesman cold-called him a few weeks prior, offering replacement windows. Expensive ones.

"Where I'm going, I won't need windows," Daddy told him.

"What do you mean, sir?"

"Where I'm going the streets will be paved with gold, with mansions of alabaster..." and so on, a glorious description of the Bible's heaven.

Papa Bear in his "jammers" on Christmas morning. Every gift he received, regardless of quality, was "just what I wanted."

"Sir, please don't talk like that," the flustered salesman said.

Daddy continued with how he was headed for a life where every tear would be dried, with no pain, no suffering... and no windows.

The salesman gave up and ended the call.

But on most days, the impulse to tease seemed to have been beaten out of Daddy.

"Don't expect much," I tell Shad. "He may come off as quiet or stand-offish."

Back in the day, my fear would have been that Daddy would hold court a little too robustly, telling stories that were off subject or dated. With Carolina struggling, he might go on a rant about lack of effort or something. On this day, my fear is just the opposite.

"My dad may not be himself," I tell Shad.

The drive down is actually entertaining. Shad is at his best, regaling me with recollections of ACC games from the 1950s as easily as I can from five years ago. He holds forth on marriage and parenthood. He quotes poetry with precision and makes it relevant. He tells me what to expect as I grow older. And all sorts of other wise things. I'm a little ashamed I dreaded this. We're at my parents' house in no time.

I'm startled to see my father almost gaunt. At the rate we're going, I may weigh more than him when Sophie, the granddaughter he's just learned about, is born in four months. That is a preposterous possibility. It's not so much that I was historically rail thin, which I was, but he was this giant of a man, with huge, rugged hands, powerful arms and a big belly he was never ashamed of. He had a large red birthmark on it, so we compared him to the planet Jupiter. He was always the largest in our solar system, the one whose centrifugal force bound us.

He shakes hands firmly, as he always has. But he's hurting. Nonetheless, he makes an effort, just as he did at that game in Charlotte eight years earlier, just like he did when we would call and he would hobble to the other phone in the back bedroom to join in, just as he always did in everything.

He and Shad make fast friends. They're the same age and both in poor health—Shad just had five heart bypasses. They both gripe a little about their teams, but the subject amuses them and this thread ends in laughter. They talk about the Depression. They talk about the annoyance of getting a physical for World War II. That's more war talk than I had ever heard from Daddy.

Shad gets up to go to the bathroom. Once out of earshot, Daddy says, "He's a bird, isn't he?"

Mama says dinner (that's "lunch" to non-Southerners) is ready. We gather around and pause, as always, until Daddy announces who will say the blessing. One of those things you don't think you'll miss about home until you do.

Point of View:
Linda Whisnant
Sister

When I was a teen, I had friends whose dads were helpful because of their jobs. One friend, whose dad had a car lot, drove a Mustang. Others had new clothes. I played my only round of golf because another's dad belonged to the Club. I left for college thinking most dads did what mine did: fix anything that broke, install water pumps, lay brick, build furniture, change the oil in the car. I soon learned better.

I thought I appreciated the advantages of an extremely skilled daddy, but one story took the cake. At 36, single, I had just bought my first house and needed a place to store the lawnmower, etc. Daddy agreed to accompany me to Lowe's to look at premade outdoor sheds.

Once there, he declared them unworthy, their materials shoddy, and asked why didn't he just build me one. I happily agreed and turned to go the car to go home and plan. He stopped me, asking, "You got anything to write on?" I did. Then he started to imagine the shed. "How big do you want it?," he asked.

He cocked his head to the side and looked off into space, not unlike Scott does when he's thinking, and proceeded to call out every 2 x 4 needed, how many treated, sheets of plywood, shingles, nails, roofing nails, how much paint, every single thing he'd need.

We bought it. When it was done, I had three pieces of 2 X 4, none over a foot or so, a handful of nails, and about five shingles.

I kept those leftovers in the corner of my fine building as a reminder of his precision and his love in action.

The meal is again a master stroke of simple Southern cooking done right. Country-style steak, too tender to sully with a knife. Velvet mashed potatoes and gravy that is nothing short of art—the right temperature and right consistency. Butterbeans. And a broccoli and cheese casserole that seemingly materializes out of air.

Shad takes a few bites and I recognize that look. Now he understands.

Daddy is moving all in on telling stories. The strawberry cobbler arrives on cue. We're all laughing. Daddy has his good stuff today. It's almost an annoyance we have to leave for the game, but we do. Shad has forgotten his handicapped tag, so Daddy loans him one. During the rest of the way to the game, Shad can't stop gushing about his new friend and how he's looking forward to the trips to Wilmington Daddy is sure to make when his granddaughter is born.

The game? I don't really remember. I think Florida State has a chance to tie it late but doesn't. I do run into several high school friends and we go out to eat with them afterward. Shad makes for good company.

Now we have to run the tag to my parents' house before heading back. We're looking at a midnight arrival in Wilmington, so I'm starting to dread this side trip. I even consider mailing it to Daddy, but he needs it now.

I pull into the carport. Shad is tired and stays in the car. Mama is running an errand somewhere. So I approach the door and Daddy is asleep in his recliner, mouth agape, at peace with the world. It's a pose his children have seen countless times.

I wake him up and try to drop the tag and leave, but he insists on coming out to the car to say goodbye to Shad. They talk about meeting again soon.

As I back out of the driveway, Daddy stands in the carport and waves goodbye.

"What a wonderful man," Shad says.

Yes indeed. So what if he griped a bit during Carolina games? Can the man not have his hobbies and passions? This won't pass muster as "dysfunction," not among those who truly have a toxic family. The good here far outweighs watching ballgames and I had let that go a long time ago. Still, seeing him through the eyes of someone new gives me a new appreciation.

"Look at that, Shad," I say, pointing at my father. "Every time I've ever left here, he's stood there and watched us drive off, just like that. We've always known he loves us."

Shad begins to get emotional, but I do not. I know he'll do it again when I see him next time.

About four weeks later, Daddy feels spry enough to load the riding mower on the trailer he built and mow my sister Linda's yard, across town in Greensboro. He finishes the yard and empties the clippings at the mulch pile.

Papa Bear doing Papa Bear things with his grandson. We all had a love/hate relationship with that harmonica.

The paramedics tell us he was dead before he hit the ground. A massive, sudden heart attack while he was doing what he loved best - mowing a yard for someone he loved. There would be no visits to see his granddaughter, no more Carolina games, no more waves good-bye.

Mama and Linda both tell me that if I had to pick a day to be around him during those final six months, I had picked the right one. Florida State at Wake Forest.

I kept the ticket stub in my wallet until, finally, it disintegrated.

February 26, 1997
North Carolina 76, Clemson 69

It's my lunch break on a Wednesday afternoon and there's not enough people to play pickup basketball at the Wilmington Athletic Club. So I lift weights, still needing a spotter to bench 135 pounds. Undoing 35 years of slovenly body care doesn't come overnight.

When Celia, five months' pregnant, shows up unannounced with our friend Gray, I suspect what it is, and I am correct. Papa Bear has left the earth.

During the four-hour drive to Route 7, the mind goes to so many things, none of them college basketball. My sisters are "home" and my Mama is devastated but holding on. Aunts and cousins are trickling in, as are neighbors and friends. The food is piling up. So much orange glop, that staple of the Southern sideboard, a weirdly appealing mashup of orange gelatin, cottage cheese and pineapple. How much orange glop can we possibly eat?

One of the underrated hassles of immediate grief is the logistics. When is the funeral? Who speaks and in what order? Will that offend someone? Which hymns to sing? Is that because I like it or because Daddy liked it?

I'm sitting in his chair, the recliner of a thousand naps, because I have to sit somewhere. And just before 7 p.m., it hits me.

The Tar Heels have a game tonight. At Clemson. We are so watching this game.

Clemson is actually having a good year by anyone's standards and a historic one by theirs. Just five weeks earlier the Tigers were 16-1 and ranked second in the nation. They have lost six conference games since then—the league is still brutal—but remain ranked 12th.

Meanwhile, something has gotten into the Tar Heels. After losing to Duke to close the first half of the schedule at 3-5, they have run off six straight in the league, winning close games and routs, even hammering Wake Forest in the rematch of that 24-point blowout.

This game has drama on its own merits. But in the Whisnant home on this night, it really doesn't matter who we are playing. To watch the Carolina game, from his chair, in his home, before his fireplace and with the people he loved, is the only way forward tonight. It's the only sensible thing we will do on a day that will never make sense.

Guests stop and stare at first. As in "are you really going to watch a game at a time like this?" And my unspoken reply is "A time like this is exactly why I am especially watching this game." The Tar Heels have been my idols, my passion, my frustration. They taught me perspective in religion and race relations. I have seen them as gods, as heroes, as fellow students and as interview sparring partners. Now as kids just doing their best to represent a school I love.

Tonight, they will be healers. They will mend the last and only fence between myself and my father, and we will put off funeral planning for two hours until we see this through.

Carolina immediately falls behind 28-15. The Clemson crowd senses the kill. Oh well. Perspective. Maybe it's just a game and Daddy happened to pick this night, when Clemson is too tough, to die. Funeral planning and meal gathering continues. I may be the only one in the house paying attention.

The Tar Heels hang in. Shammond Williams gets red-hot in the second half, scoring 14 of his 16 points. I believe it's his three-pointer that puts Carolina ahead. I do know everyone in the entire house is rapt by now, rooting the Tar Heels on. Williams scores nine points in the final two minutes.

Carolina wins it. Now I can cry for real.

March 2, 1997
North Carolina 91, Duke 85

We're still at my Mama's house. Daddy died on a Wednesday, the funeral was on Friday and now it's Sunday, the sensible day to leave and try to start the rest of our lives.

There's been a shift in momentum. Now it's about her. We have buried my Daddy, greeted family and friends and told stories. The funeral two days before had been oddly gratifying, giving us a chance to publicly say what he meant to us.

On Saturday, my good buddy Dave Willard tries to "entertain" me by having me work out with some of our friends at a gym in Jamestown. He's so well-meaning and doing what friends do, but I'm not in the mood. He thinks I don't want to talk about it, but it's all I want to talk about.

But I go anyway. They are wrapped up in bench-pressing free weights, so I slip away to the machines. Where I encounter Reggie Tice, one of the great athletes in Ragsdale history who is three years older. I've played hoops with Reggie, but never really bonded with him as I was too busy looking up to him.

He's in the machine next to me and I remember that his mother had died just a few months before.

"Sorry about your dad," he says.

"Yeah, thanks."

"He was such a good guy. He always talked to me at church. Really good guy."

I think about that for a moment. That is so like my father. He would befriend anyone, regardless of age, status or athletic prowess. And so many people, more than I had realized, saw him for the genuine force that he was.

"Sorry about your mom," I say.

"Yeah."

"My friends here, they're trying to keep me 'entertained' so I don't have to talk about it. They don't get that it's all I want to talk about."

"I know," Reggie says.

We both sit there, not lifting the weights on those machines, crying a little. That's what I need.

On Sunday, it's time to go, but of course we'll stay through the Carolina-Duke game. If ever there is a moment that Carolina basketball set the rhythm of my life, this is it. Duke is ranked 7th and Carolina 8th, but the Tar Heels are much better by this point in the season. They begin proving it almost right away. But the game's very framework creates the oddest sensation.

It hits me soon that we are about to leave our mother, who has known nothing but partnership with this man since she was 20, some 46 years ago, alone in this house. It's a heartbreaking reality. With each TV timeout punctuating a four-minute chunk of the game, we realize we're that much closer to leaving her.

Carolina is winning against our hated rival, and I can't stand it. During every commercial break, I go to the bathroom to cry. Then compose myself enough to watch the next four minutes, to ensure Antawn Jamison, Vince Carter, Ed Cota et al are keeping the Blue Devils in their place. Then the under eight-minute timeout, and I cry some more. And so on.

Dave calls me during a TV timeout in the second half—he knows better than to call during the game—and I am so overcome that I can't speak. We have to leave her. I know this. If the game could last forever, we could stay with her. But if it lasts too long, Duke might win. It's very confusing.

Finally, Carolina seals the least gratifying win over Duke in my memory. And I hug my mother goodbye and leave her in the house at Route 7.

We back out and exit onto the highway. She watches from the driveway.

March 15, 1997
North Carolina 73, Colorado 56
NCAA Tournament Second Round

It's meant to be, right? Carolina storms through the ACC Tournament, routing Wake Forest once again. Duke, the regular-season "winner," loses in the first round. Then again in the second round of the NCAA Tournament to a Providence team whose starting point guard is named God Shammgod. While defeating Duke, God is good (12 points, nine assists).

Meanwhile, Providence is also smiling on the Tar Heels. They get to play in Winston-Salem, the same place Shad and I watched our game together. The win over Colorado is fairly ordinary, except for one major detail: Coach Smith's 26th win of the season - a number that seemed out of reach two months ago—is also the 877th of his career, passing Kentucky's Adolph Rupp for first place on the all-time coaching wins list. We know other coaches have since passed him, but it diminishes our reverence for this accomplishment not one bit.

Coach Smith tries to downplay it, but his players and many former players won't hear of it. They mob him on the court after this win, making sure he celebrates.

The fact he passes Rupp, a renowned racist who refused to change when the world around him changed in the 1960s, makes it all the more gratifying. Coach Smith had long ago passed Rupp on issues that matter.

This Tar Heel team has a look of destiny to it. They win two more and reach the Final Four. I call my mother after every game, believing our late Papa Bear is somehow responsible. The '97 team is making a dreadful time in our lives bearable.

March 29, 1997
Arizona 66, North Carolina 58
NCAA Tournament Final Four

Has a great person in Arizona also died? Or is it really time to let go of the "win it for Papa Bear" theme?

Life works this way. Sports are not arranged as a salve for our hurts. They can be a wonderful distraction, but our grief is not the center of the sports universe. No one tells Mike Bibby over in the Arizona locker room about my father, and he likely has his own issues.

The Tar Heels jump to a 15-4 lead, largely through alley-oop dunks by Vince Carter, among others, on passes from Ed Cota. Then the magic just stops. They shoot 31% from the field. Bibby wakes up from a 2-for-12 start to hit five three-pointers in the second half.

The team that started the league 0-3 (and 0-4 if N.C. State could have inbounded the ball in Chapel Hill) shows up in the Final Four. It's almost like the grief for Papa Bear was too much to bear at one time. So Carolina kept him alive for four weeks, and now it's time to let all of him go.

We don't yet know this is Coach Smith's last game. He retires just before the next season at age 66, which at the time seems like a reasonable age to retire but, today, not so much.

Sophie Caroline Whisnant, 9 lbs., 10 oz., is born June 14, 1997, in a world without her paternal grandfather and one in which Coach Smith will never coach. She will not be carrying on Tar Heel traditions but witnessing new ones. If that is even still a thing by the time she's old enough to care.

22

"GO WHERE YOU GO"

February 5, 1998

North Carolina 97, Duke 73

Coach Smith has retired in such a way, just before preseason practice, that the university just about has no choice but to hire Bill Guthridge, his long-time assistant. It is widely assumed Coach Smith did this on purpose, as if there could be some other explanation, to allow his friend and partner the chance to lead the program.

Guthridge was plenty fiery during his 30 years as Coach Smith's assistant, but by 1998 he comes across like somebody's grandpa. The players love him, and he knows basketball inside and out, but he doesn't seem to have the energy for all the stuff required of a high-major college basketball coach. Stuff like media interviews and especially recruiting.

His first team in 1998 is excellent, with two All-Americans (Antawn Jamison and Vince Carter), a fantastically clever point guard (Ed Coda), shooting guard Shammond Williams and two others who are worthy starters. If you're keeping score, that makes six players.

Guthridge's answer to this dilemma is to start them by alphabet and then rotate who sits out every game. It isn't the most definitive answer, and it sometimes leaves the wrong player on the bench too long at the start of a game.

The team is fabulous, as is this year's version of the Duke rivalry. Both teams have realistic national championship aspirations. The first game is a rarity, one between the top two ranked teams in the nation (Duke is 1st) in Chapel Hill where we blow out Duke twice.

The Tar Heels lead by 20 points, only to have Duke systematically close the gap, aided by an untimely technical foul. Suddenly, the lead is four.

Carolina then ends the game on a 24-4 run that drives the Smith Center into a frenzy. Even when it's bad, it's good. On a breakout, Cota throws an alley oop off the backboard to Carter, only to have the other-wordly leaper miss the dunk. The rebound goes straight to Williams at the three-point line, and he hits from there. Three points are better than two.

We can't rewatch this enough times on our VCR, this game now a star selection in the library of videotapes I am amassing. Sometimes it takes about 10 minutes to fast forward past sitcoms and random documentaries to get to the part I want to watch. God we were primitive.

February 28, 1998
Duke 77, North Carolina 75

The rematch in Durham has lost some of its luster, as Duke is still top-ranked but Carolina has fallen to 3rd.

In the hype leading up to the game, much is written about how Coach K somehow brought a candle to a Duke practice, turned down the lights and led the team through some Wiccan chants. Or something like that. What a fantastic coach. His top-ranked team lost by 24 points in Chapel Hill, but he brought a candle to a team meeting.

It's senior night for the much-hated and pesky Steve Wojciechowski, the Duke point guard whose primary contribution to the landscape has been to slap the floor on defense for four years. The Heels lead by 16, only to get swallowed up by the Devils and their frantic crowd. Duke rallies to win by two and Wojo, who poured in one point and added some floor slaps, hugs Coach Krzyzewski as the fans storm the court.

Decent people are appalled.

March 8, 1998
North Carolina 83, Duke 68
ACC Tournament Final

Using good ol' electricity through the next week at practice, Guthridge leads the Tar Heels to a rematch with Duke at the ACC final the next weekend.

It's a 1 p.m. Sunday game. Has the ACC, still moored in the Bible-belt South, turned heathen? This is still the church hour. We can't come in midway and start from the beginning, because that's not how VCRs work. At least we can't get spoilers on our phones because they are still house-bound rotary phones connected by a coil.

We eat after church—we have to eat—at Goody Goody Omelet House, a Wilmington staple, not because it's good or historic but because it's fast. One false move could cost us the tip-off. The waffle goes down in three bites. We pay when the waitress brings the food. She doesn't even call us "hon."

It's tied in the second half when Antawn Jamison, whose oddly spelled name is a source of derision for Duke fans who speculate if his mother could spell—racism, anyone?—goes off and does what Jamison does. Carolina by 15. I think that settles it.

March 21, 1998
North Carolina 75, Connecticut 64
NCAA Tournament East Regional Final

Carolina's winning the rivalry war means we get the top seed in the East Regional, this year in Greensboro, beloved second home to the Tar Heels and just an hour from Chapel Hill. Duke is sentenced to a top seed in the South Regional in St. Petersburg, Fla., where second-seeded Kentucky is looming.

The *Morning Star* is entering an era of fecklessness that will only get worse and will be shared by daily newspapers everywhere. It has a press pass to the game, but no reporter. So they agree to give it to us and I magnanimously offer it to Celia so she can experience NCAA Tournament stress from up close.

Meanwhile, Rick, my cousin in Atlanta, had thought ahead before the season and bought two tickets for this regional, seizing the chance to also visit his mother who lives in Jamestown. Now, can I talk his wife into giving up her ticket so I can join him?

Yes, I can. I am that cousin. Sumi gracefully backs down because, at the end of the day, she really doesn't care about Carolina basketball. At least not like I do.

We spend the day before in Chapel Hill at sister Judy's house, watching Duke play Kentucky in another classic regional final, though decidedly less famous than the 1992 Laettner shot.

Here's a Duke team plenty good enough to win another title, leading by 17 points in the second half. Here's Kentucky, pressing on every possession to catch up. And here's Duke, so flustered by the press that they use all their timeouts to save possessions. And here's more of Duke, unable to call timeout as Kentucky mounts a charge. And finally here's Duke, unable to get the ball to Elton Brand, their best player, when it counts.

Kentucky surges to force overtime, then takes Duke out of the tournament. What a warm-up act for the Carolina game in Greensboro.

The Connecticut game in fascinating live because I get to see how much effort Vince Carter puts into defending Rip Hamilton, the Huskies' All-American forward. Carolina is staying ahead just enough in a taut, tense game.

At halftime, I do something I shouldn't do. I am better than this. Ever since my years as a sportswriter and my "guys in short pants" reckoning with my father, I swore I wouldn't be this guy.

But I see an older lady wearing a Duke sweatshirt as I come back from concessions.

"I'm guessing when you bought these tickets you weren't expecting to see Carolina play," I hear myself say.

Now, that's not a friendly thing to say, but in saner hands it could have been the start of some self-deprecating banter, along the lines of "no, it's not, but if I can see you guys lose I guess it will be worth it."

That's not where she went.

"I'm sorry you didn't have the SAT scores to get into Duke," she fairly screamed at me. I think it was a canned line she had been prepped to use.

"You know, I had choices on where I would go to school and I chose Carolina," I replied, turning on my heel and walking off.

Actually I never applied to Duke, would never have wanted to go to Duke and would never have gotten in to Duke. That's so not the point.

Anyway, we take control, finally, in the second half and seem headed for a Final Four rematch against Arizona, the defending national champion and the hottest team in the nation at this moment.

That's when the PA announcer breaks in.

"Your attention, please. Final score from the West Regional. Utah 76, Arizona 51."

The Carolina fans erupt, a classic example of the flawed thinking of "Carolina should win because we know nothing about the other team." Utah will come to the Final Four ranked seventh at 29-3.

I lean over to my cousin next to me.

"If they're good enough to beat Arizona by 25 points, why are we cheering?"

March 28, 1998

Utah 65, North Carolina 59

NCAA Tournament Final Four

This would prove to be a good question.

Carolina is never really in it, falling behind 26-12 before cutting it to two with two minutes left. Utes guard Andre Miller immediately scores over Jamison, Carter misses a 1-and-1 free throw and it slips away.

Shammond Williams, our best shooter who keeps defenses honest, goes 2-for-12 (and misses eight of nine three-point attempts) as he starts the game on the bench (the alphabet turned against him) and never gets in the flow. Jamison, who was uncharacteristically bad (7-for-19 from the floor), kisses the floor before he leaves.

He appears to be saying goodbye to college basketball after his junior season. A team that ranks among the all-time favorites for an entire generation of Carolina fans of a certain age has absorbed what is widely considered one of the worst five losses in program history.

Our upper hand is slipping.

March 11, 1999

Weber State 76, North Carolina 74

NCAA Tournament First Round

Without Carter and Jamison, the Tar Heels slip some more, finishing third in the league and losing to Duke three times, yet drawing a 3 seed it probably doesn't deserve in the NCAA Tournament. The reward is 14th-seed Weber State. When my N.C. State friends next see me after this game, they ask if Weber has become the 51st state. This is what they cling to now.

To say we've never heard of the Black Bears would be an understatement. Wait. Their nickname is the Wildcats? We think the Big Sky Conference is a natural park, with a water fountain that will erupt if you look at it just right.

This is when Harold "The Show" Arceneaux earns his spot in Carolina infamy, scoring 36 points, 35 more than Brendan Haywood, our NBA center, and looking like he'll make people forget Kobe Bryant. He never plays a game in the NBA. The loss is technically the worst for Carolina in NCAA history, sending Duke fans into a flurry of buying up Weber State's student store inventory.

March 24, 2000
North Carolina 74, Tennessee 69
NCAA Tournament Sweet 16

Few things are more frustrating to the good college basketball fan than to watch a verified Blue Blood program have a lousy year, especially relative to its superior talent, then catch fire, get of a ton of breaks that hyphenated schools, directional schools or various religious schools wouldn't get in a lifetime, and become the darling of that year's NCAA Tournament, even earning some misguided "Cinderella" tags.

For reference point, look at the 2014 Kentucky team, which underperformed all year but had one guard (it was one of the Harrison twins. I'm thinking "George," but I may have him confused with someone else) make a bunch of last-second shots and voila!, Kentucky is in the championship game as an 8 seed. If this were James Madison or Austin Peay, it would be charming. For this to happen to Kentucky, it's like watching the Kennedys or Vanderbilts win a scratch-off lottery.

This year we are that team.

We slide a little further in 2000. Coach Gut just doesn't have it in him to do what it takes to address the current recruiting "environment," otherwise known as "seedy underbelly." The Heels are even ranked second early in the year, but they don't fool anyone for long. In January, they lose four ACC games in a row, heresy by Carolina standards. They limp to a regular-season finish at 9-7, tied with Virginia for third. Losers of three of their last four and eight of 15 after losing in the first round of the ACC Tournament, they fall to 18-13, unranked since January.

Making this worse is Duke is really, really good again, no doubt pleasing that bitter fan I met in the Greensboro Coliseum. The Blue Devils finish 15-1 in the league, win the ACC tournament and are top-ranked most of the year, never below fourth. Their fans are measuring the drapes of their Final Four hotel.

It's actually a controversy that Carolina even gets an NCAA Tournament bid, as an 8 seed, when Virginia, our co-third-place finisher who beat us *twice* (by 14 in Chapel Hill), goes to the NIT. Pundits dare to allege favoritism. Carolina is good for TV ratings, so of course they're in.

This is largely forgotten because of what happens the next three weeks. In round one, the Tar Heels smoke Missouri ("Where was that all year?" Ed Cota is reported to have asked) and draw top-seeded Stanford. And glory be, Stanford decides to shoot 34% and Carolina somehow wins.

Next up is Tennessee, my father's alma mater though he never openly rooted for the Volunteers. They have no basketball tradition to speak of, with no regional final appearances in their history. Carolina historically wins games like this.

Tell this to Ron Slay, Tennessee's goofball of a freshman who pretends to shoot a bow and arrow when he makes a basket, calls the paint his "Boom Boom Room" and openly disrespects Carolina leading up to the game. Slay will go on to finish his career as Tennessee's 13th-ranked scorer, get his diploma 15 years later and become one of the more provocative voices in college basketball broadcasting in that region. The Internet says one reason he was considered outlandish in 2000 was that he wore a white headband. Hmmm. Did white guys wear headbands then? Is it somehow threatening when Slay does it? In any event, he is considered a first-class turkey when Carolina plays Tennessee in 2000, giving the game a back story. Mocking Carolina is in season.

We take our 2-year-old to Greensboro this weekend to watch the game with Mama Bear, who manages to put together a multi-course meal that all comes out on time, a meal that restaurants would mortgage their families to serve. We're such good children to visit her like this.

Then CBS serves up a delicious doubleheader for fans in ACC country. First up is Duke vs. Florida for a berth in a regional final. You know, top-ranked Duke against 13th-ranked Florida, loser of eight games and third-place finisher in the Southeastern Conference.

Duke lays an egg, a beautiful shiny egg that so discredits its dominant season. When the Carolina game tips off minutes later, the only ACC team still playing in the tournament is North Carolina, fresh off its most uninspiring season since, well, 1966.

For about 33 minutes, it looks like Tennessee is set to slay the Tar Heels (bad pun alert). A 22-7 run gives the Vols a nine-point lead in the first half, and it's still at nine with seven minutes left. Brendan Haywood, our 7-foot center and only chance to control the inside, has fouled out.

That's when I make the call.

"We need Woody," I announce.

This is a storied and long-held tradition among Carolina fans. Woody Durham is not just our radio play-by-play guy, but he's our rock, our foundation, our friend and our strength in times of need. He is entirely synonymous with Carolina athletics and has been since 1971.

We actually remember him as the sports guy in WFMY in Greensboro and even entertained the thought, as young fans immature in our process, that he must be a Duke fan because, you know, "Durham." But as soon as he took the mike for Carolina, we saw through that folly. He was a better game announcer than haters give him credit (in other words, he was famously a "homer" but still managed to professionally broadcast the game), but let's be frank here. Woody's calls are the soundtrack of our fandom, and even though almost all games became televised, sometimes nothing will do during a tight jam other than turn down the TV and bring up Woody to take us home.

I had personal experiences with Woody. In college, I concocted some reason to interview him and he could not have been more gracious. I told him how much the '82 championship game had meant to me and he dug out a cassette of his call of that game and gave it to me. I played it in five cars I owned ("How 'bout dem Heels!!! They are the NATIONAL champions!!!), starting with the green Camaro and all the way to a Ford

Expedition worthy of transporting a family, until the tape finally had worn slam out. I loved that tape. Whenever I saw Woody, he asked about my career and offered encouraging words.

There was also the Woody you didn't hear on the radio. Still a great guy, but not necessarily safe for family viewing.

I was with Draggon Mihavolich, preparing to help the *Chapel Hill Newspaper* cover the 1984 Tar Heels' first NCAA game in Charlotte against Temple. The first game was still unfolding, and 12th-seeded Richmond was pulling away from fifth-seeded Auburn and their rotund force of a power forward, Charles Barkley.

As Richmond made play after play, Barkley was getting visibly agitated. We watched with bemusement.

Woody then walked behind us and warmly greeted Draggon, harkening back to the days he served as Woody's color analyst in football and basketball. After asking Draggon if he was about to start a war in Sarajevo (as he was preparing to work with ABC for the 1984 Olympics at a time of impending tension in his parents' native Yugoslavia), he made an observation about the game in front of us.

You have to read this in Woody voice, the perfect baritone, the Southern voice without sounding like a hick, the staccato clips on all the right syllables. He spoke fluent Woody even off the mike.

"If Barkley gets loose," he said, "he'll tear down the fucking backboard."

Woody!!! I might have been only slightly more shocked if my father had announced he was having an affair. But everyone laughed. They were used to it. Woody is a regular guy. And as I recall, Barkley did get a breakaway and, yes, he damn near tore down the rim. Auburn still lost.

Sixteen years later against Tennessee, we use Woody as a baseball manager may use his closer to finish out a game. Back then, the TV and radio broadcast simultaneously so the synch worked. Today it doesn't work because of a network delay—ESPN is the worst—and the radio guy sounds like Nostradamus, seeing everything 15 seconds before it happens.

We need Woody this night. And we tune in just in time for the signature moment, when the Tar Heels are up against it, and the breaks are going against the boys[1] and Woody offers the magic call to Tar Heel nation.

"It's time to go where you go and do what you do."

We're with you, Woody. Three-pointer by Joseph Forte. Layup by Jason Capel. Cota with a running jumper, then a floater over Slay. Carolina by two. The house at Route 7 is rapt as we hang on every Woody word.

Slay misses a "wild layup," as the Associated Press later calls it. When Forte grabs the rebound, Slay slings him to the floor, nearly an intentional foul. Forte makes two free throws with 35 seconds left. Then Julius Peppers, a 57-percent foul shooter, makes two more. That's the same Peppers who trails only Lawrence Taylor as the school's all-time greatest football player. The basketball players had discovered him in a gym playing pickup well enough to "help" the varsity team, and help them he has. Tennessee hasn't made a basket in 7 minutes, 15 seconds.

Game over. Woody got us to go where we go and do what we do. For us and millions in Tar Heel Nation, that meant tuning in to him.

Carolina draws Tulsa, a 7 seed with even less basketball history, in the regional final and somehow makes it to the Final Four, our fifth in eight years. Fans everywhere must be thinking "how nice that the University of North Carolina can catch lightning in a bottle and have something good happen to them."

No, that's not what they're thinking.

No matter. On the way back to Wilmington, we decide to stop in Chapel Hill to see how the celebration is going.

What we get are a bunch of drunk students roaming Franklin Street shouting "Fuck Duke." I disapprove. Not on the basis of language used in front of 2½-year-old Sophie, who's just beginning to build a vocabulary. She hears that word all the time—and not from me.

---

1 "Win one for the Gipper" speech of Notre Dame lore. Woody didn't actually say this.

But the sentiment itself. We're Carolina. Must we gauge everything we do in relation to Duke?

Alas, the Tar Heels lose in the semifinal to Florida, still hot after beating Duke, and Guthridge takes a well-earned retirement. Carolina naturally reaches out to former assistant Roy Williams, who has built a formidable program at Kansas since leaving Carolina in 1989.

For reasons that confound every living Tar Heel fan, really until this day, Williams turns down Coach Smith's personal plea to come back to Chapel Hill. It leaves a mark.

Determined to keep the job within the "family" of Carolina ex-players and coaches, one possibility after another fades until the school reaches out to Matt Doherty, a starter on the '82 championship team who used to give me good, albeit unauthentic, quotes for my stories.

He has one year of head coaching experience at Notre Dame, finishing with a middling 22-15 record that includes four wins in the lowly NIT. Naturally, he jumps at the job—and fires all the current assistants (including Phil Ford!!!) and much of the admin staff, some of them long-tenured motherly figures, at the UNC basketball office. So that's how it's going to be.

This is either going to work out in a big way, with a young coach modernizing the program and injecting needed energy, or it's headed for disaster.

23

THE NEWEST SCHMUCK

January 19, 2002

Connecticut 86, North Carolina 54

It's all I can do to keep from turning on the TV.

Every instinct I have within me says the Tar Heels are playing, therefore I watch. But this is a season for introspection. Must I drop everything in my life for two hours just because Carolina is tipping off?

The team is objectively terrible this year. Oh sure, the year before we were pretty good— for a while. There's a hilarious upset of Duke at Cameron and even a No. 1 ranking for two weeks, which is funny right up until the moment Duke wins the national championship. Then it all falls apart at a road game at Clemson. The season fades quickly from there and everyone who can leave does. The 2002 team shapes up

It's never too early to indoctrinate a child. Especially one as cute as this.

to be bad, yet Carolina still manages to underperform, losing to Hampton and Davidson at home to start the season.

The games are brutal. We're on our way to an 8-20 record, a level of futility unthinkable through my first 40 years on this earth. Must I watch every game?

There are other things to do. On this Saturday afternoon, my 4-year-old daughter wants to play a board game. Sophie doesn't care that the Tar Heels are on national TV against a really good Connecticut team, a program that is turning into a national power - the kind of game that could turn around a lousy season. She just wants a play date.

The board game, "Survivor," based on the then-fledgling reality show, is meant for groups to play as teams—otherwise the "challenges" have no point—but we don't have groups on this winter day. We just have us and our imaginations.

The Carolina game will have to wait. Sophie and I concoct ways to make the challenges, well, challenging. Then it's time for the final tribal council. How to avoid a 1-1 vote?

Usually at this point I just vote for her. Then I walk a few feet away, turn my back and give my "concession speech," as they do on the TV show, just loud enough for her to hear. ("I just want to congratulate her on the way she played the game...") Even at age 4 she knows it's silly.

On this day, she votes me as winner. We tie a few times, then I let her let me win. And when she turns the corner, faces the hallway and gives a fake "concession" speech to the imaginary camera, well, I realize I've won today, regardless of what the Tar Heels are doing.

Still, I can't help just getting a score. Maybe today is the day. Jawad Williams is shooting free throws for Carolina as the picture comes on. That's a good sign.

Then the score pops up. Carolina is behind by 40. Off goes the TV and we set up another game of Survivor, the Tar Heels having been voted off this island long ago.

March 1, 2003
North Carolina 67, Georgia Tech 66

It's time to introduce Sophie to how we do things around here. We need to visit the Dean Dome for a game. She's almost 6, for crying out loud. She has to be brought up the right way and this falls on her mother and me.

Carolina has better players this year but is really crappy again and will not make it to the NCAA Tournament, a two-year mark of shame. Based on internal reports, we can't imagine Matt Doherty will still be employed after the season ends. But, still, they are our Tar Heels and she is our daughter. And she needs to see them before she starts first grade.

She may or may not understand how many points a basket is worth, but there we are, scalping our way into the cheapest seats.

Now comes the learning lesson. We have no intention of sitting up there. As much as it pains me to admit, at any game in the Dean Dome (absent the Duke game), you can move to a million-dollar seat with impunity. Some donors literally give that amount for the privilege. The ushers not only turn a blind eye, they almost encourage it.

Try this at Fenway Park, or Madison Square Garden, for example, and you will be lucky to still be inside the stadium once the usher busts you. Here, they almost seem glad to have the seats filled so as to make a better impression for the TV audience.

This move is not without its shaming. Many is the time when Celia and I "bounce" four or five times in a section, after late arrivers ("The traffic!" they always say) come for their rightful seat. Everyone in our section knows we're up to no good, but the trick is to refuse to bow your head. Instead, we act like there's been a misunderstanding. We belong here somewhere. Typically, our section-mates see us as comrades and begin to volunteer helpful hints like pointing to seats and saying, "I know these people aren't coming today." We have Stockholm Syndromed them into sympathizing with their captors.

There's an algorithm, not articulated but clearly known within our heads, that proportionately increases our indignation the later someone comes to claim their seats. If you arrive after the under 12-minute media timeout and find us in your seat, expect a glare, a harumph and reluctance to move bordering on "I need to get an usher." One couple shows up for a Wake Forest game midway through the first half. My wife glares at them and barks "Are you kidding?" At some point, you don't deserve the seat.

We pick a seat five rows behind the Georgia Tech bench, at the row's end so we can easily enjoy the other amenities. Sophie, her new Carolina blue suede coat reaching her knees, senses we don't belong. Her preschool teacher has famously warned us she has "a high sense of justice," so we walk a delicate balance of morality here as we explain it's ok to sit here as long as no one comes to claim them.

We're introducing her to our schmuckery. Just as we get to a place where she no longer wants to turn us in, an official-looking well-scrubbed man with a radio walks across the court directly toward us.

Have we so violated decorum that the program itself has sent someone to eject us? Have we landed in the seats meant for the Georgia Tech coach's parents? Can we crawl to our upper deck seats and promise not to misbehave again?

The man introduces himself. He says there will be a pregame "drawing" for the seat number of a lucky fan who gets to walk across the court and collect a bag of McDonald's goodies from the Ram mascot himself. And the winner of that "drawing" is going to be our 5-year-old, because she has been spotted in that light blue coat and is unabashedly cute.

This flips the morality of the matter on its head. Sitting in these seats is not so bad. Sophie "wins" the rigged drawing and overcomes her

Is it any wonder the UNC basketball staff rigged its pregame "drawing" so this 5-year-old could meet the Ram mascot at center court?

bashfulness enough to prance across the court for a hug from the mascot. The crowd cheers its youngest schmuck.

No one claims these seats. We can almost smell the panic in the Georgia Tech players, including borderline Hall-of-Famer Chris Bosh, as the Yellow Jackets blow a five-point lead in the final minute. Carolina surges ahead to win by one point, an outcome worthy of the bygone Dean Smith/Carolina Piss Factor days.

The students even "storm" the court to celebrate this win over an unranked 12-12 team.

"Where are we going, Daddy?" Sophie asks.

"We're storming the court."

"We're not supposed to go down there."

Oh but we are. We are schmucks at the highest level. We're all in.

She gets over it and joins me. One Carolina game. One lottery win. One midcourt meeting with the Ram in front of 10,000 people. One comeback worthy of the program's legacy. And one midcourt storming.

We're off to a good start here.

24

ROMPING THROUGH
THE YARD

March 6, 2005

North Carolina 75, Duke 73

We're in another Duke rut. The Blue Devils have put together the most successful seven-year run in the history of the league. This does lead to one national championship, but, given the Blue Devils' talent, they have precious little overall to show for it.

The 1999 team had been as good as any I can remember in the league, even compared to the David Thompson teams at N.C. State. Duke won every league game by an average of 24 points. They romped to the national final with just one loss and met what should have been an overmatched Connecticut team. Yet the Huskies led most of the way, and the defining moment came with Connecticut up by one in the final minute. Five-foot-10 Khalid El-Amin drove to the hoop and encountered Duke's Shane Battier.

I imagine Battier growing up standing in front of tricycles and drawing charges on the playground, or establishing position and flopping in the grocery store aisle as distracted shoppers try to maneuver their carts through canned vegetables. Drawing charges is especially his thing. A gifted 6-foot-8 athletic forward, he had the ability to swat El-Amin's shot to kingdom come. But what did he do? He did what Duke does. He planted to draw the charge.

El-Amin simply pulled up, shot over Battier and hit. Duke lost. A great team came to naught, ending up 37 and 2.

In 2002, Duke lost what would have been the most embarrassing game in NCAA Tournament history, if not for the fact they had won it all the year before. They led a middling Indiana team by 17 points in a regional semifinal when Jayson Williams, their All-American guard, blew a breakaway layup.

We were vacationing at Bald Head Island, one of the premier secluded beach resorts on the East Coast. I had found a TV in a bedroom wired for cable, and, despite Celia imploring that we, you know, should enjoy the beach or have "family time" with our 4-year-old, I couldn't turn away. Williams' blown snowbird gave me hope.

She reminded me Duke was 17 points ahead. Sticking with this was futile. But I had to see it through.

Watching the ensuing Duke collapse was like sitting over Shakespeare's shoulder as he composed a sonnet. Indiana rallied and took a four-point lead, against all reason. In the waning seconds, Williams threw in a three-pointer while being fouled. With 4.4 seconds left, he had a chance to tie the game.

He missed, but it got worse. Duke's Carlos Boozer rebounded and was in position to win the game. I winced, forming the same expression you make right after your girlfriend says "we have to talk." Boozer put up an errant shot and there appeared to be contact, but no call. Game over.

But not for everybody. Duke reserve Matt Christensen, standing a thuggish 6-foot-10, charged the referee, former Atlanta Braves catcher Bruce Benedict, and had to be physically restrained from mugging him, an utterly graceless way to end a season. Had Christensen not been a departing senior, his suspension may have lasted past the birth of his first child. Yet this prompted no *New York Times* columnist to remark on the "renegade" state of college basketball. It may be relevant at this point to mention that, yes, Christensen is a white guy.

I called my buddy Dave Willard, no doubt minding his own business with his own family when he picked up and heard a long "FUUUUUUCK DUUUUUKE."

I missed a wonderful sunset, but there's one of those every night. Watching Duke lose in the Tournament is special.

Anyway, while Duke was enjoying this run of historic talent, Carolina was withstanding the Doherty years. After internal reports leaked that he abused players, violated their trust and treated former players and valued program employees like so much dirt, it was clear he couldn't continue as coach. After the 2003 season ended with a 19-16 record and an ignoble home loss in the NIT, the UNC leadership gathered and Doherty was executed.

Oh, the talking heads in the sport and fellow coaches tried to defend Doherty, saying he didn't get enough time, it's the players' fault and the "inmates are running the asylum."

Dick Vitale was a chief defender, but let's defend him for a moment. His genuine enthusiasm for the sport did as much to lift college basketball from 1980 on as anybody or anything. In those early years, he was a prescient, concise commentator with the demeanor of a kindly golden Labrador on speed. The game needed that. Yes, he loved Duke, but he loved all great programs and their coaches, to the point of fault in this case. He has since become somewhat of a parody of himself, and age started to catch up with him. But, come on. He has turned his own cancer battle into a huge fundraiser against the disease, he has been steadfast in championing the Jimmy V Foundation and when he crosses Jordan, the sport cannot build a statue big enough to correctly honor him. It's just that in this case he supported Doherty without really knowing the background and I'm willing to bet he'd do it differently if he could now.

Lost in this discussion was a vastly under-reported quote from the Doherty press conference by none other than Dean Smith, who retired just six years earlier and still hovered over the program.

"I was pushing to give him more time, very much so," Coach Smith said, "and then some people shared some of the problems and then you could see where they were coming from. You can put it that way."

It was a fairly shocking lack of support for a former player from a coach who famously supported all of them. But that's where we were after three years of Matt Doherty.

That brought us to the Roy Williams era and the worm started to turn. We all remember Williams, the long-time Carolina assistant, moving to Kansas as head coach in 1989 and enjoying tremendous success. When Bill Guthridge retired in 2000, the obvious move had been to hire Williams as UNC's next coach. Dean Smith had personally invited him.

But he stayed at Kansas, saying he had developed roots and obligations there. In the process he inadvertently bequeathed us three years of Doherty. During that time, Celia did not allow the name "Roy Williams" to be spoken in our home.

Three years later, he was ready to leave Kansas. Coach Smith invited him again and he couldn't say no this time. Celia and I immediately loved him like a son, or maybe a favorite uncle. We were all in.

The 2004 season was fairly nondescript. Two more losses to Duke, but in reality Doherty had recruited some really good players. They all returned for the 2005 season and Carolina quickly emerged as a national championship contender.

That still couldn't beat Duke. In Durham, the Tar Heels trailed by one with the ball as time wound down but couldn't correctly run a play. The clock expired without Carolina getting off a shot.

So the return game in Chapel Hill is for our immortal soul. We need the win to clinch first place, but we actually need it for so much more. We've lost 15 of our last 17 to Duke. My child cannot be raised in such a world.

Somehow, on this Sunday, we have other obligations. It may have even been church. Given that we have entered the 21st century, we tape the game on TiVo, which we had somehow mastered during its brief relevant reign on this earth, and watch it on our terms.

This requires us to remain "pure." Texting isn't yet commonplace, but we still have a house phone. And, while still about 15 minutes behind real time, Duke takes a nine-point lead with less than four minutes to go and the phone rings. Who calls during the Duke-Carolina game?

I have no Duke friends who are big enough assholes to taunt me after the game, which would be ending about now. We still have an answering machine, and I hear the strains of our sweet 80-year-old neighbor, a grandfather figure to Sophie who brings her fresh flowers and vegetables from his garden.

He's a Carolina guy. He must be calling with good news. Or maybe to bitch about a world where Duke reigns again. Either way, my purity is taken from me. I will spend the next 15 years counseling friends and family to never, ever text or call during a Carolina game without first confirming that I am in "real time."

The ensuing Carolina rally is glorious, nonetheless. As Duke falters, missing free throws, turning the ball over and generally panicking, Raymond Felton has the ball with Carolina down two in the final 20 seconds. It was Felton in Durham who botched the final play.

He goes hard to the basket this time and draws a foul. He makes the first, then bricks the second so badly that the long rebound comes to Marvin Williams, who then scores while getting fouled. From all accounts, the Smith Center crowd, once mocked as wine and cheese, is the loudest it has ever been.

When J.J. Reddick misses at the other end—capping a second-half outburst of zero points—it's over, the fans storm the court and Billy Packer tells the TV audience that "college basketball is on fire."

And just like in 1993, it feels like a Duke-shaped cloud has lifted.

April 4, 2005
North Carolina 75, Illinois 70
NCAA Tournament Final

This team restores our dignity. Not only have they conquered Duke but they have rolled into the Final Four. Just as Sophie is figuring out college basketball at about the same age I was when I equated belief in God with Tar Heel victories, Carolina has actually given her something to be proud of.

On the Monday before the semifinals, I'm in Raleigh for a meeting of the North Carolina Hospital Association, our state's hospital advocacy group. Bill Pulley, the NCHA leader, pulls me aside with a stunning offer. He knows I'm a Carolina guy. Hell, everyone I know knows this.

Bill says he's got two tickets to the Final Four he can't use. Would I like to go?

I've been dreaming about returning to a Final Four as a Carolina fan since 1982. I especially want to take Celia, who would appreciate this like no one else—assuming we wouldn't need cardiac resuscitation during a close game.

However, Pulley's generous offer has some problems. We have no way to get to St. Louis. Plane tickets out of Wilmington have long been sold out, and we're not driving that far. We have nowhere to stay. Forget hotels, and we don't know anyone in St. Louis. And just who will take care of a 7-year-old?

We can't do it. Celia and I hunker in our bedroom, still the site of the best TV in our house. Carolina swamps Michigan State in the second half to earn a date with top-ranked Illinois, loser of just one game all year. This is the rare year when truly the best two teams in college basketball meet for the championship.

Going to work that Monday is painful. The hospital, what with its illness, pathos, death and tragedy, seems so trivial on a day like this. The hours agonizingly pass by. The game doesn't start until 20 past 9 p.m. What do you do until then?

We put Sophie to bed and finally - the first championship game for Carolina in 12 years. Carolina takes control early and leads by 13 at the half. In the second half, we fall deeper in love with Sean May, who scores at will.

Yet Illinois is top-ranked for a reason. The Illini start popping three-pointers like M&Ms, rallying from 15 down to tie the game. May puts us ahead, but Illinois ties it again. Jim Nantz and Billy Packer are ominously predicting the public reaction if Roy Williams' team blows a 15-point lead in the national championship. As successful as he had been at Kansas, he never won a title. Apparently, this game has become a referendum on his legacy.

We just need something to go our way. About a minute and a half left. Rashad McCants, who had previously compared playing basketball at North Carolina to being in jail and later becomes the program's anti-hero, drives from the left side and throws up a silly shot that doesn't come close to the rim. But it's right where Marvin Williams can tip it in. The break we needed. Illinois misses several chances to go ahead before Felton steals a pass and starts making foul shots.

Carolina is national champion again. As confetti falls, Williams huddles with his seniors who were freshmen on the 8-20 team and outlived the Doherty regime. We're so excited we don't quite know what to do. Just three years ago I feared turning on the TV because I knew the rout would be egregious. Now we're national champions.

Celia solves our dilemma. She runs downstairs and into the backyard. It's dark out there, but we live in a city and we have neighbors. No matter. She takes off her top and streaks the back yard.

It's an unorthodox yet appropriate response. Let's just hope our 7-year-old doesn't wake up.

25

BLOODY HANSBROUGH

March 4, 2007

North Carolina 86, Duke 72

Ok, there's this guy, Perry, who lobbies for a construction company and tries to get large organizations, such as our hospital, to hire his client for projects. We've used him enough to qualify him as one of our "vendors."

He also runs his mouth a good bit. We're at the North Carolina Hospital Association Winter Meetings and he brags to me that he can get tickets to any college basketball game in the Triangle area. Any game. So I have to call this bluff.

"What about the Duke-Carolina game?

Any game, he says. Give him some time, but, yes, he can do it.

No, he cannot. He is full of shit. I call him out.

"Get me two to that game," I tell him, referring to the game just two weeks ahead.

"I'll get back to you."

I think I have committed some kind of kickback fraud. He's our vendor, for goodness sakes. I can't send him on personal errands for my benefit and let him think we'll hire him for our next $200 million project.

The good news is, I'm certain I won't hear from him again. The bluff has been called. I do refer this to our hospital's in-house lawyer, a do-gooding hippie who takes a "liberal" view when she can to help us get things done. As long as I pay for the tickets, and only at face value, and make it clear that this is my personal business, we can live with this, she says. And don't speak of it again.

A week later, Perry calls. He has two in the lower deck. He apologizes they are skewed toward the end zone.

I tell him it's ok. Will he take a personal check?

The Tar Heels have already rebuilt from the 2005 championship season behind wondrous sophomore center Tyler Hansbrough. Last year, as a freshman, he led a hilarious upset of top-ranked Duke, ruining J.J. Redick's Senior Night game. At one point, with Carolina ahead by eight but still plenty of time remaining, Hansbrough found himself with the ball 20 feet from the basket and the shot clock running down. He hoisted a three-pointer and it swished, one of his two three-pointers for the entire season.

Duke went down, then faceplanted in the NCAA Tournament. By now, the tables have turned. Carolina is clearly the better team and has even already defeated Duke again in Durham. They are expected to win the rematch in Chapel Hill and are legitimate championship contenders.

Celia and I decide it's time for Sophie, at age 9, to get a taste of the Duke-Carolina rivalry in person, which we think will accelerate her passion for the Heels. It's like giving a 13-year-old her first cigarette tailored to taste like candy, certain it will develop a lifelong habit. We want her hooked.

Once inside the arena, I'm in full Dad mode. I buy one of those light blue wigs for Sophie at a booth on the concourse. It fits perfectly. We note the dance team, the pep band and the sights within the Smith Center. We get indulgent concessions.

Then the game tips off and Sophie, who has been to four or five games by now, immediately notices this one is different. This game has no down time. Every shot, every whistle, every move draws a reaction. It's a lot for a 9-year-old.

The game is tight, even tied midway through the second half. Duke has no answer whatsoever for Hansbrough but manages to make up for it in other ways.

Finally, Carolina pulls away, as Ty Lawson is too quick and Hansbrough too forceful underneath. Carolina is up 12 with 17.5 seconds left when Hansbrough is fouled and sent to the line. He already has 26 points and 16 rebounds. I'm not sure why he's still in the game, but Duke is playing its starters so I let it go.

Up until now, I'm content Sophie has tasted the rivalry. By most standards, this game is intense, hard-fought and distinctly elevated from the others. But by the standards of this rivalry, it's an almost forgettable instance of one team being just a little bit better than the other, a difference that eventually plays out on the scoreboard.

Hansbrough misses, then misses again. The rebound comes right back to him, as a dispirited Duke has forsaken the most elementary fundamental of blocking out the free throw shooter. Hansbrough being Hansbrough, he gathers in the lane and rises for two more points. We're not passing this out to a guard and dribbling out the clock. That's not Tyler Hansbrough.

As he rises for two meaningless points, Duke's Gerald Henderson, an extremely athletic guard, attempts to "block" the shot with the same care you might use to swing a bowling ball on a chain to drive a tenpenny nail. He's all fist and elbow and where they land is irrelevant to him.

They land on Hansbrough's nose. Not sure if Henderson meant to do that, but if he had, he could not have done more damage. Hansbrough goes down in a heap.

Point of View:
Sophie Whisnant
Daughter

Even though I'd been to games before, this felt like an entirely different experience, really from the moment we sat down.

I was so amazed by how "in" on every play every single person in the Smith Center was, and it was by far the loudest thing I'd ever heard. It was like every dribble was life or death. I'd never seen anything like it. Something was just in the air and everyone was... rabid.

And then of course, with the injury, I remember being stunned for a while trying to process what I had just seen, while the ball boys were literally wiping up Tyler's blood (I later found out one of those ball boys was my UNC buddy Charles).

I remember having a moral quandary for a second. I'd never really booed anyone before because I thought it was mean, but when I saw how literally psycho Tyler looked and felt the adrenaline of the crowd, I felt safe to just let my boos FLY and threw my whole self into it.

Looking back on it, that was probably the first game where for me it got TRULY personal. Before that I think I just enjoyed and followed along with what I was supposed to do, but it really all clicked after that and my own hatred was formed.

A respectful hatred I'd say, but hate, nonetheless.

"Whoa," I tell Sophie. "That's not good."

Then Hansbrough gets up and tries to charge Henderson. His face and jersey famously bloodied, he looks like a zombie who has just awakened and must eat flesh. If his teammates do not restrain him, the brawl with Henderson would be epic and one-sided.

Welcome to the Duke-Carolina rivalry, Sophie.

"That's how this game is going to be remembered," I tell her, masterfully grasping the obvious. I am a former sportswriter.

The emotion in the Smith Center, already heightened in a celebratory mode, switches to pure fury. Henderson is kicked out of the game and his perp walk to the locker room is booed as lustily as any moment ever in that building. Or any building.

I offer my boos, and notice that Sophie has joined me. I've never been prouder.

In a misguided attempt to defend his guilty player, Coach Krzyzewski later proclaims that Henderson is the "real victim" in this incident. Duke doesn't win another game the rest of the year. In the ACC Tournament, without the suspended Henderson, the Blue Devils lose to 10th-place N.C. State. Then they lose to Virginia Commonwealth in the first round of the NCAA Tournament on a buzzer beater. Where was this karmic correction when Christian Laettner went open-court stomping in the Kentucky game?

Hansbrough suffers a broken nose, from which he will recover. Sophie is hooked on Carolina basketball. She will not recover.

March 25, 2007
Georgetown 96, North Carolina 84 (OT)
NCAA Tournament East Regional Final

Our good friend from church, Tom Morris, is a world-renowned philosopher and made a living in that field. Actually, more than just a living. A former Notre Dame professor, he wrote a gazillion books, ruminating on what Aristotle, and later Harry Potter, would do if they ran General Motors, and deep questions like that.

One thing he is not is a terribly passionate college basketball fan. In the early winter of 2007, he gave a motivational speech, as he is often wont to do. As part of his payment, he received four tickets to the 2007 Final Four in Atlanta.

They may as well have given him tickets to Willy Wonka's chocolate factory. Tom appreciated the tickets, but he didn't need them. But he knew someone who would appreciate them a lot more.

That would be the Whisnants, who consistently occupy the front pew in his section and wear their Tar Heel love on their sleeves. In an act of Christian charity, he offered us the tickets.

"Well, yes," we say, "as long as Carolina makes the Final Four."

It's understood. Without North Carolina, we aren't driving seven hours to Atlanta to watch four other fan bases live out their dream.

But this is not some distant fantasy. Carolina is good enough to make it. With Hansbrough wearing a mask to cover Gerald Henderson's act of shame, Carolina is marching toward Atlanta. They falter in the regional semifinals against Southern California, but overcome a 16-point second-half deficit to draw Georgetown in the regional final.

A Final Four in Atlanta is a much different proposition than the St. Louis Final Four two years before. Atlanta is drivable, so plane tickets are not the issue. I have college friends and cousins who live there, and my good buddy from UNC has already offered her house. We have four tickets at our disposal this time, and our daughter, almost 10, is old enough to want to go. Just a few weeks before she had witnessed what is already known as the "Bloody Hansbrough Game." Sophie is all in.

All we have to do is beat Georgetown, a plenty worthy opponent, though it's apparent early the Tar Heels are just a little bit better. At halftime, with Carolina ahead by six, we pause the recording of the game and attend the ballroom dance class we have been attending, an unusual burst of erudition on our part.

We're not worried about maintaining "purity" as it is unlikely the ballroom dancers will suddenly interrupt a foxtrot with an updated Carolina score. We master the "open left" and "hockey stick," then return to our game, the three of us huddled on our bed watching our inevitable glory.

Carolina just gets better and better. Hansbrough is dominating Georgetown's Roy Hibbert, a 7-footer with an NBA future. The Tar Heels lead, 75-65, with six minutes to play. Celia is plotting where we will stop on our way to Atlanta. Maybe lunch in Columbia...

What in the immortal fuck has happened to Carolina? The Tar Heels are spraying shots all over East Rutherford, treating the ball as if it were gaseous matter too toxic to handle. The Hoyas move closer, and closer, and closer. They are within three in the final half-minute with the ball. Carolina allows their best shooter room to fire, and the game is tied. Carolina has time for one more shot, but it's a bad one. We're headed to overtime.

Complete silence in the master bedroom. We know, and we suspect millions of viewers know as well, that overtime is not really necessary. Not after a collapse that epic.

Georgetown scores the first 14 of overtime. Carolina's only points are a meaningless three-pointer in the final seconds. In 11 minutes of game time, Georgetown outscores Carolina by 24 points. The Tar Heels miss 22 of 23 shots down the stretch.

College basketball is many things to many people through the years. Exhilaration, joy, sadness and despair. On this day, it's just pure cruelty.

March 15, 2008
North Carolina 68, Virginia Tech 66
ACC Tournament Semifinal

The Tar Heels are better still in 2008. Top-ranked at the start and top-ranked at the end. Just two regular-season losses and, for the third straight year, a win at Duke.

I decide to return to my childhood home to watch the ACC Tournament with my mother, who hangs on every Carolina game. She doesn't bitch or moan like my Daddy did, but she seems to have taken over his passion for the Heels. It is no doubt a connection to him, and to me.

So my arrival warrants home cooking and a strawberry cobbler. I am, after all, the only boy who's ever been born. Selflessly, I queue up the Carolina game so we can watch together with me sitting in Papa Bear's favorite chair.

Despite Carolina's pedigree, the Heels are struggling with fourth-place Virginia Tech in the semifinals. The game is a slog, points scoring with the ease of extracting confessions. Mama asks what's wrong with them and I don't have a good answer.

I do know what's right with them. That would be Tyler Hansbrough. He makes several plays that keep Carolina in it—an offensive rebound of a missed free throw here, a steal there and a deflected pass over there.

Somehow the Heels are tied in the final seconds when they set up a play for Ty Lawson, who gets off a terrible shot. The rebound leaks out to the right corner, and Hansbrough beats all nine other players on the court to it. Then he turns and puts up a baseline jumper at the buzzer.

As it goes in, he breaks into the goofiest celebration dance, a celebration of unbridled joy. And that's what we also have in my childhood living room.

My mother, living alone without her husband and too rarely in the company of her children, is happy. Giddy as a schoolgirl, chanting "goodie, goodie, goodie," which is about as profane as she gets.

I text my niece, currently a student at UNC. Why in the world aren't you dating Tyler Hansbrough?

She replies, not that I should mind my business, not that she currently has a boyfriend, not that she's in college to get an education and set a course for her future, and not that this notion is borderline inappropriate. She says he already has a girlfriend. And we curse her. For no good reason. Tyler should belong to all of us.

April 5, 2008
Kansas 84, North Carolina 66
NCAA Tournament Final Four

We have no illusion of going to San Antonio for this Final Four. But we have every notion that Carolina is the team to beat. The Tar Heels are 36-2 heading into a match with Kansas, Coach Williams' former team.

The three of us gather on the bed to watch the coronation into the finals. This Final Four features four top seeds for the first and only time, but there are top seeds and then there is Carolina's 2008 team. This could redeem the flameout last year against Georgetown.

So we're slack-jawed by what actually happens. Kansas has no intention of playing any role in our ascension. The Jayhawks are active, they're trapping us on defense and they're making every shot.

I try not to be one of those fans who believes a time out will cure all ills when an opponent is running hot. Roy Williams certainly doesn't believe that either. But there comes a time and place... It's 7-2 Kansas. Now it's 15-10. Now it's—wait—33-10! Call a time out, Roy. Please God, make it stop.

There's two official TV timeouts but they don't help. Roy lets them keep playing. Brandon Rush makes a layup and it's 35-12. Then Rush hits a three-pointer and it's 38-12.

Billy Packer offers this analysis on CBS: "It's over." Which must come as a disappointment to the network's advertisers, given there's still 7½ minutes left in the first half.

Time out, Coach Williams. Finally. By now, we're questioning who kidnapped our Tar Heels. That is, when we're actually able to speak.

It reaches 40-12 before it turns, an embarrassing round number that will be flung in our faces for a full year.

Now here's the thing: Almost no one remembers that Carolina gets back in this game, cutting it to four in the second half. With just over eight minutes left, the margin is five when Danny Green puts up a three-pointer. The ball dips in, rolls around and spins out. Every Carolina fan alive who watched that game will tell you for certain that if Green's shot stays down, Carolina wins this game.

And we will rub it in Billy Packer's face from now until eternity. Instead, it's another humiliating defeat.

The question immediately becomes "will this team stay together?" Hansbrough announces he's coming back for his senior year, but what about Green? And the guards, Ty Lawson and Wayne Ellington, both excellent and with NBA options? Unfinished business remains here but usually when the NBA beckons, players leave.

The following June, a Chapel Hill police officer cites Lawson for driving after drinking (as he is not yet 21, the law has no tolerance for any alcohol in his system, not even the paltry .03 they measured) and driving without a license.

This officer has given us a wondrous gift. Lawson's NBA stock plummets after this news, as he may be the only 20-year-old who has ever driven after drinking.

Carolina is having a historic run of talent but no title to show for it. But now Lawson is returning. Everyone is. The band is together for one more show.

April 6, 2009
North Carolina 89, Michigan State 72
NCAA Tournament Final

The idea of entering the lottery for Final Four tickets in the Silverdome in Detroit crosses my mind, but I give in to another encroaching reality. My advancing age is outstripping my desire to negotiate the logistics needed to make this happen. I especially don't want a seat in the hinterlands of a domed stadium. In New Orleans in 1982 I lucked into the fifth row, courtside, and was forever spoiled.

One variable I can be certain about: North Carolina is definitely going to the Final Four. Oh sure, when the Tar Heels lose their first two ACC games, this provokes stress and panic, but this gets righted quickly. We beat Duke at Duke again, a sweep for Tyler Hansbrough's four-year career in Cameron Indoor Stadium. Snarky Carolina fans immediately photoshop the sign outside the old barn to say "Hansbrough Indoor Stadium," and good Carolina fans to this day refer to Hell's outpost in Durham as "HIS."

Ty Lawson's toe injury late in the year passes for drama on this team. His father mistakenly has him soak the toe in Epsom Salts, which makes it much worse. Lawson, now the best player on the team as Hansbrough, the reigning college basketball Player of the Year, graciously makes room, misses the first game of the NCAA Tournament and some question if he'll return. And if so, when?

He does come back. Carolina wins every tournament game by double figures on its way to Detroit and to the final game against Michigan State, eighth-ranked and hardly one of the two best teams in the nation. The teams met earlier that season in the same Silverdome—and Carolina won by 35.

With a national recession hitting Detroit particularly hard, the media dreams up a fantasy where Michigan State is playing for the oppressed working man in Michigan. So much nonsense. As if poor people aren't hurt by the economy in North Carolina.

I am eager for us to enjoy a national title as a family, a development I consider as necessary as middle school graduation, church confirmation and puberty. We now have a flatscreen TV in the living room, a nod to modern times, and I have a patriarchal chair, a soft purple armchair that's wide enough for napping.

I settle into Purple Boy and watch something unfold that I cannot remember previously happening in my Carolina fandom. The Tar Heels play exactly to their level in a big game and wipe the floor with the Spartans, leading by 23 at the half and coasting from there. No one is late to the pregame meal, no food poisoning, no sudden inability to make a shot. No drama. The three of us soak it in, a ritual rite of passage that bonds us.

We somehow talk Sophie into going to bed and step out the back door. It's time to observe the new ritual. Instead, we find two of Celia's mom friends sitting in the porch swing, huddled in the cold eating popcorn and "waiting for the show."

Evidently, they heard about the 2005 celebration and want to witness. We shoo them away. This is not a spectator sport, but a sacred rite that must be done correctly to honor the Tar Heels.

As soon as they leave, Celia and I both fully streak the back yard. The Tar Heels deserve no less. They are kings of college basketball and, again, it feels like this could last awhile.

26

A VERY BAD DAY

April 5, 2010

Duke 61, Butler 59

NCAA Tournament Final

The Tim Hennis story has taken an unprecedented turn.

The murder trial, the subject of my book *Innocent Victims* published 17 years earlier and an ABC mini-series airing in 1996, is headed for a third capital trial, the first time in American history a defendant is tried three times for his life after getting guilty and not guilty verdicts in the first two. It's essentially a best-of-three series playing out over 25 years, with the third and deciding trial on the government's home court.

Tim Hennis is among those wondering how the hell someone can be hauled back in court after being acquitted on the same charges. It's a legitimate question that no one seems to want to seriously consider.

After his acquittal in 1989, Hennis went back into the Army for 15 years, fighting two wars and compiling an admirable record. He raised a second child with his wife and took part in an impressive list of volunteer duties that included driving the van for his daughter's Girl Scouts troop. He retired in 2004. Less than two years later—a key phrase—a Cumberland County detective ran the case's lone semen sample through the state's DNA lab, as DNA had become a thing since Hennis' acquittal.

The DNA matched Tim Hennis. Because he's within two years of retirement, the Army "reinstates" him, charges him with triple murder and court martials him for his life. The military is a different court, you see. And as the case now has a DNA match, no one much cares about Hennis' "double jeopardy" rights. In the minds of 98% of the public, he slashed the throat of a 5-year-old girl and her 3-year-old sister.

So a court martial he shall have. It's set to play out on Fort Bragg, very near the scene of the murder and about 90 minutes from my home. I make arrangements at work to take days and half-days off to cover this trial, which promises to be a one-of-a-kind judicial moment bringing me back to my reporting and writing roots.

Except I feel crappy all the time and just can't make it on most days. Among the days I miss are those when Hennis is convicted and sentenced, again, to Death Row. My days instead are marked by long naps after work and a level of sorriness that's scandalous even by my standards. My running partner makes fun of me because I whine about being tired. My basketball buddy lectures me during car rides home about not playing hard. A high fever creeps in, then breaks all at once, leaving me drenched in sweat.

On a Saturday in April, I'm at the job that pays me, meeting with the head of a non-profit and a doctor, a friend of mine, who's interviewing for the new role of medical director. We're sitting at a table on the sidewalk, during that fragment of Wilmington time between overcast winter and stifling summer heat. Perfect 75 degrees.

And I feel horrible, struggling to keep myself from reaching for the doctor's hand, guiding it to my steaming forehead and to this lump near my collarbone, and asking "what do you make of this"? But this is a professional job interview. I hold it together, then go home and sleep away the rest of a weekend day off.

Two days later, I decide to make like a privileged white American with insurance. I go to see my doctor, who works me in and feels that lump near the collarbone.

"Let's get Scott in for a CAT scan," he calmly tells his aide.

"How soon do you think I need one?" I ask.

"You're going today."

This malaise hasn't interrupted my viewing of the Tar Heels' NCAA Tournament march because there hasn't been one. After the Hansbrough/ Lawson group finally won an NCAA title, everyone who was anyone left for the NBA. The only players who are any good are hurt. The season is truly terrible—5-11 in the ACC and not even considered for the big tournament.

Duke, on the other hand, has put together a team that is the last of its breed. Coach Krzyzewski had already remade his program after the "back pain" year, recruiting players more liable to jump to the NBA when ready. Gone are the Bobby Hurleys, Christian Laettners and Grant Hills who stay all four years, causing the fan base to believe Duke players just love their school a little more than the others and that's why they win. And not because Hill, for one, is a generational talent.

Players like Elton Brand are part of the new order. He's on that dominant 1999 team and is good enough to leave after his sophomore year to become the top pick in the NBA draft. So he leaves. Which gives us the greatest and most revelatory email exchange in fandom history, an exchange that plays out every reason why Carolina, and most college basketball fans, cannot stand Duke.

As a public service, I will summarize it here. The fan's name isn't Karen, but in another, more global sense, it is. Here is what she basically said in 1999, long after great college players had begun leaving for the NBA:

Karen, a Duke graduate who holds the basketball program and its accomplishments in high regard, is "disgusted" Brand would leave after two years of representing Duke, which is "first and foremost" an academic school.

If Brand was not more committed to Duke than this, he did not belong there or at any college. He has insulted current students and alumni who "realized the value of a Duke education" and "what an honor and privilege it was" to attend there four years.

And therefore, if Elton Brand didn't realize the opportunity to not only graduate from Duke but play for Coach K, then that is his loss. But couldn't he have "spared us the notion" that he was continuing the Duke tradition of excellence in academics and athletics.

Brand will not "be considered part of the Duke family," Karen writes, having not proven himself "worthy of that title."

Karen "sincerely" signs off.

Brand not only verified the authenticity of this email, but dignified it with a response, earning the respect of Duke-haters for history. Here's his reply:

From: Elton Tyron Brand
Sent: Sunday, April 25, 1999 8:05 PM
To:
Subject: Re: Leaving Duke

Thank you very much, for reminding me of the reason why I left Duke. People like you can not and will not ever understand my situation. I'm sure daddy worked very hard to send your rich self to college. While real people struggle. I would also like to extend an invitation for you not to waste your or my time ever agin. Never being considered a part of your posh group of yuppies really hurts me to the heart. Yeah, right. Because I don't care about you or your alumni.

Sincerely,

Elton Brand #42 NBA

The best part, among this rich smorgasbord, is signing it "#42NBA." Yeah, lady, I'm getting paid to play, and paid a lot. Deal with it.

Brand is a big part of Duke's historical seven-year burst around the turn of the century, but the program has started to wane. In a year, Coach K will take out a second mortgage on his soul and invest in the "one-and-done" model.[1] All vestige of Duke fans preening about their program's purity will be forever gone.

But the 2010 team is the last of the old-school kind, built on juniors and seniors who fill a role and play together. They are much like the 1993 Carolina team that won it all. Perhaps the most crucial piece is 7-foot-1 senior center Brian Zoubek, who forfeits any dream of playing professional basketball to take on a role of setting screens and rebounding. He's ridiculously good at it. The team, by Duke championship standards, is tolerable.

In an NCAA Tournament without North Carolina, UCLA, Indiana, and Michigan, among other blue bloods, where top-seeded Kansas loses in the second round to Northern Iowa and Villanova in Duke's regional bows out to St. Mary's, Duke has reached the final against Butler, a scrappy team from a small conference that's probably better than most of us remember.

The game is the same Monday as my impromptu doctor's appointment. Just hours before it starts I learn the CAT scan lit me up like a Christmas tree. Dr. Musselwhite tells me I have Hodgkins Lymphoma. We're looking at 12 rounds of nasty, nasty chemo, featuring a chemical known as the "Red Devil."

---

1   In 2005, the NCAA ruled that high school players couldn't jump to the NBA, as many were doing, until one year after their class graduated. This led to an annual group of elite teen phenoms who were essentially forced to play one year in college. Duke and Kentucky, to name the top two, began recruiting these players almost exclusively, building their program on one-year rentals who never had any intention of staying in college (to be fair, Carolina recruited most of these players, and they simply chose to play somewhere else - often Duke). It is alleged, though I haven't seen it proven, that many stopped going to classes after the first semester. Somewhere the writer of the Elton Brand email is apoplectic.

I settle into Purple Boy and ponder how much worse this day can get. As it so happens, I'm about to find out. Duke is playing for a national championship.

I have hope in Butler, though. The Bulldogs hang tough, but they can't quite make enough shots. Down two in the final seconds, their star, Gordon Hayward, heaves a final try from halfcourt.

I think we established during the Laettner years that God was not then a basketball fan. He's had almost 20 years to take up this hobby, but, alas, He has not.

The shot banks off the board and barely rims out.

Instead, we have Coach K's fourth national title. In a year when Carolina doesn't even make the tournament. So much for Carolina ruling college basketball for a while.

For the rest of my life, and counting, my story on the day I was diagnosed with cancer ends with "and that's not even the worst thing that happened that day."

But was it? Let's make the case for cancer:

Over six months, I'll lose about 40 pounds and my hair. My body will accelerate its aging by about 10 years. I'll spend the better part of those 24 weeks either nauseous or on the verge of nauseousness, carrying a bucket with me at all times, because you never know.

But then there are precious moments that only come when people show you how much you are loved. When it becomes apparent my hair wants to fall out in ghastly clumps, my good buddy Kenny takes me in the back yard and shaves my head, while Sophie and an 8th-grade classmate make a video for a presentation due the next day. Hundreds and hundreds of cards eventually line the fence on our back yard as part of an "I'm healthy" party. My college roommate's mother, herself a survivor, sends me a card every single week. The first lesson of cancer: There is no such thing as a "small gesture." They all matter.

There's the guy from my Sunday School class who hasn't attended in years but likes the fact that I've been teaching since 1995. So he mows our yard every week, doing it better than I ever would. Lesson No. 2: If you're doing something for someone else, give it your best.

There's the meal chains from work and church. The kindnesses from people we don't know. When my good friends take me to a UNC football game, one of them asks the football office for special on-field access in honor of his friend recovering from cancer. In return, we get the access and I get a personal email from Carolina football coach Butch Davis.

My good buddy Dave Willard comes to visit and brings his daughter, then a senior at UNC-Wilmington. I tell them that after the nausea debacle that followed my first chemo treatment, my oncologist asks if I have any problem with marijuana.

"Can you prescribe that?" I ask him.

"No, silly. It's illegal."

But marijuana is one thing proven to settle nausea and build appetite. That last part I'd known for 30 years but had no idea that was a positive. But by now I'm hopelessly uncool on how to find it.

Natalie Willard listens to this, pulls out her phone and types a text.

"I'll be back in a minute," she says.

Ok. We talk some college basketball, about Dave's wonderful brother Pee-Heed who has sadly become so morbidly obese he's practically housebound. Dave can't know then that, later in 2010, Lee Willard, an icon in Jamestown who sang, tap danced, acted and led church music ministries, will stop breathing, his body no longer able to sustain his powerful presence. RIP, Pee-Heed.

And... Natalie's back. With a healthy sampling of weed, fresh from Wilmington's streets. I'm touched. Lesson No. 3: When people ask "How can I help?" find a way to let them.

The cancer cements a bond with Celia that I didn't even know could be tightened. It's humbling to have to turn your entire life over to someone while she puts hers on hold, including suspending the humor column she had written weekly, without fail, for 20 years. You realize you will live the rest of your life in someone's debt without being asked to pay anything and wonder how people can live on their own.

Then there's special moments with Sophie, who at age 13 has been asked to come to grips with what this means. She walks me around the neighborhood every night. All I can stand is one square block, but it's enough to find out who's "talking" (middle school-ese for dating), which girls are creating drama (you'd be surprised) and juicy family dynamics, otherwise known as "gossip."

Sophie gets up her nerve and joins the cast of *Godspell*, a musical performed by our local children's community theater. She practices her angelic voice in the shower, unaware her mother and I can hear her. It may be our tenderest memory of her growing up in our home. On opening night, one of the leads who performs the show's signature number can't be there, so Sophie, with almost no time to rehearse, nails it.

I find an excuse to attend every show, arriving just in time for her first number. A healthy me may have been too busy.

The entire experience is humbling on many levels as so many people show they care. During the height of it, I must have been a sight - rail thin, bald, dull eyes and pallid gray. Once I start to recover, I

During the season I gave over to cancer, Celia and I took a trip to nearby Bald Head Island. My hospital boss would later say "You look like shit." He was being kind.

find myself in the office of our CEO, Jack Barto.

This would be the CEO who tells me the day I'm diagnosed, "take whatever time you need. The next six months are on me." That only inspires me to work as many days as I can, even when I'm not contributing much, because who wouldn't want to work for that man?

"Jack," I tell him, "I must have really looked bad there for a while because everyone is saying how good I look today."

Jack, a Yankee from Pittsburgh, is not given to mincing words or beating around the bush.

"You looked like shit," he says.

I'm sure I did, but no one would let me feel like it. It's an honor to be so loved, yet it's an honor you would wish on no one.

So what was the worst part of April 5, 2010?

Well, the cancer is curable. In fact, the kind I had is the most curable you can have. Before the 2011 season begins I will in fact be cured. Duke winning another title is not, the image of that program raising another trophy indelible in all the wrong ways. If that tells you which direction I am leaning.

27

WE WILL LOVE AGAIN...

February 8, 2012

Duke 85, North Carolina 84

Watching a Duke-Carolina game comes with rules in the Whisnant home.

First, everyone needs to understand: We're doing this in private. For many years, we would be invited to "game-watching" parties that start as well-meaning efforts to focus on the game at hand but drift into conversations about children, parents, dreams, hopes, aspirations and other nonsense.

We're not there for that. For two hours, we need every bit of mental energy we can muster to put toward the Tar Heels. This is actually true of all Carolina games, not just the ones against Duke. We don't want to hear your prattle and you don't want to see this side of us. It's called "mutual respect."

We have turned down so many of these gatherings over the years that it has become a running joke among friends who still think group game-watching is a good idea. Yes, we'll go to sports bars when the cable is out

Point of View:
Celia Rivenbark
Wife

"So, I'm thinking of getting lowlights. What do you think?"

I stared at my friend's innocent face framed by hair that honestly could use chestnut lowlights and felt nothing but unbridled rage.

Yes. My Tar Heels are on a TV I can barely see behind her pretty head in front of me and she wants to talk about her fuckin' lowlights. I can't even.

"And then I was thinking, well, maybe I should just go red! You know just this once......"

Was I just going to say it? I wanted to say it so bad.

"Can we table this? I'm trying to watch the game."

No, of course I couldn't say it. I'm Southern. We are incapable of that level of rudeness. But wait. Wasn't she the rude one, ignoring my considerable body language? I mean, I had done everything but place her head in my two hands and twist it toward the screen.

Or off her shoulders. Whichever seemed most likely to SHUT HER UP.

When I say I want to watch the game, I don't mean I want to watch a few possessions here and there while you talk about your hair or your mama dying or whatever. I'll be the best friend you ever had in exactly two hours, more if we go into overtime. See, I'm actually nice.

Don't assume because I'm female we're going to head to the kitchen and hang out during the game. We are not. Not now. Not ever. No apologies.

or no other options are available, but even then we're not there to talk. We have responsibilities.

The Duke game takes this to another level. We turn off every light in the house, assume our seats, take care of all bodily needs (food, bathroom) and focus, focus, focus. During the game, game-related banter is permitted, such as encouragement for one of our scholar-athletes, questioning the parenthood of a Blue Devil, and so on.

Then during the TV timeouts, I mute the sound and we sit in silence, thinking of ways we can hate Duke more. We're dealing in very small increments at this point, as the hate has just about reached the max. I imagine spreadsheets, PowerPoints, lab values, absolute values—some way to conjure up more bile against these rivals.

It's a fine line between agonizing tension and unadulterated joy.

With this grim determination, we watch the 2012 version of the Tar Heels host Duke. Sophie at age 14 has earned the right to join this ritual and knows the rules without asking. To do so would be needless banter. There will be no "Can I invite my friend over?" or similar folly.

Carolina has put together another national contender, but Duke, now fully in the throes of the one-and-done era, is pretty good, too. We're ranked 5th and Duke 10th, led by this year's freshman of choice, Austin Rivers, the cocky son of a professional coach who has many skills, the most salient of them being swagger.

Carolina is the better team this night, leading by 10 points with just over two minutes to go. We relax a little. Will the fans storm the court? No, that's too much of a nod to our fear of Duke. Of course we're going to win. No need to act all shocked about it.

Tyler Thornton, the prototypical Duke scrub who succeeds only when he annoys, lines up a three-pointer, and it goes in.

We fart in his general direction. Carolina by seven.

Then we throw it away. Mason Plumlee, one of about 14 Duke-playing sons to emerge from the same tortured uterus, recovers and throws it cross-court to Seth Curry, who travels long enough to recite the Pledge of Allegiance. Then he nails a three, and ESPN treats us to yet another reaction shot of Sonya Curry, his attractive, photogenic and irrelevant mother. (As opposed to four years' worth of reaction shots of Tami Hansbrough, attractive mother of Tyler, during his four years that were warranted and added to the viewers' overall understanding of the game).

Sonya's reaction? She's happy about it. The lead is four. Whatever passed for jocularity in the Whisnant living room has turned to grim silent reflection. This can't be happening.

Harrison Barnes charges for no good reason with 1:23 left. Duke's ball. Ryan Kelly misses a three, but the rebound ricochets right back to him. Why wasn't he blocked out? As if to emphasize this oversight, Kelly puts in a short jumper and the lead is two.

Tyler Zeller makes one of two free throws for Carolina. Then, with 14.2 seconds left, Kelly misses a three. Under the basket, Plumlee pushes Zeller so blatantly—to his credit, what does he have to lose at this point?—that Zeller can only get one hand on the rebound. And that one hand guides the miss back into Duke's basket.

That's what we're up against. Carolina's ACC Player of the Year just scored two points for Duke to cut it to one.

Zeller is immediately fouled and again makes one of two. Duke clears the rebound and gives it to Rivers. And we have this feeling, sinking, sinking, sinking. This isn't good. This won't end well.

Duke runs Rivers through a screen and Zeller switches on him. Zeller is 7 feet tall. He's worried about Rivers going around him, so he plays back a little. I'm worried he's too far away.

"Get up on him, Tyler. Get up on him."

There's no good way to lose to Duke, but there are gradations of loss. Sometimes Duke is just better and controls the game from the start. Sometimes the teams are evenly matched or Carolina is a little better, but a Duke player goes out of his mind, or the home court is too much.

Sometimes Duke is better, but we play really well, hanging in or even leading long enough to create hope where there was once none before faltering—a pattern all too common through much of the 2010s. They hurt a little more.

But the worst, by far, is when Carolina has the better team and controls the game, yet still manages to lose. These are unnecessary, reducing one's overall lifespan by months and sometimes years.

And this is what we're looking at. Rivers waits until two seconds remain, rises over Zeller, who's in fact is too far away. The shot goes in, the buzzer sounds and the backboard lights up. Duke dogpiles Rivers, the last guy we can stomach having this moment. It won't help that, in the rematch three weeks later in Durham, the Tar Heels will jump to a 22-5 start and lead 48-24 at the half before cruising to an emphatic win that no one will remember.

The Whisnant living room is silent. For maybe a minute. Somebody needs to say something, and as leader of the family, at least on this front, that is me.

"We will go on," I say bravely. "We will go to school, to work, to church. We will continue to live our lives. We will find love and learn to laugh again."

Celia and Sophie wish I would shut up.

March 16, 2012
Lehigh 75, Duke 70
NCAA Tournament First Round

Our smallness knows no bounds. Carolina has dispatched with Vermont in its NCAA first-round game in Greensboro. Duke, as its region's second seed, has also been rewarded with a trip to Greensboro, just an hour from its campus, to play 15th-seeded Lehigh. Among Lehigh's seven losses are those to Holy Cross, Bucknell and Cornell.

I've been dispatched to PTs Grill to pick up burgers. It's a Friday night and this is what passes for a date. The Duke game is on TV in the restaurant and two things are apparent.

First, Lehigh has an NBA-caliber guard, C.J. McCollum, for whom Duke has no answer. Second, playing in Greensboro is no reward for Duke. The Carolina fans have stuck around and joined forces with every other fan in the building not wearing royal blue. Turns out the backlash against Duke that started in the late 1980s has come around full force to haunt this version in its backyard.

Once home, I turn on the TV.

"We have to watch this," I tell Celia. "Duke is struggling with this team."

"Don't do this to yourself," she says. She knows better. So many times we've been down this road only to watch Coach K smugly chest-pat the opposing coach in the handshake line to honor a worthy but unsuccessful effort against his superior troops. It's hard to watch.

But I have hope. This might be the time.

And glory of all glories, it is. Duke flails down the stretch, as McCollum is too good and the Brown Bears make their free throws. Austin Rivers will jump to the NBA, as they all do now, and this will be his last college game.

The best day of the year. When Duke loses in the NCAA. The earlier they lose, the better this day becomes. This one is the best, even producing a great meme for Carolina fans. Whenever a Duke fan tries to brag about something, the retort becomes "Are you serious LeHigh?"

Yet that damn Rivers shot in Chapel Hill is all anyone seems to remember.

February 20, 2014
North Carolina 74, Duke 66

I can't believe it's come to this.

My niece, still living in Chapel Hill, and then-boyfriend have arranged to buy four tickets to the Duke game in Chapel Hill. I will join my sister and the couple for the first Carolina-Duke action in person since the

Bloody Hansbrough game seven years earlier. I am giddy, glad to pay the $130 on StubHub for this upper deck seat.

The problem is, it's snowing. And that's an issue in the South. It's actually a credible snowstorm, which means the hospital where I work as communications director must activate its storm team for all-night activities. Panicked communications must go out, and nurses must be cajoled to report to work. Try not to laugh at us, Northerners and Midwesterners. We can't help it.

The chances of my leaving Wilmington for this game are Zero Point Zero. I am bound by work but also by common sense. There's snow piling up on the road. We're not wired for this.

Now, Duke University is all of eight miles from the UNC campus. You would think someone who has coached in the South for 33 years, say Mike Krzyzewski, would know to leave a little early to ensure they get to Chapel Hill on time during a snowstorm. This would not be the case.

A couple of hours before game time, I get a warden's reprieve. Duke can't make it to Chapel Hill. The game will be postponed a week, on a day I'm actually in the Triangle area on other business. Sometimes it just works out.

This is a Duke team with a classically great one-and-done player in Jabari Parker, and a transfer in Rodney Hood, who played a year at Mississippi State before prostituting, er... transferring to Duke for one year. They come in ranked fifth. Carolina is middling along, unable to recruit the great players and not yet quite able to rebuild with juniors and seniors. The Tar Heels are not ranked.

But they do have the great Marcus Paige, having one of the best seasons as a sophomore in UNC history. His special knack is hitting key shots late in the game, earning him the nickname "Second-Half Paige." I didn't say it was clever.

This is the wildest Smith Center crowd I've seen. Duke leads most of the game, but when Carolina pushes to tie, and then lead by two, the crowd is relentless. Paige scores twice with heroic drives to the hoop to keep Duke from getting back in it.

The four of us pose for selfies. We sway arm-in-arm to *Hark the Voices*. The crowd storms the court. I consider jumping the rail and freefalling to the deck below to join them. Everything goes this night. The team is not really headed anywhere, but we have this Duke win.

There was a time when I would be embarrassed to say that. We're supposed to be better than this. But I'm learning to enjoy the moment for what it is.

February 26, 2014
North Carolina 85, N.C. State 84 (OT)

By this point in our lives, Celia is a brand.

Her career as a humor writer and speaker has reached the point where she jokes with our friends that she is, in her words, a "fucking brand," a bit of a faux brag she does for laughs. But her friends love it and refer to her as "the brand" in public. As in "Can the Brand get some extra salsa."

By now she has written a weekly humor column for 25 years, only missing when I had cancer, and seven humor books, with titles like *We're Just Like You, Only Prettier* and *Stop Dressing Your Six-Year-Old like a Skank* and *You Can't Drink All Day If You Don't Start in the Morning. You Don't Sweat Much For a Fat Girl* landed on the *New York Times* bestseller list—we have that week's list framed if anyone should question it—and the *Skank* title landed her an interview on the *Good Morning America* show. Because she hit a major truth on that one. Look at the clothes they try to sell young girls next time you're in a store.

In town, she often is approached by fans.

"Are you her?" they ask.

"I am she," she tells them.

I am but a recurring character in her prose, and a doofus one at that. She refers to me as "Duh-Hubby" in the columns. Despite a career in hospital outreach founding programs for the uninsured, the homeless and the hungry, even winning UNC-Wilmington's Albert Schweitzer award in 2011 (Mother Teresa joins me on the roster of winners of this award), the language on my tombstone is set. "Here lies Duh-Hubby..."

I can hardly count the times I worked alongside hospital directors and clinicians, addressing issues of inequities, social determinants of health and the like, only to have a peer look at me and say "aren't you married to Celia?"

"Yes. Yes I am," I will say, dreading what's coming next.

"That makes you... Duh-Hubby."

Then they laugh, quite pleased with themselves. And another person no longer takes me seriously.

Celia is a good get. A local retired TV host, an endearingly sweet man named Wayne Jackson, asks her every year to attend a UNC-Wilmington basketball game, offering his season tickets. I come along as the date.

On this year, we agree on a game against... I don't remember. But I do remember our shock and horror when we realized it was the same time as the UNC-N.C. State game in Raleigh.

Coach Williams has a particular hatred for N.C. State. He remembers, as those of us around this age all do, when State was the actual rival. But it goes beyond that. The players and coaches maintain the State fans are the rudest, at a personal level, in the conference, and it's State fans who seem to have the personal phone number of everyone in the ACC compliance division, as their grievances about Carolina are long and weighed down by animus.

State finally won the ACC Tournament and even made it to the Final Four in 2024, its first regular season or tournament win in basketball or football since 1990. Many of their fans had synthesized this into the greatest of conspiracies, all at the hands of the University of North Carolina at Chapel Hill. They love to add the "Chapel Hill" part.

Coach Williams' record against N.C. State, when he retires, is 33-5. Yet it never gets old. We're not missing this one. Through the magic of digital recording, we can attend the UNCW game, make nice with Wayne, and return home and start the State game. We just have to remain pure.

This means turning off the car radio before it can default to the game broadcast. Not engaging in small talk with anyone who's tracking the game live. And most of all, it means putting the iPhone down and out of sight.

This particular game is the most amazing chapter of the season of Second Half Paige. State is bringing it tonight. Their star, T.J. Warren, is on his way to 36 points, scoring at will whenever the Pack needs a basket.

But Paige is doing a Jerry West imitation. He matches Warren basket for basket, whenever the Tar Heels need one. Midway through the second half, Celia's phone is buzzing and she can't help but look. It's a classic mistake that we'll discuss in the film room when we review our performance. It's one of her fans, a growing occupational hazard.

"Paiiiiiiiiige," the text says.

Something Paige has done is wonderful. She has the decency not to tell me. While I'm six inches from the screen egging Paige on, Celia slumps in her chair. She doesn't know exactly what will happen, but purity is shattered. Our immediate circle of family and friends know not to do this, but her circle is too big.

The game goes to overtime. Back and forth. Paige and Warren. With 90 seconds left, State leads by six. Three-pointer by Paige. State hits a free throw. Two free throws by Paige. Carolina steals in the backcourt and James Michael McAdoo ties the game. Just 29 seconds remain and Celia is muted in her chair. What is wrong with her?

State works it to Warren, of course, and he is fouled with 8 seconds left. Oddly, he misses the first. After the second make, State lets Carolina do exactly what it can't allow: Get the ball to Paige.

Marcus drives the length of the court, gets a screen to send him to his natural left-hand and puts up a layup high off the glass over a defender. The degree of difficulty is close to 8, maybe 9.

It banks in, Paige's 35th point, 31 of them after halftime. The game runs out. Carolina by one.

"Paiiiiiiiiige," indeed. We love him like a son. Like a son, I tell you.

28

FAREWELL, COACH

January 31, 2015

Louisville 78, North Carolina 68 (OT)

We have no idea what we do to our kids.

High school should be an idyllic time for coming of age, for beginning to figure out who we are, for first kisses, first beers and prom dates. However, those of us who believe college is the end game tend to hover that goal over our teenagers, a cloud of angst that isn't quite visible but is always there.

Girls, in my experience, are more susceptible to this than boys, who at this age tend to be unable to plan beyond the next video game or, later on, the next kegger. From the moment Sophie entered ninth grade at New Hanover High School, every course, homework assignment, pop quiz and after-school activity was filtered through one lens: How will this help me get into college?

Celia and I didn't dream this up or actively promote it, but we damn sure didn't stop it or even mitigate it. Ballet, acting, singing, church youth group, yearbook editor, senior class officer, AP classes and grade point average, grade point average and grade point average—all of that will look good on the ubiquitous entrance application we imagine.

And there's really only one place to send it. We tried not to direct our daughter to the University of North Carolina, other than taking her to basketball games throughout her childhood and regaling her with endless stories of my time there.

During her sophomore year in high school, a year earlier than typical, I took her to the "college tour" of UNC on a 75-degree day in mid-October and damn near re-enrolled myself. My favorite corny bit: the tour guide ran into a friend on his bicycle and shared that they were part of an impromptu "ukelele group" that met on the steps of the graduate library.

"You hear that?" I told Sophie. "A group of people just happened to have the same hobby, they found each other and they formed a club. Don't tell me Carolina is a big school. It's just a matter of finding your tribe within that school. It can be as small as you want it. I remember when..."

"Dad, you are embarrassing me." There were cute guys around. She needed me to pipe down.

Carolina could do no wrong. Oh sure, we took her to other schools, notably the University of Georgia, which has a Journalism program ranked higher than Carolina's. Sophie applied and was accepted at Georgia, as well as Missouri, where she applied sight unseen. Celia and I tried to wrap our heads around driving seven hours to Athens to see our daughter and trod the same grass where Hershel Walker had played "between the hedges," and pretending that mattered to us.

One school left to hear from. On January 28, 2015, the acceptance email from UNC hits her inbox. Sophie calls me while I'm traveling back from a hospital meeting in Raleigh with a bunch of husky, manly paramedics.

We have a Tar Heel. I can't cry in front of the leadership of the Emergency Medical Services Department, so I'm stoic. I'm happy for her and proud. And other Dad stuff.

But once home, bedlam. The main thing is the relief. Celia and I had no idea how much it meant to our daughter to get accepted to the school of her childhood, her roots and her essence. We would have loved her anyway but having her as a Tar Heel is so much better.

We do a group hug in her bedroom, the three of us plus high school bestie Gracie. Then we sway arm-in-arm as we hum the alma mater, even banging the footboard to match the drum solo.

Sophie is going to a place where she already knows the words.

Three nights later, we play at Louisville, new to the ACC, as underdogs. And lose a gut-wrencher in overtime. Welcome to life in the UNC family, Sophie.

February 21, 2015
North Carolina 89, Georgia Tech 60

It's Sunday morning and we're getting dressed for church when the news comes. It's not exactly "news" because it's been expected for a while. Still, the passing of the great Dean Smith is a sad moment. A part of all of us died right there.

The saddest part was the decline that preceded his death. Coach Smith seemed to be cruising along in old age and had even agreed to partner with his writer friend, John Feinstein, on a memoir where he might even share what he actually thought about players, opponents and games. I seriously doubt he would have dished dirt, but with his legendary memory, he may have remembered details about Carolina basketball in the last half century that no one else could know.

His decline started from a simple orthopedic procedure, after which he struggled to wake up from the anesthesia. When he did, he was never the same. The memory that produced names and occupations of spouses and children he had met just once, the analytical mind that revolutionized much of the way college basketball would be played, was gone.

The book project was abandoned. As Coach Smith's condition worsened, former players were encouraged to come see him, but cautioned not to be shocked if their coach did not recognize them. The universe had cruelly taken the greatest gift from this great man.

On the day he died, church was a bummer, as were the following days. The mood lifted a little when it was revealed that, in his will, Coach Smith bequeathed a $200 check to each of his former players, with instructions to spend it on dinner or on themselves and their families. That was so Coach Smith to give Michael Jordan the same $200 check he gave every reserve or walk-on who made the roster.

Players like Jimmy Moore, a reserve on Smith's third team that finished 12-12 in 1964, the last time Coach Smith failed to have a winning season. Moore moved back to his hometown Wilmington, became a success as an insurance broker and carried with him the same pride in UNC's basketball as the seven Hall-of-Famers who played under Coach Smith.

When I moved to Wilmington in 1984 at age 23, I looked for things to do during the day before my sportswriter shift. Some days I went to the YMCA, where I met a man in his 40s wanting to play me in a game of one-on-one hoops.

I hate one-on-one, especially when I'm bigger, at 6-foot-4, than the opponent and can simply just back him down and score inside. It's not fun. I tried to turn down this guy, but he persisted. So we played.

I couldn't move him. I couldn't turn the corner on him, or even shoot over him. He wasn't great on offense, but he tracked down his misses and beat me every time we played.

That was Jimmy Moore, still carrying the humility his college coach obviously taught him. I learned a little humility myself.

Moore and hundreds of other unknown lettermen got that same $200 check from Coach Smith's will. Rather than cashing it, many framed it instead.

When Coach Smith died, Carolina was in the middle of a three-game road trip. The first game post-death was a loss to Pittsburgh, then a trip to Cameron Indoor Stadium to play a very strong Duke team (again). To their everlasting credit, Coach Krzyzewski and Coach Williams worked together on a tribute before the game. All 10 starters knelt in a circle at midcourt, a solemn, powerful moment.

I guess at some level, we really are family.

The fourth-ranked Blue Devils were less hospitable during the game. They jumped out to an early 10-point lead but this was one of those games where Carolina, with less talent, played well enough to instill false hope. The Tar Heels led by 10 with 3:33 left and still by five with less than a minute left. They were on the verge of a signature win for Coach Smith, but turnovers and missed free throws were too much.

As was Duke. When the Blue Devils forced overtime, the outcome was fairly certain. National media stories would describe this as college basketball's game of the year in 2015.

At this point, I'm morally obligated to report that the 2015 season ended in another national championship for Duke, its one glorious year in the one-and-done era. My pastor is a Duke guy and a reasonable one, so as an act of Christian charity we buy him a specialty basketball commemorating all five Coach K titles, a vulgar idea some capitalist wished into existence.

I wrote Bob a poem to go with it. The first line: "First they came for Robert Morris, but they were a 16th-seed so we didn't care." It went downhill from there. Needless to say, Duke's title turned out to be fascist.

Anyway, the Heels finally return home to play a fairly awful Georgia Tech team headed for a 3-15 conference finish. Coach Williams has a tribute up his sleeve for Coach Smith in the building named after him.

Carolina opens the game in the Four Corners offense, a symbolic tribute to the stall offense that made Coach Smith and the program famous, and sometimes infamous, in the 60s and 70s. It is "symbolic" because the 30-second shot clock renders it useless. You can only stall for so long.

Yet Georgia Tech chases the ball as if it's a real stall. Marcus Paige picks up his dribble, the one thing you can't do in Four Corners. Still, he finds Brice Johnson on a backdoor cut for a layup as the shot clock expires, as Dean Smith of a basket as is possible. Carolina goes on to a rout, but one sour note soils this play.

Coach Williams is pissed that a large portion of the Carolina crowd, per usual, had not found its seat for the game's first possession ("The traffic is terrible!"). His Four Corners tribute is wasted on many of those who bought tickets.

I'm here to tell you: If Celia and Scott Whisnant had attended this game, our fat asses would have been sitting. In somebody else's seat, way better than the one on our ticket stub.

29
THE CRASHING
OF HELICOPTERS

February 17, 2016

Duke 74, North Carolina 73

Freshman orientation is hilarious. As maybe a thousand parental helicopters hover over their precocious children, the UNC adults in the room are relieving them of their hopes and expectations.

Your child will binge drink. Like, lots of alcohol. Raising the drinking age to 21 has effectively relegated underclassmen to drinking copious amounts in their homes through drinks they mix themselves. They have a phrase "black out or back out," which means if you're not committed to passing out, don't bother to party with us.

Your child may or may not attend class. It's none of your business. If you haven't heard from your child in a few days and call to ask, "is everything all right?" the school has no choice other than to have "the po-po roll up" to check on your child's wellbeing, mortifying the student and creating lasting relational damage.

Your child will choose his or her classes. Your child will arrange advanced placement testing. Don't even ask us about your child's grades.

Or try to argue that "you're the one paying the bill." It's not about the parents anymore.

In the face of this unyielding reality check, as one parental helicopter after another crashes into the metaphorical hills, a parent stands up and asks if "*we* can retake our Mandarin placement exam, because *we* missed placing out by two points."

There is no "*we*." The school has another agenda. During a presentation from, of all people, the band director, a parent asks how music classes will help his child get a job.

"Your child is not here to get a job," the band director says, rather high-handedly. "Your child is here to get an education."

I'm loving every second of it and ready for Sophie to experience

Sophie going back to the well, so to speak. This time as an undergraduate.

all of it. Even though I am widely mocked for being that guy who asks questions of the tour guide—Celia and Sophie both shudder from memories of tours of museums, historic landmarks and mansions, of my asking the tour guide in her antebellum outfit "tell me about the slaves' quality of life," - I don't have the guts this time to ask what I am thinking.

We're in the AfAm scandal phase of UNC's life as an institution of higher learning. The best possible version of this is that a well-meaning professor in the African-American Studies Department, and his assistant, devise Independent Studies classes where all that is expected is one paper by semester's end.

That in itself is not terribly unusual, and many schools offer these courses. It's not that the papers are not done, or someone else does them for the students. The issue is that the papers are not graded with any integrity. Apparently just about anything goes.

And the greater issue is that athletes through the UNC Athletics Department have "found" these classes. Are athletic advisers "encouraging" players to take these less-than-rigorous courses? Do the coaches and leaders know about them? Do they exist for athletes' benefit?

It's all murky. The only thing that saves what's left of UNC's reputation is the fact that the NCAA, the governing body of college athletics, has no jurisdiction, per its own bylaws, over the academic curriculum at a member school. You can't pay players, cheat at recruiting, hire tutors to write papers for players, etc. But the NCAA can't tell a school what courses it offers. Other accrediting bodies monitor that, and Carolina has somehow survived whatever overview those groups provide.

Still, it's not enough for me. With every fiber of my being, I want to grab the lapel of the university official who's talking about his solemn job to protect my child and tell him how this administration has shamed my alma mater and cheapened the value of my diploma. Can he promise, guarantee and swear that this will NEVER, EVER happen with my daughter's education?

Alas, I am a coward. The elephant in that room lumbers off while parents worry about Mandarin AP exams.

Sophie is lucky to attend just as the AfAm cloud lifts and basketball starts to return to normal after a malaise, no doubt caused by negative recruiting from teams expecting Carolina to go on probation. This hovering scandal contributes to Roy Williams being

My precious Sophie and I at the Dean Dome during her college days. By now she had fully bought into her parents' clever habit of snagging someone else's seats.

unable to land the significant "one-and-done" freshman that Duke and Kentucky always seem to get.

Nonetheless, the team has unintentionally taken another route to power. By recruiting "four-year" players not good enough to turn pro early, Carolina now has a roster of juniors and seniors who have played together and grown, evolving into a national contender leading up to the home game against Duke. Somehow, all three of us end up with tickets, a political favor here and a social favor there, and witness what could have been a classic. Carolina trails by one with the ball in the closing seconds yet is unable to run a play and get off a decent shot.

We gather outside the Dean Dome to process what just happened. I assume it's the AfAm karma still haunting us. Are we getting what we deserve?

March 12, 2016
North Carolina 61, Virginia 57
ACC Tournament Final

We have made a colossal scheduling error. In violation of our own rule about not scheduling trips, visits, weddings, funerals or illnesses in March, we decide to go to New York City during Carolina's Spring Break to amuse our daughter, now a freshman, and her childhood friend and fellow Carolina student, Alice.

We're flying up on the day of the ACC Tournament final, an event in recent years that has not concerned us. Carolina, ranked 7th and the league's regular-season champion, is playing fourth-ranked Virginia, long evolved from its "zebra" days to a formidable program. The team pulls together behind the wondrous Marcus Paige and Brice Johnson, having an all-American senior season. The only game Carolina has lost since the first Duke game is to Virginia. We've grown used, to some degree, to being unable to beat Duke. We can't tolerate futility against another program. And certainly not Virginia.

Our first night in New York is a no-brainer. We're watching the Carolina game. We could hole up in our hotel room, but this is New York City, for crying out loud. We find a "Carolina bar" in the city, Slattery's Midtown Pub on 36th Street. We jump into a cab.

Sure enough, this place is jumping. There's a giant inflatable Ramses out front, and upstairs every TV is tuned to ESPN and the Tar Heels. The place is selling giant beers in blue cups like you get at He's Not Here, a quintessential college dive bar on Chapel Hill's iconic Franklin Street. They even have a deal going where if you buy one, they give you a shot of Jameson whiskey for free.

Celia and I line up our "He's Not" buckets and shots at our table, then notice the hang dog looks of our two 18-year-old freshmen next to us. No, we're not those parents who will blatantly buy our underage children beer. But maybe giving them those shots wouldn't be so bad. This is a celebration, after all.

We offer the shots. They accept. We're expecting them to sip a little, put the glass down and wiggle their heads as the pure whiskey causes their systems to backspin.

That's not what we get. Sophie and Alice knock back the shots with the same effort it would take to eat a Peanut M&M. These girls have been in college for seven months. This is not their first shot.

Celia and I try to not tease out what all this infers and focus on the game. It's a typical Virginia game of this era, as the Cavaliers render Carolina impotent on defense while employing an offense more suited to the Victorian era. It's a slow grind of a watch, which only makes every possession more taut.

This tougher version of the Tar Heels stays together, goes on a late 7-0 spurt and hangs on, the first ACC Tournament championship since the Tyler Hansbrough days. Virginia is finally vanquished.

Slattery's is bonkers, as total strangers bound by just one common denominator dance about and hug one another. Then the bar plays a recording of *Hark the Voices,* the school alma mater, and we all line up, arms around each other's shoulders, and sway in unison.

For me it's right up there with the Final Fours during my college days. Not sure how many schools' fan bases could pull this off as emissaries in a foreign land. Never prouder of Tar Heel nation. This team is headed for something special.

April 4, 2016
Villanova 77, North Carolina 74
NCAA Tournament Final

Maybe something "unforgettable" is more like it.

This Final Four is all about my daughter. Within seconds of Carolina's regional final win over Notre Dame, I call Sophie and ask if she's going to the Final Four. Like her Daddy did at her age.

It's a bit of a haul. The Final Four is in Houston, where we know no one. But some things are looking up. Sophie has joined a sorority and has all sorts of "sisters" (even though sorority girls don't call themselves this anymore), and one of them lives in Houston and wants to go to the game. She's offering lodging.

But Sophie points to barriers. She has a sorority function she has to attend early on Saturday. And there's this:

"One of our professors is giving us a test on Tuesday. I wouldn't be back in time."

Well, well, well, well. Perfect words to provoke a rant in the old man. No daughter of mine is going to put academics ahead of an experience like this.

"Sophie, a month from now, no one will remember this test. You'll pass this class and graduate regardless. But you'll remember the Final Four the rest of your life."

The professor would certainly recognize the folly of his efforts to improve the minds of young adults and reschedule (and, in fact, this is exactly what happens). You're in college to get an experience, not a grade point average.

I am fairly indignant. She says she'll think about it.

And she pulls it off. She has just enough time after her event to hop a flight to Houston, arrange for an Uber to her friend's house to drop off her stuff and make it to the stadium in time for Carolina's semifinal against Syracuse.

Regarding the friend's "house," I assumed this would resemble my trip to New Orleans, when four of us slept on the floor of an apartment of one of the guy's girlfriend. We were grateful to have it. But, no. Turns out this girl's family lives in an upscale neighborhood, the same one where the Bushes live. You know, Poppy and W. Those Bushes.

Continuing in true Whisnant schmuck fashion, at the game she manages to outflank her fellow students and get to the second row behind the basket. Where she will be seen on camera multiple times during the Tar Heels' win.

She didn't see the first semifinal and maybe it's just as well. Villanova destroys an overmatched Oklahoma team, as bad a beating as I can remember at this level. I have some concerns about the final game, but the Heels are on a mission.

And as with all tragedies, it's the small things that stick out as the metaphorical car flips over and over. There's Carolina outplaying Villanova in the first half, up by seven in the final seconds, when Justin Jackson makes a clever steal and has a run out for a layup.

Someone is chasing him. Dunk it, Justin. Go in hard.

No, he tries a reverse layup, using the rim as shield. The Villanova player slams the ball against the backboard. They have time to recover and get off a shot at the buzzer, which goes in. Instead of nine, the halftime lead is five and it feels like we're behind.

Soon we really are behind. The Tar Heels crumble a bit, falling behind by 10 with three minutes left. Then Paige, known for his late-game exploits, starts doing the Paigeiest thing of all, hitting a three, setting up Joel Berry for a three, forcing a turnover and turning the course of the game.

But still down six with 1:30 left. Paige hits another three from the deep corner at an impossible angle. Villanova turns it over against a trap and Johnson scores to cut it to one. Villanova's Phil Booth travels, travels—call it, ref—but no, is finally fouled with just a few seconds left and makes both.

We're three down with about 15 seconds left. We get it to Paige, but Villanova expects that. Paige rises to shoot but has to hang in the air to shed a defender. All he can do is fling a double-pumped three-pointer at the basket, but this is Paige and it goes in.

Tie game. Bedlam. Timeout Villanova with 5 seconds left. I'm so happy for Sophie. She's watching not just a national title but a classic that will be long remembered after Carolina seals this in overtime.

Just keep Nova from scoring.

Then it happens. Villanova's lead guard rushes upcourt and drops it to a trailing Kris Jenkins, a shooter of such skill and grace that it looks like he's taking a routine jump shot. Watch the replay sometime. He's a good six feet behind the three-point-line. This is a 25-footer.

Jenkins' shot strips the net at the buzzer, a replay that will haunt a thousand future tournament promos.

After some initial swearing, all we can think about is "what have we done to Sophie?" This will leave a mark. I text her to "get the hell out of there as soon as you can." Nothing good will come from watching Villanova celebrate.

I imagine Sophie in her mid-30s, with children, when Carolina finally makes it back to a Final Four and wins a title. She will excuse herself from the room to cry a little. Her children will ask their witless father "What's up with her?"

"She was in Houston," he'll say. And that's all that will need to be said.

Turns out I'm off by about 17 years.

March 26, 2017

North Carolina 75, Kentucky 73

NCAA Tournament Southeast Regional Final

Celia is an exacting Carolina fan. She expects the players to produce to a level worthy of the honor of wearing the uniform. We're not talking about belly-aching if they don't, but we have expectations.

The Tar Heels of 2017, despite losing perhaps their two best players from the year before, again have the look of a title contender, again led by a line-up of juniors and seniors such as Justin Jackson, who likely returned for another year because of weakness he showed in the Villanova game. Now he's on his way to winning ACC Player of the Year.

The Tar Heels have a strong starting five and more than adequate subs in the frontcourt, the wing and at guard.

The "ninth man" is Luke Maye, a sophomore forward who literally walked on to the team the year before, though this story is more lore than fact. Maye was fairly heavily recruited and was offered scholarships at many major programs. He attended UNC because his father had been a star quarterback in the 1980s and they were able to pay his way when it didn't look like a scholarship would be available. Turns out, there was an opening, and Maye was on scholarship all of his four years.

Me and my game-watching pal overseeing our boys. We didn't belong in these seats, by the way.

Unmoved by this detail, our non-UNC friends mock Maye, saying he resembles the missing link to our Neanderthal ancestors ("Fire bad!!" they quote him as saying).

Celia operates on a higher plane than that, but not by much. As Maye struggles in his limited minutes in 2017, she resorts to a bit she developed earlier in her fandom.

She pulls his metaphorical scholarship out of the file drawer and places it on the table. It's up for debate. After he struggles again, she pulls the trigger. Luke Maye's scholarship is revoked, joining a pantheon of forgettable players through the past 20 or so years whose career just didn't work out.

Maye regains his scholarship quietly in the Sweet 16 game against Butler as he scores 16 points, including a stunning 3-for-5 on three-pointers. Who knew he could shoot it?

That brings us to the Kentucky game two days later.

Kentucky has three freshmen who will be drafted in the first round by NBA teams in less than two months. The Wildcats have already beaten Carolina this year, as one of those first-rounders went for 47 points. Kentucky is the one program whose history rivals Carolina, and their fan base is universal and obnoxious. Without doubt, there's a Kentucky bar in New York City.

Losing to Kentucky on a stage as large as a regional final is intolerable. Especially when we have a team good enough to win it.

Yet, there we are, five points behind with 5 minutes to go after a Kentucky role player—not a first-rounder—has an out-of-body experience and hits several jump shots in a row. Coach Roy Williams takes the unusual step of calling time out.

He switches the defense to a zone. Carolina scores two baskets on fortunate bounces and Kentucky starts turning it over. Soon we're seven points ahead with less than a minute to go. But before we can really taste it, Kentucky hits a three, we turn it over, and Malik Monk, the 47-point guy from earlier in the year, hits another three-pointer. The lead is one.

We score two more and get the ball back. Jackson, our all-American, is fouled with 15 seconds left. And he promptly misses. Kentucky gets it to Monk, and he makes an even more difficult three-pointer.

We're tied with 5 seconds left. I sag into Purple Boy. This will head to overtime and a replay of the Georgetown debacle from 10 years before.

I cannot believe we're blowing a game of this magnitude to, of all teams, Kentucky.

However, Carolina does a curious thing. Instead of calling timeout and having Coach Williams draw something on a white board, Carolina quickly inbounds to Theo Pinson. All five players are headed downcourt in an organized fashion. They know exactly what they want to do. No panic or self-flagellating. This is what a well-coached team does.

Pinson leads a charge up court against a scrambling Kentucky defense. He shields the last defender with his body as he turns to drop it off for one last shot to... Luke Maye, still just freshly scholarshipped. The Carolina season will basically hinge on whether this "walk on" can hit an 18-footer against Kentucky.

Oh, he can. It's beautiful to watch, in real time, in slow motion, on You Tube and on an Instagram post a college friend sends me, the shot synched to the *Titanic* theme song. Somehow that is the best of all.

Maye is further cemented into Carolina lore when he shows up the next morning back in Chapel Hill at his 8 a.m. Business class, receiving a standing ovation from his fellow students.

April 3, 2017
North Carolina 71, Gonzaga 65
NCAA Tournament Final

Sophie can't, or won't, go to this Final Four in Phoenix. The PTSD from the year before still fresh, she cannot karmically afford to make the effort to go to another one and watch us lose. She decides to take it in on campus, where the aftergame parties are legion.

The semifinal win against Oregon, by one point, tests every nerve ending in our bodies, but we survive, nonetheless. The final game against Gonzaga is an ugly, foul-marred slog, but both teams make big shots down the stretch.

Isaiah Hicks, the senior forward who played so poorly in the regional that Luke Maye was allowed on the floor in clutch time, makes his first big shot in weeks, putting Carolina ahead by three with less than a minute to go. The Zags run a play for their best player, who makes a weak spin move that Kennedy Meeks blocks.

Joel Berry picks it up and hits a streaking Justin Jackson. This time he slams it home. Redemption is Carolina's.

We do our usual bit, streaking the back yard and toasting champagne *a la mode*[1]. But this night belongs to Sophie. She later sends us a photo of her in the middle of the mosh pit that became Franklin and Columbia streets, arms raised high wearing the UNC road jersey we bought her, a few blue cups in her, smiling the smile of genuine joy,

A few blue cups in, Sophie celebrates the 2017 title on Franklin Street riding the shoulders of someone we're not sure she even knew. Proud moment for any father.

riding on the shoulders of someone we don't know and we're not sure she does either.

It's what every father wants for his daughter.

---

1   That's Latin for nekkid, right?

30

THE BARGAIN

February 8, 2020

Duke 98, North Carolina 96 (OT)

Sophie has graduated and is teaching kindergarten at a high-poverty school in Charlotte through Teach For America. She's home for spring break and we're observing the ritual of the Duke game.

That's about the only reason to watch this one. Carolina is terrible this year. The Heels were pretty good the two years after the championship but lost early in the NCAA Tournament, the success metric that matters. For 2020, Coach Williams just couldn't put together the right mix of players.

The Heels stand at 10-12. Duke is ranked 7th nationally. That's a fairly accurate representation of the gap. The late-season advent of COVID will spare the Tar Heels from the embarrassment of missing the NCAA Tournament, as that event will be canceled.

We decide on a new strategy for this Duke game: Drinking heavily with our 22-year-old daughter.

I'm averaging about one beer per TV timeout, and Celia and Sophie are finishing a bottle of Rose' and eyeing a second. It seems to be working.

Carolina is inspired, the home crowd is wild and role players better suited to junior college are having a moment. We're up an absurd 13 points with 4½ minutes left. I believe I need a fresh cold one.

We start missing foul shots. Poor Andrew Platek. Never has anyone been more overmatched at the foul line as he misses two with 57 seconds left and Carolina up five. Anyone who has seen *Monty Python and the Holy Grail* and remembers the foibles of Sir Robin knows what we mean here.

We're up three in the final seconds and we foul Tre Jones on purpose with 4.4 left so Duke can't get off a three-pointer. See how smart we are? Jones, wretched brother of Tyus Jones who played on the 2015 championship team, makes the first free throw. We applaud his efforts.

Then Jones does something ridiculous. He throws a vicious line drive straight at the rim, hitting it dead on. The ball ricochets toward the three-point line, where only Jones can recover it and, with two defenders on him, gets off a shot that ties the game.

The mood is not as glum as you might think, as this just means Happy Hour continues. Carolina even manages to take a five-point lead with 21 seconds left in OT, but Jones scores another layup and is fouled. He misses, but naturally Duke rebounds and scores again.

One-point lead with 12 seconds left. All we have to do is inbound the ball, but we can't (Platek!!). Jones gets fouled again and makes one to tie the game. Then he misses, which will only make what he has to say after the game more of a farce—that the line drive free throw that bounced back to him at the end of regulation, something he couldn't do in an empty gym with 10 racks of basketballs, is a move he *practices* and can accomplish about 75 percent of the time. Ok. Yet with the game in balance in overtime, he misses a normal free throw even ordinary humans can make.

No matter. None of it will matter this day. The rebound comes to Duke, Jones tries another jumper, misses, and Wendell Moore tips it in at the buzzer, setting off the greatest celebration you'll ever see over beating a 10-12 team.

And the truth of it all is, it doesn't matter. We have had the times of our lives, the three of us drinking as adult friends and laughing all the way. There comes a time in your child's life when she morphs from needy child to adult friend.

I say this carefully and fully considering the ramifications: This is more important than losing to Duke. Especially for a team that wasn't going anywhere anyway.

January 20, 2021
North Carolina 80, Wake Forest 73

Lord knows, Mama tried.

Almost 24 years since her husband and North Star died, she has tried to make a life of it. In the early days, she was that healthy grandmother who visited us after Sophie was born, not to hold the baby but to fix every meal, wash loads of clothes and clean every nook and crevice of the house, sometimes on her knees, so that *we* could hold the baby.

She still had her health then, at 65. She would walk Sophie in her stroller for miles, sometimes across the park to the neighborhood grocery store to buy food she would cook that night. Mama was a committed walker, at home through the neighborhood cul de sacs or on vacation.

Then the surgeries started. Back fusion, then a procedure to correct where that one went wrong. Three surgeries in the next couple of years, with one setback after another. The arthritis flared up, and every day was marked by pain and more pain. Before long, doctors would put her on morphine that barely touched the pain.

She spent her 70th birthday in a hospital. A few years later, we—my sisters and I—took her car keys after one too many minor wrecks. She compared living at home without a car to living in jail. Holding on to the house was becoming more of a struggle. Too many times my sister Linda or a neighbor would catch Mama trying to pull the garbage can to the curb, a wrestling match the garbage seemed favored to win. But that's what homeowners do, and Mama wasn't giving in.

What she had were Carolina basketball games, a final connection to her late husband and her son. My sister Judy got her a calendar every year that listed each game and, most important, where to find it on TV. She kept up with it really well for a while, and we often timed visits to her house around Carolina games.

Adapting to 'smart" TV proved a challenge, but she had bigger issues. Finally, just before her 83rd birthday, we moved Mama to the "home," an independent living facility nearby in Greensboro.

We sold Heritage Greens to her as an opportunity to live a less strenuous life and meet new people. In reality, it was a death of sorts as we said goodbye to my childhood home since age 5, where Daddy, because of his prodigious skills and desire to save money, laid the brick, made the cabinets, put up the roof and practically built the whole thing. The house brimmed with him from every wall, every cabinet, every crevice.

On a sweltering July day in 2015, I had the somber duty of cleaning out the attic with my two brothers-in-law. After they left, I stopped by my old bedroom one last time.

A simple square room where I slept on the double-bed my grandfather had preserved from his in-law's home, along with the cherry dresser and table. This is where my brief burst of "decorating" interest meant cutting photos from my *Sports Illustrated* collection and taping them to the wall.

Above the bed was the cover of Phil Ford leading Carolina to the 1975 ACC championship ("Upset in the ACC. Phil Ford Kicks Up His Tar Heels"). On the wall was a grinning Dudley Bradley leading the Heels to the 1979 title ("Stealing the ACC Title. Dudley Bradley Dunks Duke).

Several pieces of art involved rare UCLA losses, notably the 1974 team losing twice in three days at Oregon and Oregon State ("UCLA's Lost Weekend"). For a 13-year-old 3,000 miles from Los Angeles to care enough about two losses in routine Pac 8 games tells you something about UCLA's dominance of college basketball at that time.

All this and so much more from this room swelled up inside of me. Here's my mother checking my fever with the back of her hand. Here's her earnestly praying over me, not realizing I have awakened enough to hear her. Now I hear Daddy's footsteps down the hall to wake me for school, but not before a breakfast of eggs, bacon, fruit and unlimited toast courtesy of Mama.

"Goodbye room," I said. We told Mama this would open new opportunities, but who were we kidding? Things would never be the same.

At Heritage Greens, also likened to jail, Mama was her same sweet self, but she ebbed from us in a cloud of pain and, later, confusion. Too often I would call and ask her if she had watched the Carolina game, only to find she didn't realize they were playing. She would forget she had the schedule on her refrigerator.

We went through the usual stages adult children endure. We printed lists giving her channel numbers for different ESPN outlets and other sources for Carolina on the air. We bought her simpler and better TVs. I even tried teaching her how to record games ahead of time and watch them on her schedule. I might as well have asked her to split an atom.

It became my job to call her just before every game and tell her to turn the TV to a certain channel. And that worked for a while. She didn't know the players and often forgot who had won by the time I called again. But it gave her something to do, something to look forward to, and a connection to us.

In the fall of 2020, we were starting to think about her 90th birthday the following July. But then, on the day after Thanksgiving, she fell one more time—maybe crawling up on a chair to fix a clock or a light bulb, as she never gave in to our pleas to let the maintenance crew do these things. Mama broke her hip and went to a hospital in Greensboro.

This was the height of the COVID pandemic, so we couldn't visit her. We put the staff up to Facetiming with us, and, though frustrated, she improved enough to be discharged to a rehab facility.

For this frail, sweet woman to be in such a foreign land, with crappy food, no one she knew and therapists prodding her to exercise, was heartbreaking. Still, she was well enough to be home, or back to her regular jail, by Christmas.

Sophie was home in Wilmington for Christmas with full-blown COVID. We were staring at a Christmas day of communicating with her from the living room to her bedroom via Facetime. We even opened gifts that way, a uniquely 2020 experience.

I decided to go see Mama, a four-hour drive up Interstate 40, and surprise the family with my presence, certain that this would inspire Mama to greater heights and start her road to recovery. I planned how I would sneak up on the crowd, how I would make my entrance and how Mama would declare, again, that I was the only boy who had ever been born. This was a Christmas movie in the making, the script just needing a few tweaks from here.

I posed as a pitiful old man huddled under his coat in 18-degree weather until the family gathered at the front of Heritage Greens right around lunchtime. Yes, they all agreed after my "reveal," I was convincing as a doddering old man. Isn't family so funny?

Mama was confused and didn't understand why I was there. We were not allowed inside, of course, so we scurried to the nearby gazebo under blankets and exchanged gifts, or more accurately, bestowed them on Mama. She wasn't herself, but Lord she was sweet.

Then she offered a prayer. This devout, humble woman had never volunteered to lead a prayer out loud. I used to tease her about what it would take for her to speak up and join the discussion in Sunday School, and the conclusion always landed on "nothing." But now we bowed our heads and this confused, addled woman cut loose a prayer as righteous as anything Jesus mustered in the Garden of Gethsemane. The only time my thoughts strayed was when I wished I had recorded it on my phone.

We left her that night and hung out at Linda's. The next day I went to see Mama, just the two of us. Linda had taught me how to sneak past the desk at "jail" and go to her room.

And she had almost nothing to say. After a short while, she asked if I could put her to bed. She didn't feel so well.

I did that and returned to Wilmington. My sisters had the Heritage Greens staff check on her, and she had COVID, either from the hospital, one of her rehab stints or from the home itself. She went back to the hospital, this time the one designated for COVID patients. Her condition worsened, with her kidneys and digestion functions joining her lungs in deserting her. We Facetimed, but the image we got was not my Mama. She seemed agitated and terrified and so, so lonely.

She had given it all she had. The hospital saw what was coming and discharged her to hospice.

Sophie and Mama Bear. So sweet.

That Wednesday night, the same night Donald Trump officially stops being president (the first time), Carolina hosts Wake Forest. Right at game time I think about calling Mama again, but she is way beyond watching ball games at this point.

I watched the game, of that I am certain. And I remember nothing about it. I had been a Tar Heel fan for 55 years at that point, but they are no match for my mother. They play Wake Forest every year.

I tell my sisters I will work on Thursday and be there on Friday. Because I have something important to do at work on Thursday.

They call me just before noon. Mama had slipped away peacefully, her daughters and grandson with her. She likely believed he was me.

I have no idea what it was I was supposed to do that day at work.

March 5, 2022

North Carolina 94, Duke 81

We're sitting in Rey's Restaurant, a toney Raleigh steak house, on a Friday night to celebrate my brother-in-law's 75th birthday. We agree to do this with the understanding we will drive two hours back to Wilmington immediately after, as we don't want to risk being late for watching the Duke game on TV the following day. At 6:20 p.m.

We're not taking any chances. It's not that we're looking forward to playing at Cameron Indoor Stadium. Quite the opposite. We dread it as we might the hangman's gallows. But it's in our contract as lifelong Carolina fans to be there. We'll stand with our boys as they endure this ritualistic slaughter, almost Christ-like in taking on the suffering that is at least partly ours.

Carolina has been lousy for a while now. The 2021 season is meh at best, barely making the NCAA Tournament with players so disinterested and generationally distant that Roy Williams decides he's too old to coach them anymore.

Before an N.C. State game, we stalked Hubert Davis in the parking lot. "Nice to meet you," Celia told him. "No, nice to meet you," he said, as though he meant it.

So we get Hubert Davis, former player, current assistant, who may be the nicest person on earth. Whether he's much of a head coach, able to lead perhaps the most famous basketball program in the nation, is a question very much up for debate.

The Tar Heels of 2022 are lethargic and disjointed at times, with mortifying blowout losses at Miami and Wake Forest, the Heels down by more than 25 before halftime, and another one at home against Duke, as the Blue Devils go easy on us and only win by 20.

Yet, some hopeful signs emerge, as Carolina wins four in a row heading into the final Duke game. The game before, Senior Night at the Dean Dome, required an absurdly long three-pointer by Caleb Love in the waning seconds to avoid a loss, and two more by Love during overtime, to beat a pedestrian Syracuse team. As we head to Durham, we're sitting at 22-8 and all is not exactly well. There's even talk about Carolina being a "bubble team" that may not reach the NCAA Tournament, a once-foreign term that has been our lives the last three years.

All of which is to say the final Duke game is sooooo not about Carolina. This is the last game for celebrated Duke coach Mike Krzyzewski after 42 years as head coach. As my former boss Jerry Hooks once said about Carolina and Dean Smith, I cannot count how many times this man has personally hurt me. Which is to say he's been outrageously successful.

The spectacle of his last game in Cameron would perhaps be matched by the second coming of Jesus Christ only if ESPN could run a few thousand promos leading up to Holy Week. Coach K made his retirement plans known before the season, causing a season-long run of self-pleasuring anticipation, with "ceremonies" at all the ACC stations where he tormented the home teams so many times, though not in Chapel Hill. Carolina gave him a plaque, or something, after he won his 1,000th game but opted against the hypocritical route of concocting a ceremony no one believed in.

The road to the final game burned more intensely among the Duke faithful. (I would say "in Durham" but in reality more Carolina fans live in Durham than Duke fans. Duke basketball is a national brand in much the same way Hades is.) Tickets reportedly hit $10,000 on the secondary market. Celebrities with tenuous Duke ties—Jerry Seinfeld (his daughter goes to Duke); NBA Commissioner Adam Silver (Duke grad); actor Ken Jeong (went to Duke and Carolina, so he actually had a choice)—will be there. About a hundred former players I regard with varying levels of personal animus will attend, though, oddly, none of the one-and-done players who left after their freshman year. All of them wear a special Coach K sweater-shirt.

ESPN has pushed the start time to 6:20 p.m. to keep the 4 p.m. game from running long and bleeding into the pre-game ceremony, where Coach K will walk onto the court as the adoring thousands wave palm branches, or something, and the Worldwide Leader will broadcast this nationally. A post-game fete is scheduled for ESPN's primetime slot at 8:30 or so p.m., so that we can hear from Coach K one more time from the seat of his throne.

This didn't happen when Dean Smith retired, or Roy Williams for that matter. Both had the grace to retire after their last game and avoid the year-long circle jerk. In fact, this hasn't happened for any retiring coach. Krzyzewski said he did it so "recruits will know what to expect" and professed discomfort over the year-long fawning. As if he couldn't have put a stop to it at any time.

At any rate, what the pregame buildup is *not* about is North Carolina. The Tar Heels are the perfect lamb to serve up for mighty K's last game. They aren't very good to start with, but even a good Carolina team would be assumed to fall in the last game in Cameron. Humiliating Carolina in K's last game is the perfect salve for this fan base.

Carolina is the Washington Generals to Duke's Harlem Globetrotters. And Carolina has never, ever been relegated to a role like that.

At the steakhouse in Raleigh, my sisters, their husbands, Sophie and her boyfriend, Cole, and we consider our fate the next day.

"We can't win," I tell my sisters, delivering the news with as much grace as I can summon and still remain a stinky little brother.

"Would you rather win this game or the national championship?" Cole asks.

"Oh, this game," we all say, fairly in unison.

Someone at the table poses a hypothetical.

"What if we win this game but play Duke again in the tournament? Which game do you want?"

"This game."

"You would trade winning this game for losing to Duke in the national final?"

Yes, we would take that trade. Beating Coach K in his final game would be a stain no other game could remove. It's a dreamy hypothetical because 1) we won't win the game and 2) we won't win enough tournament games to play them again. But it's fun to fantasize.

Once home, Celia and I, as well as millions of Tar Heel nation, settle in expecting the worst. Our fondest hope is that the game doesn't devolve into a blowout.

Right away, karma fires back at Duke. The Texas-Kansas game on ESPN runs long and goes into overtime, eating up that 20-minute window of pregame silliness. Coach K's triumphant last walk onto the court is shown on split screen, sound down, while Kansas fends off the Longhorns to win the Big 12 title, an actual breaking news event. The start of the game has to be pushed to the netherlands of ESPNNEWS, where UNC's Armando Bacot starts the game with a dunk.

Carolina actually manages to hang around. With about three minutes left in the half, Duke eases to a nine-point lead, and we're thinking "here it comes." But Carolina on this day has brought something it didn't have all season. Resilience. Toughness. The Tar Heels claw back and when R.J. Davis hits a bomb at the halftime buzzer, the Duke lead is only two.

Duke regains some control in the second half, as each basket gets a reaction shot from wife Mikki Krzyzewski, seated with their daughter; Jerry Seinfeld; Christian Laettner; J.J. Redick; or various other former Duke rascals. But around the 10-minute mark, Carolina channels a Dean Smith team from the early 1980s and starts making every play, defending every shot and grabbing every rebound.

There's Bacot scoring to give us the lead. Cue Mikki Krzyzewski crying for a traveling call. There's Brady Manek scoring on the end of a fast break. Six in a row for Carolina. Cue former player Jayson Williams, motioning desperately for his coach and mentor to CALL A TIMEOUT.

"This is happening," I tell Celia.

"Too soon. Don't talk about it."

Manek hits another three. Cue disgust on the face of Shane Battier. We're inching, no barreling, toward Carolina porn.

Then with an eight-point lead in the final minute, Love drives the lane and dishes to Bacot for a thunder dunk, a play so spectacular and definitive that Bacot celebrates as he dunks it, Manek raises the rafters on court and Love grins toward the Carolina bench and makes his best happy face, sticking out his tongue.

Duke is done. Coach K is taking an L in his last home game.

Against all odds, it gets better. Now even ESPN is piling on. We're getting one of our favorite scenes from any Carolina win in Cameron: Crowd shots.

Sad guy in overalls and no shirt, his blue paint starting to rub off. Two redheads in overalls, one sobbing into the other's chest. A couple dressed as Bert and Ernie, disconsolate and unaware that neither Bert nor Ernie went to Duke. Guy in pink toboggan and no shirt, giving the "cobra surrender" signal (hands behind head, elbows out). Three guys in feathered boas with blue paint below the eyes, one of them in full-on cobra.

Perhaps the best is a girl, possibly a cheerleader, wearing a Duke mask as if still carrying COVID, eyes full of tears. She sees the camera on her and enters into a death stare contest, glaring as if to say "I'm not going to cry for you."

When it's over, Duke assistant coach Chris Carrawell in the post-game handshake line ignores the hand of Hubert Davis, suddenly elevated to Carolina coaching icon. ESPN has no choice but to carry on with the post-game "celebration," which features Coach Kzyzewski taking an unscheduled turn at the mike.

He tries to apologize for the game. When the crowd won't hear it, that's not what he wants from them.

"Be quiet!" he says in his most Midwestern twang to the adoring fans, some of whom spent $10,000 thinking they would get Romans vs. Christians, not this.

"Today was unacceptable," he says.

Meanwhile we can't believe we lived long enough to see this. Within a week we both own T-shirts with the final score that say "94-81. Acceptable." We have forgotten all about our "bargain." The chances of these teams meeting again in the NCAAs is almost nil.

Surely this is the pinnacle of our Carolina fandom. It can't get better than this.

31

THE SONG WE ALL SING

April 2, 2022

North Carolina 81, Duke 77

NCAA Tournament Final Four

Just win one game. Beat Marquette. That's really all we need from the NCAA Tournament.

It won't get any better after that glorious win in Cameron. We've watched the replay countless times, laughing a little harder with each viewing. From the 10-minute mark on, it's pure comedy gold.

The 2022 Tar Heels have nothing left to prove. We lose to Virginia Tech in the ACC Tournament, deftly avoiding Duke, who then loses to Virginia Tech in the final, another unexpected burst of comedy.

We draw an 8 seed for the big tournament, a little on the embarrassing side but about right for this season. Our first-round game is with a plebian Marquette team seeded ninth. Losing in the first game would not be disastrous, but let's get one win. Just for the hell of it.

We beat the living snot out of Marquette. Caleb Love inhabits a superior alien's body for one half, hitting six three-pointers. The next draw is top-seeded and defending national champion Baylor. R.J. Davis loses his mind, making shots from all over in the first half, and Brady Manek joins the delirium in the second half.

We're up 25, defying all logic, when Manek elbows the most annoying Baylor player and is ejected from the game. The final 10 minutes are a shit show at the highest level, as Carolina revisits every flaw it exhibited during the year. Love fouls out, we can barely inbound the ball against the press, and we keep fouling Baylor as they score.

All I can think about is what my father would be doing had he lived to see this. Never mind that he would be 98 years old. I still see him in his prime, hands raised and shouting "nothing!" He would be asking why Carolina went into the Sorry Game Plan, and I'm wondering that myself.

Baylor forces overtime, setting up Carolina for the biggest choke in history. Then the oddest thing happens. The first possession of overtime is another tentative slog, dribble, dribble, dribble, no one seems able to get a shot. The ball finds Dontrez Styles, a seldom-used freshman with potential who has spent most of the season not developing it on the bench. Down two starters, he is forced to play.

He decides now would be a good time to squeeze off a three-pointer, perhaps unaware that he is 2-for-17 for the season. It goes in. Armando Bacot finds Leaky Black near the basket for two more, then makes a series of trips to the foul line.

Celia can't look, literally a first in our 35 years of watching the Tar Heels together. She stands with her back to the TV, staring out the window, while I begin to channel the great Woody Durham, who died four years earlier after meeting a fate as cruel as Dean Smith losing his memory. Complications from Primary Progressive Aphasia left Woody, the silky-smooth voice for a generation of Carolina fans, unable to speak.

"Ok, he's dribbling, dribbling, dribbling—he looks nervous," I say. "It's up... No good."

"SHIT," Celia says. "I can't stand it."

For the game, Bacot tortures us by making seven of 15 free throws, though I'm certain he felt worse about it than we did. But he makes just enough and his teammates make just enough plays in overtime. Carolina steadies itself and wins, 93-86, a tough-as-nails game over a top seed.

Now we have something. A very good UCLA team is next, and Love goes off into the stratosphere again, scoring 27 points in the second half, including the tying and go-ahead three-pointers in the final two minutes.

"Love him like a son," Celia says. "Like a son, I say."

Carolina has somehow managed to reach a regional final. Against a 15 seed. How can we be this lucky?

St. Peter's University has taken out Kentucky and Purdue, but as so often happens to teams like this, the Peacocks invariably revert back to their seed. Carolina starts 9-0, then goes to 27-9 and the game is never in question. The Tar Heels are headed to another Final Four, this time as an overachieving 8 seed.

So why do I spend the final 10 minutes of this game in utter dread? Because the Final Four opponent will be Duke. The Blue Devils have put together four wins and await the East Regional winner.

We've never played Duke in an NCAA Tournament. Many is the year when this would be fine. Let's play the Blue Devils with James Worthy, Sam Perkins and Michael Jordan. Maybe the Antawn Jamison/Vince Carter teams could run into Duke. Or we find Duke in the Sean May year, or Tyler Hansbrough era.

But not this team. Duke has five players who will be picked in the upcoming NBA draft, four of them in the first round and one, the vile Paolo Banchero, will be chosen first. They have the greatest coach in the sport, or so they believe, in his final year. They are loaded.

Carolina has no one who will get a whiff of the NBA. Well, maybe Bacot and Love will one day catch a faint odor. The Tar Heels have a first-year coach with no head coaching experience prior to this year. We're an 8 seed for a reason.

And now we're served up to Duke in the Final Four, giving the Blue Devils a golden opportunity to pay us back for the Cameron debacle. Yes, I know we made a bargain over this very scenario, trading a win in K's last game in Cameron for a loss in the NCAA Tournament, but now it doesn't look so good. Watching Duke "redeem" itself and go on to a national title in Coach K's final year is beyond repulsive.

I don't think any living Carolina fan is honestly excited about playing Duke again.

We tell ourselves it doesn't matter. The win at Cameron will still be glorious and can never be taken away. Right? And why did we make this bargain in the first place?

The week inches toward Saturday. If possible, we dread this game more than the one at Duke. They have better players, more experienced coaches. They have a cause. This will be K's legacy game. I can't stand it.

Finally, tip off. Black opens the game with a three, always a good sign. And as the game progresses, it turns out we are Duke's equal. It's going to come down to little things. The little things will stick out.

After Banchero dunks early in the second half, inordinately pleasing CBS' Bill Raftery ("Leave the chandeliers, big fella!"), Duke leads by seven. Heaven help us. Carolina then puts on perhaps its greatest three-minute stretch in memory. Three-pointer by Love. Another by Love. Manek hits from the corner and lets Banchero hear about it, cutting loose with his infamous "Bang bang, mother-fucker" comment. To the top draft pick's face. From a guy who will be playing in Australia next year.

A lay-up by Love and Carolina leads by four. Coach Krzyzewski calls a time out. This is a traditional "stop the run" timeout that no one will question. It doesn't exactly stop the run as Love scores again, capping a 13-0 run. But Duke quickly stabilizes, goes back ahead, and the teams begin swapping the lead.

Were we not certain this would end badly, we would marvel at the back and forth for these rivals. But Celia and I are not marveling. We're terrified. This is playing out like one of the worst types of Carolina losses to

Duke, where we play well enough to inspire hope, only to have it dashed. We're inching up the top of the roller coaster, knowing the downhill part could be glorious but unsure the work crew has finished putting together the track. We believe we're headed for a crash.

"I'm glad we're not there," says Celia, a play on a comment she usually makes. Historically, when Carolina has done something great, she'll say "It's your fault we're not there," even though the game is hundreds of miles away and we never discussed going.

This time, no such interplay. "If we were there, the paramedics would be on stand-by," she says.

Manek hits another three from the left corner, a shot he launches from his toes that, had his heels been on the floor, they would have been out of bounds. Instead of contesting the shot, Wendell Moore points to the floor, trying to tell the referee to call a violation. The replay proves him wrong and a little bit foolish. Just play defense, Wendell.

Carolina by two. Banchero scores to tie the game with 10:53 left and Coach K calls another timeout. Why? I guess he would say he wanted to talk to his team, but the teams were trading baskets, Duke seemed to be scoring well and now he's down to one timeout.

Duke responds to whatever K said by falling behind five points. The first three of these are classic and epitomize the one-and-done era in one play.

R.J. Davis gets Banchero to switch onto him and drives around him for a lay-up. But Banchero, almost a foot taller, is too nimble and skilled for this. He blocks it and makes a play to save the ball from going out of bounds, two seconds of action that show why every NBA scout so desperately wants him.

Then Banchero does something you're taught not to do from the second you begin organized basketball. He saves the ball by throwing it underneath his own basket, a reprise of the AAU brand of sloppy basketball that still haunts one-and-done freshmen, even at this level. This is the deal you make when you build teams around skilled but fundamentally flawed freshmen, as Kentucky and Duke have both been finding out the hard way since 2015, the last year either made the Final Four before this one.

The ball goes right to Bacot, who not only lays it in, but draws the fourth foul on Duke's Mark Williams, their best big man and future lottery NBA pick. The added free throw gives Carolina a three-point lead.

Still, the lead goes back and forth. Bacot rolls his ankle and appears lost for the game. As he hobbles off, the Whisnants question the fairness of a world in which this could happen. We sit in silence, preparing for a five-minute dose of Puff Johnson in the biggest game of his life.

"That's just not right," I manage to say, though unsure to whom I lodge this complaint.

Johnson, the seldom-used reserve, comes in, and hits two free throws to tie it with 4:36 left, as stunning a development as any we've seen during this entire run. The camera pans to Bacot, jogging near the locker room like a modern-day Lazarus. With just 42 seconds of game time elapsed, he somehow returns.

The teams continue trading the lead. Manek's third cold-blooded three puts Carolina ahead, 73-71, with 1:44 left, but Duke rebounds its own miss and Moore hits a three to give Duke the lead with 1:18 left. The teams are fully in rhythm, trading blows. Jim Nantz on CBS marvels how rare it is for a game with this buildup to actually deliver more. And Coach K responds by calling his last timeout.

Why? Again, he's won 1,100 games and I haven't. He apparently had something to say to his team. But he's out of timeouts.

As the timeout nears its end, CBS cuts to Mickie Krzyzewski, making her way past the Duke students to get to courtside. They reach out to touch her like the bleeding woman who touched Jesus, hoping her mere physical being can cure them. Mickie returns their affection with high-fives, smiling like Cleopatra leading her Egyptians into battle.

We're not responsible for our actions or thoughts at this moment. Where does she think she's going? Does she know something we don't?

Has CBS already told her the outcome of the game and she's getting into position for maximum camera time?

Carolina scores—two Davis free throws—so whatever was discussed didn't work. Duke gets it inside to Williams, their big center, and Bacot responds by committing his fifth foul. Just 47 seconds left. Williams at the line for two.

Now, of all the Duke litany of bastards, preeners, show-offs and reprobates, Mark Williams is not among them. As best I can tell, the only objectionable thing he's done was deciding to attend Duke University. He apparently had other options. I hope he has a decent pro career, finds love, has a family and achieves his slice of the American dream.

Right now I need him to miss a free throw.

"He's got a miss in him," I tell Celia. He's at 72 percent for the year and has a smooth stroke. But 7-footers typically have trouble making big free throws.

Williams dribbles, inhales and sends a missile off the back rim. The worst he can do now is tie the game.

After missing one, Williams now has the sphincter in play, as we like to say. You couldn't pull a toothpick out of his ass with a team of horses. He gathers for the second one, and some genius director at CBS isolates a camera on his face.

The shot bounces around on the front rim and falls off. Puff Johnson and Manek are so committed to blocking out, wiping out two future Duke pros, that Love is able to easily gather the rebound from the third spot on the lane. And the replay we later get of the angst on Williams' face is priceless, but for the fact that we harbor no ill will against him. Why couldn't this have been Christian Laettner?

Carolina has the ball up one. The ball is in Love's hands. Celia and I, and I presume all of Carolina nation, are standing mere inches from the 60-inch screen. Our proximity won't help us see it any better and it certainly won't help Love and the Heels. But we're needed in that spot. In heaven, a celestial Woody Durham is asking us to "Go where you go and do what you do." That's what we have done.

It's soon obvious that this will be Love's play to make. He's liable to make an incredible shot or miss the entire goal. We've learned to live with either result. What he's not liable to do is pass. Not in this moment.

Carolina calls the simplest play possible. With just under a half-minute left, Love dribbles left toward the middle of the floor. Leaky Black sets a screen that eliminates Trevor Keels. Love now belongs to Black's man, Mark Williams. What Williams can't do is allow Love to pull up and hit a three.

But that's exactly what he does. In his defense, he probably can't believe Love will try to shoot over a 7-foot-2 defender running at him. Neither can Celia and I. But that's what Love does.

All of Carolina nation remembers the ball stripping the net, the elation and joy of a four-point lead—two possessions. Most Carolina fans will rank the shot right up there with Luke Maye and Michael Jordan.

My mind goes back to my childhood living room, the smell of paint still permeating from the back bedroom. All the way back to when this Carolina affair started—Charlie Scott scoring to beat Davidson and send the Tar Heels to the 1969 Final Four.

But there's still time remaining. Duke's Jeremy Roach scores a driving layup to cut it to two points with 21 seconds left.

Here comes my favorite subtle moment of this game. Anyone who watched the Baylor game, or paid much attention to Carolina all year, knows we are historically bad at inbounding the ball against pressure. A press defense by Duke's top-notch athletes would have a high probability of working.

But Duke is OUT OF TIMEOUTS! Coach K used the last two at the 10 minute and 1 minute mark for God knows what reason. And the Duke players on the floor, four of them headed to the NBA next season, don't have enough savvy to automatically set up a press.

Instead, they drift downcourt as if to hunker down against Carolina's next possession. There's 21 seconds left and you're down two. What can they be thinking? Watching the replay, as we have an embarrassing number of times, you see future coach Jon Scheyer motioning frantically for his players to get in the backcourt to apply pressure. To no avail.

Carolina gets an easy inbounds pass to Love, their best foul shooter. Duke takes a foul, and Love does them a solid by making just one of two.

But it's too late for Duke. They draw a foul on the other end, and Trevor Keels makes one of two. Love rebounds the second miss, adds two free throws and Carolina has the greatest non-championship win in its history. By far. Maybe better than some of the championships. Apparently the bargain we made has no downside. We couldn't have hoped for this.

Coach K walks off the court having lost his two biggest games against Carolina. Duke's record against UNC during his 42 years stands at 50-50, a wonderful symmetry. Can you be the best coach in the sport without a winning record against the one team your fan base wants you to beat? Did John Wooden have a losing record against Southern Cal? Did Dean Smith have a losing record against Duke? (No, of course not. 59-35 against Duke, 24-14 against Krzyzewski). Against N.C. State? (Pause for laughter. 60-30 against the Wolfpack)

It's almost too much to put into perspective. I have been a Carolina basketball fan since the age of 6, wondering why God let other teams win. Actually, it goes beyond fandom. The milestones of my life are marked by Tar Heel games, many of them wins but not all of them.

They saw me through my awkward pre-teen years, when my overbite fed my flagging self-esteem and blunted my ability to make lasting friends. I then believed Carolina won games because they were Carolina.

They saw me through the teen years, past confusing racial stereotypes and into lasting friendships. The Tar Heels taught me that color was meaningless as long as it wore light blue. They guided me into college, as I began to see the players as peers more than heroes. They provided much-needed and lasting perspective as a sportswriter, allowing me to return as a fan and not as an entitled owner.

They were the drumbeat of my first serious relationship, with my wife as we built a shared life together around their winter exploits. They became my daughter's passion and later her school, even providing the framework for us to become friends at an adult level.

They were the one hurdle in my relationship with my father, forcing us both to reconsider what was important and come out better on the other end. They connected me to my mother and helped us move forward rather than dwell on what we missed.

They provided the greatest joys in our lifetime, as well as some of the most sorrowful moments. Not to compare to marriage, birth and death moments, but most of the other ones.

My journey is not so different from that of thousands, no millions, of Carolina fans and even fans of ACC basketball. This love of college basketball, the way it permeates our lives, the common denominator that binds even those of us who grew up cheering for others—it's unique to those of us who grew up in the ACC South.

College basketball is a national game now, secondary to college football. But tell that to someone who remembers the "Sail with the Pilot" ad, then the cut to teams in layup lines, getting ready, then the voices of Jim Thacker and Billy Packer falling in - and you're about to share a cultural moment the next two hours with an entire region. It didn't much matter who was playing but it meant so much more when your team was on.

The fireplace is crackling, and you sit by it so long your shirt almost catches. Then you sit on the couch and let the heated shirt warm all of you. Mama finishes puttering in the kitchen and takes her chair. Daddy is in his recliner, feet up and hands on armrest. My sisters take their place on the couch. We're peeling late season tangerines, and Mama has made a pie.

If Heaven is indeed a mansion with many rooms, then surely this is one of them.

All of us have this story. The words differ but the song is the same.

As soon as the Duke game is over, the texts start flowing in. A thread from Sophie. One with my sisters, nephew and niece. Another with my Sunday School class. Here's my best buddy from work. And here is a thread among my fellow Carolina grads at work.

College friends weigh in on another one. Here's Dave Willard, my childhood friend. A note from our "foxhole" friends who have children our age. And random other people in my various circles.

We are all congratulating each other. It's as if all the work we've been putting in, others joining at various stages, has paid off in ways more glorious than we could have imagined.

"I wonder if they will show up in class on Monday," I say out loud.

It's a profoundly stupid statement. Celia quickly reminds me they have a game Monday night, the national championship. It's like I've already looked past it. And, in fact, we will lose that game, blowing a 15-point halftime lead. As an 8 seed playing a top seed, a truly good one in Kansas, we had no right to expect better.

No, it's the Duke Final Four game where 55 years of this journey reaches its nirvana. To have lived to see such a moment is an honor. These six decades worth of investment in this team, this school, this sport, this cause, have come together, a moment as pure as we will ever see. I wish I could call my Mama and ask if she saw it. I wish my Daddy were here to ask why can't they do this every year.

I wish the camera could pan to Dean Smith, in his prime wearing a sports jacket and pointing to the passer. Or Charlie Scott, different from the others only because he is more skilled. I want to flash a straight-toothed smile for Dr. Hershey and take a bow for Pee-Heed.

It's coming together faster than I can text, speak or even think. God must be real because he has allowed a moment such as this. Fandom doesn't have a theoretical "peak," yet here we are. Can it ever get better than this?

I can't wait for next year.

EPILOGUE
SO *THAT* WAS
THE BARGAIN

While putting together the thoughts on the previous pages, the 2023 season happened.

The Tar Heels were terrible. Actually worse than terrible. Had they been terrible, they would have benched the starters and tried something else. They were just good enough to invoke the glory from the 2022 tournament run and make everyone—Coach Davis, players and fans— believe we were just a few tweaks away from it happening again.

The media was certainly fooled. The Tar Heels were ranked preseason No. 1, a heady honor for a team that struggled most of the previous year. But they had four starters returning, some transfers, a freshman or two and none of it worked.

In most of their 13 losses, they led in the second half but couldn't finish teams off, the mark of a team with something going on besides Xs and Os. Caleb Love? Bless his heart. He sprayed shots all over every arena, apparently licensed to do just that as playing time never diminished. By season's end, he had (mostly unfairly) earned the fan base's enmity, despite hitting one of the biggest shots in program history a few months before.

In retrospect, the four weeks that ended the 2022 season were the aberration over the past four years of Carolina basketball. Something got into them that couldn't be captured again. Maybe, if you squint hard enough, you appreciate that run, and the two Duke wins, even more. Something magical was happening.

Carolina didn't make the NCAA Tournament, a first for a preseason No. 1 team. They declined a bid to the NIT rather than prolonging the misery. Within three weeks, six players, including Love, had transferred out of the program.

Evidently, this was the terms of the "bargain" Carolina nation made in March 2022. Give us two amazing wins that will historically thwart Duke, and in return, you will stink at a historic level for God knows how long. If given that scenario in that Raleigh steakhouse, we'd still take it.

The 2023 season included two losses to Duke, both games winnable but it was that kind of year. Duke went on to win the ACC Tournament. As top seeds failed everywhere early in the NCAA Tournament, Duke seemed poised to fall into the Final Four and perhaps win it all.

We steeled ourselves for a "redemption" argument that tried to minimize the two catastrophic losses to UNC the year before. We weren't going to have it.

On March 18, we were invited to the wedding of a dear friend, albeit not a basketball fan. Duke was playing a second-round game against Tennessee, the type of program with a history of failure in large moments, a team Duke always beats in games that matter. Nonetheless, the game was close as we left the house.

As communion was offered during the service, and attendees came forward seeking salvation, restoration or some other form of God's grace, Celia and I sought ESPN.com for the Duke game tracker. Tennessee was actually winning. The game went final just before the benediction.

Best day of the year. Still. I leaned over to our pastor and fellow Carolina fan as we filed out. He was perhaps expecting me to say I had recommitted my life to Christ, but instead he got "Duke lost." Which may have been just as satisfying.

At the reception, Celia and I asked the DJ to play *Rocky Top*, Tennessee's ubiquitous fight song, which is actually more about drinking moonshine than the Tennessee Volunteers' exploits. He said his daughter was friends with Duke's team manager and refused to do it. We asked again, because we are that small, and he reluctantly gave in.

So there we were, just the two of us, dancing to *Rocky Top* the day Duke lost. Carolina was bad in 2023 and may be again in 2024. But we'll still be with them. We can't help it. And we will still beseech Duke to "go to hell" whenever our band plays the fight song ("I'm a Tar Heel born and a Tar Heel bred and when I die I'm a Tar Heel dead...")

The dance will go on.

www.ingramcontent.com/pod-product-compliance
Lightning Source LLC
Chambersburg PA
CBHW051338120626
46547CB00016B/2604